Reproduced by permission of the Radio Times Hulton Picture Library.

Workers' Control

by Ernie Roberts
Assistant General Secretary
Amalgamated Union of Engineering Workers

London · George Allen & Unwin Ltd
Ruskin House   Museum Street

First published in 1973

ISBN 0 04 321013 9 hardback
0 04 321014 7 paperback

DEDICATION

This book is dedicated to my many employers in the engineering industry, who, by their actions as capitalists, convinced me of the need for Workers' Control.

Printed in Great Britain
in 10 *point Times Roman type*
by Clarke, Doble & Brendon Ltd
Plymouth

Contents

Acknowledgements

I should like to thank all those whose books and documents I have
used and referred to in writing this book, and also Fred Wright, my
American cartoonist friend. Special thanks are due to Miss M. J.
Leonard for her valuable assistance in preparing the typescript and
compiling an index. I should make it clear that what follows are my
personal opinions, and they do not necessarily express the policies of
the AUEW.

Chapter 1

Why Workers' Control?

. . . you take my life when you do take the means whereby I live.
Shakespeare: *The Merchant of Venice*

The control and direction of the lives of the common people have always been to a great extent in the hands of landlords, industrialists and bankers.

It is they who decide whether the workers will have a job: whether a worker will have the right to till the soil, manufacture goods, or provide essential services for his family and fellow workers.

Control of society and citizens is in the hands of the owners of wealth and property. This control has meant poverty, unemployment, misery, fear and insecurity, and wars, for the working class.

Today, the working class show by their actions that they understand more clearly the meaning of the above statement by Shakespeare, by striving in many ways to achieve control over more and more aspects of their own lives.

Anthony Sampson, in his book *The New Anatomy of Britain*, while he claims that 'few workers really *want* control', still admits that the working-class movement has been able to 'limit the scope of the men at the top'. He writes:

'In the meantime, from inside the institutions and companies, the authority of those at the top is increasingly questioned. "Democracy is breaking out all over," not only in the trade unions, but in universities, in communications, among scientists, backbenchers, and even civil servants. The clamour for workers' control may often be cooked up or half-baked (for few workers really *want* control); but the rebels often have enough bargaining power to limit the scope of the men at the top. The vice-chancellors, the editors, the chairmen, the general secretaries – they all suffer from the "King John syndrome"; they have all had to give in to their barons.

The search for the centres of power leads over the horizon, to the workers on the shop floors, the middle managers in the bureaucracies, the consumer groups, the customers and shareholders, and, perhaps most important, the agitation groups all over the country.'

Furthermore, the workers who invest their lives in industries and services (whilst the employers only invest money – money gained by the exploitation of labour) are realising that the working people are making the greatest investment, and that they have more to lose. Therefore they are claiming the right to greater control over those places in which they work. The idea of workers' control is on the march, and 'no army can withstand the strength of an idea whose time has come'. (Victor Hugo)

'Workers' control' of their own lives and security has now become the demand of millions of workers in a variety of ways – for example, in the call for the right to work, more union democracy, shop-floor control, public ownership, etc.

Workers' control therefore has a many-sided meaning for the working class, and the workers' control movement, with its conferences and publications on all aspects of the struggle, is developing with great force in the labour, trade union and student organisations in Britain.

At a conference of the workers' control movement in October 1970, I made the following statement:

'We must fight for workers' control. It is a political struggle. It is the very essence, in fact, of socialism. I'd like to refer you to a resolution which was put up at the last TUC by the EETU and the PTU, in which they challenged this idea of workers' control, virtually saying that it is the job of trade unionists to look after wages and conditions only, and that "workers have no part in management, because they would confuse their role, and confuse the issue of trade unions and employers". A load of nonsense. This is the same line which has been put up by the Tories and the right-wing Labour and trade union leaders – that the workers are not fit to govern, are not able to govern.

But we are not only fit and able, we in fact do govern quite important organisations in this country, such as million-strong trade unions, political organisations, co-operatives, etc. And we can and will one day govern the industries and the services in which we work . . .

The concept of workers' control presents both immediate and long-term solutions to the people's problems, whether the problem is to fight with the engineering employers on the procedure agreement to replace the infamous York Memorandum, the rights for shop stewards on the shop floor, or the fight for public ownership of industries and services. Workers' control is concerned both with the first level of achievement that we have in industries and unions at the moment, and with the achievement ultimately of workers' power: the power to control our own lives, our industries, and the country in which we live.'

The object of this book is to examine the extent to which the working class have been able to make advances in their efforts to control their own lives in industry and society, and to consider future actions and organisations which will extend workers' control to the point where complete workers' control is achieved.

WHO CONTROLS OUR WEALTH?

The control of the British people's economy is in the grip of the Stock Exchange. In that rich man's bingo hall, £80,000 million of share-values are gambled with each day.

The British workers' livelihood is in continual danger and under continual attack from the gambling antics of the Stock Exchange manipulators. The power exercised over the economy of the country by the Stock Exchange is greater than that exercised by a Labour Government. (A Tory Government is always the executive of Big Business.)

The Young Socialists, in their *Fighting Programme for Labour* (which was carried at the Young Socialists' National Conference

From *The Observer*:

'Butterwick House, which has 750 beds at about 50p a night, caters for derelict and homeless single men. About 150 of them have lived there for at least 20 years.' Butterwick House is to be pulled down by the council "to make way for a massive airport hotel", and the council claims "no statutory responsibility for any of the inmates".

'The council's statutory responsibility only extends to the "elderly and infirm", and apart from them it is a question of priorities.'

on 12 April 1971), illustrate the power of the Stock Exchange to defeat government measures which they consider 'threatening':

'The attempt to trim the fingernails of the capitalists through the 1965 Corporation Bill, provoked a furious campaign of resistance by the ruling class. The proposal to limit the income of company directors to a "mere" £25,000 a year was greeted with baying and howling in the City of London. It was condemned by the capitalists as a "Bolshevik" measure.'

Here is a vital area in our life where the principle of democratic control must prevail. The will of the majority of the people must be made paramount.

Action must be taken to take control of the economy away from the blind, selfish forces of shareholders on the Stock Exchange, and replace it with the planned economy of a Socialist Government, based on the social priorities of the common people of Britain.

The immense power wielded by the Stock Exchange over the economy is far from being broadly based: in fact, it is concentrated in the hands of a very few rich people. It is estimated that 75 per cent of ordinary shares are owned by a mere 2 per cent of the population. Furthermore, the TUC in its *Annual Economic Review* states that 'the top rich 10 per cent own 90 per cent of the total personal wealth in Britain'. And the total personal wealth in Britain is approximately £85,000,000,000, according to the Economic Progress Report of the Information Division of the Treasury.

	No. of retirement pensioners	No. of pensioners in receipt of supplementary benefit
1969		
February		1,661,000
March	7,015,000	
May		1,685,000
June	7,066,000	
November		1,662,000
December	7,180,000	
1970		
August		1,661,000
September	7,347,000	
November		1,694,000
1971		
March		1,758,000

Source: *Monthly Digest of Statistics, Central Statistical Office*, May 1971.

APPROXIMATELY 22 PER CENT OF PENSIONERS ARE RECEIVING SUPPLEMENTARY BENEFIT!

The people who own the bulk of this are in the main also those who own the majority of the National Debt of £33,000 million. They receive the interest on this colossal sum, for which the mass of the people are taxed.

Yes, this is an extremely rich country – but the wealth is grabbed by the few so that the majority remain poor. The market value of shares in industry and commerce rose by over £10,000 million in eighteen months recently. The shareholders had not been working overtime. Oh no! This increase, caused by financial speculators, was the source of real inflationary pressure; yet the speculators would have us believe that wage-drift was responsible for inflation.

It is by this type of financial manipulation that the workers are cheated, day in and day out, all the year round.

---

1. *The average wage-increase for workers in the lower-paid industries during 1970 was 7·7 per cent. The cost of living rose 8·5 per cent in the same period.*
2. *The ten lowest-paid sectors of industry achieved their 7·7 per cent rise more than 20 months after their last settlement. But the 'top ten' sectors had to wait only 10 months between claims.*
3. *The average basic rate of the 'top ten' is something like £18·50. The 'bottom ten' average about £10.*
(At £18·50 a week, the 'top ten' haven't much to crow about!)

Each year the working class produces about £40,000 million wealth. The size of the National Income for 1970 was £42,328 million (Economic Progress Report, Treasury, May 1971). The trouble is that the twenty-five million workers and their families take only 40 per cent of the National Income in wages and salaries, while those who manipulate the wealth the workers have created take 60 per cent. This has been approximately the position since statistics were first kept in 1873.

ATTEMPTS TO REDISTRIBUTE WEALTH

The stupid mistake we make as trade unionists is that we allow ourselves to be divided, by believing that any increase in wages by one section of the workers must be at the expense of other workers. We don't have to fight each other to decide how the 40 per cent of the National Income should be divided. Rather must we unite to make a combined attack on the 60 per cent which is grabbed by those who don't earn it!

The trade unions were created for the purpose of winning more and more of this wealth for the benefit of the working class.

'What gives the unions and the strikes arising from them their real importance is this, that they are the first attempt of the workers to abolish competition. They imply the recognition of the fact that the supremacy of the bourgeoisie is based only upon the competition of the workers among themselves; i.e. upon their want of cohesion. And precisely because the unions direct themselves against the vital nerve of the present social order, however one-sidedly, in however narrow a way, are they so dangerous to this social order.'

Engels, *Conditions of the Working Class in England in 1844*

In addition to the work of the unions, the Labour Party was also brought into existence to conduct a political struggle, and bring about a redistribution of the national wealth in the interests of the working class.

This will not be done, however, unless the rank and file trade unionists and the ordinary members of the Labour Party take control of their unions, the Labour Party, and the co-operative movement.

Here is where the fight for workers' control must first be won if we are to succeed in achieving workers' control in all other areas of our national life.

Who are the present controllers of industry? According to *The Observer*, there are some 10,000 public companies (that is, companies whose shares are quoted on the Stock Exchange), most of which could be controlled by a handful of men – the top investment experts of the giant financial institutions. In 1970, these 'faceless giants' ploughed over £400 million of the nation's savings into the stock market.

'The insurance companies, investment trusts and merchant banks could [and do! – E.R.] pull the strings in almost every company in the country . . . Together,' continues *The Observer*, 'they hold about 30 per cent of the nation's shares, and control about half the deals done on the stock market.' Where is the democratic control here?

The Tories claim they are for a 'property-owning democracy'. Quite so! Property *does* own democracy in the capitalist system. I am for 'democracy owning property' – and that, to me, means workers' control under socialism.

> *In 1968 the average assistance for Exchequer and rate sub-*
> *sidies to council tenants was £35, of which £23 was direct*
> *Exchequer aid. The average tax-relief going to owner-*
> *occupiers with mortgages . . . was about £46 . . . At the start*
> *of the rent rebate scheme it was estimated by the GLC that*
> *43,000 tenants would apply for the rebates, and that by 1970*
> *70,000 would be eligible. The number who actually applied*
> *fell very far short of this. Today only 17,000 of the GLC's*
> *quarter of a million tenants receive rebates, i.e. only about*
> *7 per cent.*
>
> *Child Poverty Action Group Journal,*
> Spring 1971

> 'There are large numbers of working-class families who are
> too proud to have their poverty examined by hordes of offi-
> cials. Proof of that: the government family income supple-
> ment. Only 4 out of every 10 whom they expected to apply
> have done so. 200,000 council tenants in the GLC and only
> 15,000 have applied for a rebate.'
>
> Frank Allaun, MP, Labour Party Conference,
> October 1971

Under the present system, a few men wield a lot of power.
And are very handsomely paid for it. Not satisfied with per-
mitting grossly inflated incomes to flow into the pockets of
'Britain's Top Earners', the Tory Government in its recent
budgets has given them income tax relief amounting to pay-
rises of, in some cases, £7,000 a year.

Because of income tax relief, for example, Sir Henry Johnson
(British Rail – gross pay £20,000) had a 25 per cent increase in
his take-home pay; so did Lord Melchett (British Steel – gross
pay £25,000); Jocelyn Hambro (Hambros Bank – £30,565 gross)
is taking home 41 per cent extra in his wage-packet, and Lord
Stokes (British Leyland – £46,060 gross) gets 56 per cent. But
all those are outdone by Sir David Barran (of Shell) whose gross
pay is £72,809, and who nets an extra 80 per cent in take-home
pay, just through the Government's 1970–1 income tax changes.

Wealth Tax
Mr Sillars asked the Chancellor of the Exchequer what is his estimate of the income to the Exchequer of a Wealth tax at the rate of 5 per cent per annum, on the assumption that personal wealth up to £20,000, £40,000 and £100,000 respectively, would be exempted from such a tax.

Mr Patrick Jenkin: On the assumption that the charge was confined to the slice above the suggested limits, the estimated yield for a full year is as follows:

Exemption limit	Yield of 5 per cent Wealth Tax £m.
£20,000	1,000
£40,000	700
£100,000	350

House of Commons Hansard, Written Answers, vol. 810, col. 262. Monday 1 February 1971

How does your 9 per cent to 14 per cent wage increase compare with that? Especially in view of the fact that these tax changes for most workers mean no more than a few pence a week.

HOW 'THE OTHER HALF' LIVES

Pity the poor stockbrokers! As the *Sunday Telegraph* has pointed out, 'stockbrokers who over the years have successfully pressed for the disclosure of company directors' pay are often reticent about their own remuneration'. I wonder why?

Stockbroking – unlike weekly-wage jobs – is recognised as a highly-paid profession. A few of the top brokers clutch a gross pay of £100,000 a year (their clerical staff are probably greedy enough to take £1,000!). The commissions earned by the top dozen or so companies are each estimated to be over two million pounds each year. Such rich gains can be a problem. As the *Sunday Telegraph* continued: 'In the exceptional cases it is sometimes an "embarras de richesse", forced on to partners by laws which call for the distribution sooner or later of all the profits.' (And you workers think *you've* got problems!)

Free enterprise could not continue to exploit your labour efficiently without these chaps.

Directors of big companies have their problems, too – how to hold on to what they have gained. Here are a few examples, taken from *The Sunday Times* (30 March 1969):

In February 1971, the TUC's 'minimum wage' demand was £16·50. In the February edition of Labour, *the TUC published a list of 112 major sectors of British industry where workers are employed at a basic rate below £16·50. The list included engineering manual workers (£13·85 basic), municipal busmen (£15·40), coal and coke distribution (£12·00), and Licensed Residential Establishments Wages Council (£8·65). The TUC's 'minimum wage' demand currently stands at £20.*

Company	Director	Personal Holdings
Gestetner	J. A. Barnett	£20,300,000
	Mrs H. Gestetner	£6,600,000
Montague Burton	R. M. Burton	£9,900,000
	A. J. Burton	£11,100,000
Plessey	John Clark	£3,180,000
	Michael Clark	£3,000,000
United Biscuits	Hector Laing	£3.670,000
Firth Cleveland	John Hayward	£4,100,000

There is also our rich friend Paul Getty. A real saver. He puts his pennies where they multiply, on the backs of the labour and skill of millions of workers. He is estimated to be the richest man in the world, worth over £300,000,000, give or take a million. He certainly won't miss the one-and-a-half million pounds or so that he spent recently on a Titian painting to fill a blank space on his wall.

'Comrades, it is intolerable that tonight 11 million men, women and children will go to bed in a house without a bath, hot water or inside lavatory in the year 1971 in a so-called affluent society.'

Frank Allaun, MP, Labour Party Conference, October 1971

There are many others, too, who exercise 'directors' control', yet they have no time for this nonsense of 'workers' control'. Why are you so poor? Because they're so bloody rich!

And why are they so rich? Because people have it fixed in their minds that it is morally right for a man to take possession of a lot of money, to invest that money, and to reap the financial benefit of exploiting the labour of the working class. Once this morality of exploitation has been accepted, the rest of society is built on that foundation.

An illustration of this is the recent success-story (*The Sunday Times*, April 1971) of a bright lad who made hundreds of millions of dollars out of faith. His name? Bernie Cornfeld, of International Overseas Services Limited. He told his company associates that they too would become dollar millionaires, and so they did. A bank in London received 5,600,000 common shares in IOS Ltd; in return they handed over $52,400,826. International capitalism was involved in this great operation of exploitation – French banks, twenty-four British financial concerns, and Japanese, Swedish, Norwegian, Swiss, Finnish, Belgian and Australian interests. This huge parasitical growth creating pieces of printed paper depended for its vast wealth on the industry and skill of the working people.

Compare these activities with the statement of Mr John Davies, Minister for Trade and Industry, on 24 September 1971. Speaking to businessmen at a 'working' (?) lunch in Preston, he attempted to explain the highest unemployment figures for thirty years as the result of 'too much manpower achieving too little output'. He was not, of course, referring to the stock-brokers, company directors, and money-market manipulators (whose total manpower is vast in proportion to its total output of nothing).

The working class can well do without the operations of these people. *Workers' control* at all levels will make such operations redundant.

What does industry itself have to say about the incomes of its top men, while you and I are being told to tighten our belts? A survey conducted by the Associated Industrial Consultants shows that the average director's salary has gone up to £3,842 a year. A managing director of a company with a mere £3

"OUR EXISTENCE AS A GREAT CORPORATION DEPENDS UPON YOU LOYAL UNDERPAID EMPLOYEES"

million annual turnover, however, could expect to get £8,745 a year, while those who run £15 million outfits can look forward to £12,208. The survey also points out that over the past four years, the top salary increases have gone to heads of development, who have had a 52 per cent increase, followed by sales managers, who got 46 per cent, and personnel managers, who managed very nicely on 44 per cent.

Associated Industrial Consultants go on to say that British

Executives also enjoy a number of benefits which go with the job: one third of them get a bonus, 64 per cent have sole use of a company car, and 20 per cent get a car allowance; 70 per cent have four weeks' holiday on full pay.

How are you getting on with *your* wage-demands? No doubt you will be told by the press, television and government that your extortionate demands will wreck the economy, and your employers will say that you are too greedy – taking out more than you put in. As Alan Fisher, General Secretary of the National Union of Public Employees, said: 'We have reached a situation where a worker seeking a wage increase can be bullied by a television interviewer into accepting personal responsibility for the country's economy.'

Contrary to Labour Party objectives, the number of persons in the population who are dependent in whole or in part upon the means-tested benefits of the Supplementary Benefits Commission had increased rather than decreased, to 4 million by the end of 1968, compared with 2·8 million in 1965 . . . [the Ministry of Social Security's 1967 report] showed that, out of about 7 million families with children in Great Britain, some half a million families, including up to one and a quarter of a million children. had incomes below *the supplementary benefit scale . . .'*

Child Poverty Action Group,
Poverty and the Labour Government

The *New Statesman* (26 May 1971) summed up the position with clarity: a pay-claim from the municipal dustmen is 'an attempt to hold the nation to ransom, but a pay-claim from the Queen (with private assets estimated to be around £50 million) is termed "Her Majesty's Most Gracious Message".'

NOTHING TO LOSE BUT OUR CHAINS

Well, I have a message for her and the rest of the Establishment: it is that workers' control with a genuine Socialist Government will put an end to the autocratic financial control of our lives by those who take most from the country, and give very little value in return.

The Young Socialists take the same stand, in their 1971 *Fighting Programme for Labour*:

'The simple facts and figures, the stranglehold exercised by the handful of exploiters, if hammered home would generate over-whelming support for the demand for nationalisation with minimum compensation on the basis of proven need of the 250 major monopolies. On the basis of a planned nationalised economy, democratically operated by the Trade Unions, the housewives, the shop-stewards, the small businessmen and the working class as a whole, it would be possible to begin to organise society in a way that would guarantee that poverty, hunger and war would be something of the dim and distant past. Such is the programme, such is the battle cry of the Labour Movement.'

It is to be hoped that the Young Socialists keep this aim firmly fixed in their minds, and continue to fight for it. It is all too easy to wander away from one's ideals, on the attainment of personal honour and power.

Here is a comment from an ex-Young Socialist:

'A Socialist is a person who believes that the State should own the whole of the means of production, distribution and exchange, and in my teens I believed that was right. I don't believe that is right today. I think it's a nonsense.'

Lord Robens

In December 1970, less than 2,000 of the estimated 200,000 eligible, working, low-income families claimed their right to free welfare food. In April this year, a further 150,000 work-ing families with children became eligible.

Child Poverty Action Group Journal,
Spring 1971

The facts show that the society in which we live is in a crisis – a crisis which is seriously hurting the working class in many ways.

This is the fundamental crisis of monopoly capitalism, under which the technical and scientific developments which exist cannot be fully used, and used to social advantage, because of the class character of present-day society.

Realising this, thousands of millions of workers and peasants are bringing the world into a state of revolutionary change by fighting international monopoly capitalism, which deliberately perpetuates poverty, misery, hunger and domination in order to accumulate colossal wealth and to assist in the exercising of power by a minority class in a minority of countries. The monopoly capitalists have in their hands the military power to destroy humanity through thermo-nuclear, biological and chemical warfare.

We must end this system before we are destroyed by it. Otherwise, we shall go through worsening crises, entailing endless waste of human resources, and even greater human suffering, misery and frustration than exists at present.

What is our alternative?

The alternative is to struggle and overturn the present system and establish a new social structure – socialism which is national in content and international in form, and firmly based upon workers' control.

Chapter 2

Participation?
Industrial Democracy?
Workers' Control?

*The final role of the trade unions must be to change
society itself, not merely to get the best out of existing
society.*
Hugh Scanlon

The arguments about the meaning of 'industrial democracy',
'workers' control', 'workers' participation', 'joint consultation',
and so on, can be quite fruitless unless we relate our viewpoint
to the facts of life.

A great number of different terms exist to describe varieties
of workers' power, and there are probably as many meanings
for each term as there are people who use it. But in the last
analysis, it is the workers themselves who must decide the
'meaning' of any action they take by deciding how far they are
prepared to go in the class struggle. Whatever name we choose
to give the struggle is purely academic – simply a shorthand
way of talking about the aims and activities of the working
class.

Bert Ramelson (Industrial Organiser of the Communist
Party), in his contribution to *The Debate on Workers' Control*
(a booklet published by the Institute for Workers' Control),
regards the 'diversity in terminology' as 'a fairly good measure
of the confusion and illusions that are being sown, of the utopian
as well as class collaborationary and diversionary ideas that
surround this subject'. It seems that I and others who use the
term 'workers' control' are the utopians; while those who go in
for 'joint consultation and participation' are the class collabora-
tionists.

Certainly, the Liberal Party and the right wing of the labour and trade union movement hide behind 'participation', and use it as a cover for ideas of profit-sharing and co-partnership. Co-partnership schemes offer an illusory sense of security and involvement to workers; they are an attempt on the part of the employer to show that the lion is prepared to lie down with the trade-union lamb – providing that the lamb gives an undertaking not to eat the lion! The 1968 Donovan Report makes the same point:

'We have also received evidence concerning profit-sharing and co-partnership schemes. We do not doubt that in the right circumstances such schemes can be useful, and there are a number of well-known concerns which operate them successfully. There are also dangers which should not be overlooked. In particular, schemes of this kind have suffered in trade union eyes from a suspicion that they have in some cases been designed to attract the loyalty of workers to their employers at the expense of the unions. It is evident that such schemes cannot be an acceptable substitute for the reform of industrial relations through comprehensive factory and company agreements. If they are to play a part in the wages structure of an undertaking we believe that this should be decided by negotiation through the relevant collective bargaining procedure along with the other elements in wage-structure.'

Tackling the problem of involvement (a paper prepared by Nigel Vinson, Chairman of the Industrial Co-Partnership Association, and presented to the Adlerian Society of Great Britain in September 1971) gives some concrete examples of the level at which co-partnership operates.

CO-PARTNERSHIP–PARTICIPATION– WORKERS' CONTROL?

'Co-partnership is an attitude of mind,' says Mr Vinson, 'dwelling on those aspects that people have in common, rather than concentrating on their differences.' The 'aspects that people have in common' include birthdays, a common need to eat and

respond to the calls of nature, and so on. The differences presumably include the difference between £15 and £150 a week,
the difference between making decisions and being told to carry
them out, and 'the differentials necessary to encourage the
taking of responsibility'.

Included in the list of 'Aids to Employee Involvement' are: a
common canteen, common toilets, and a common entrance.

'Human Dignity' is preserved, providing the powers-that-be
remember your birthday, deliver 'rises and rockets' privately
'with due sense of occasion', and offer 'special privileges after
ten years' service' – a possible example being to have a holiday
on your birthday.

The section of the paper entitled 'Letting People Know' is
based wholly on the principle that decisions will be made by
management who, out of the goodness of their hearts, will
permit the workers to share the information before it leaks out
unofficially. In fact, 'letting people know' is a euphemism for
telling them!

All this is designed to make the present system more tolerable
by the condescension of management. The job of trade unionists
is not to accept the system, even in its 'improved' form, but to
change it. Yet this type of scheme. disguised as a significant
advance in participation, is passed off by the right wing as a
development in the right direction in the furtherance of the
workers' struggle for power.

'Participation is a catchword of the Right,' says Ramelson.
'It aims to create a façade to give the impression that workers'
representatives at all levels have been party to decision-making,'
while the actual power to make decisions remains vested in
management. Yet, Ramelson goes on, 'I am not arguing against
joint consultation or increasing workers' participation at every
level.' Why not, if these things are a mere façade and a trap?
They must be fought tooth and nail.

'Workers' control' is viewed by Ramelson as an equally
dangerous development at the opposite extreme – dangerous,
because it envisages *complete* control by workers over their own
lives, which, he says, is 'incapable of being realised'. He proceeds
however to chart the future development of workers' control in
some detail, though he prefers to call it industrial democracy.

His account of industrial democracy falls short of workers' control in one main feature – in that it gives the State the final say in matters of pricing, investment, and other 'management' aspects of industry.

Will Paynter (former Secretary of the National Union of Mineworkers) expresses a similar opinion in his book, *British Trade Unions and the Problem of Change*:

'It has to be accepted that the final authority on what has to be done in the day to day running of any enterprise must be that of the person appointed to manage. Efficient management is a highly skilled job and while it is proper that the views of unions should be constantly sought on matters of general policy and taken into consideration, final authority and responsibility must be upon the manager. An industry cannot be run on the basis of a popular vote or by majority rule . . . The most advanced state of union involvement in management is in nationalised industries, and it would seem that the first step to be taken in the private sector would be to adopt the same system of formal consultative machinery.'

Neither Bert Ramelson nor Will Paynter says who this skilled and all-powerful manager is to be, or how he is to get his job; they do, however, envisage him continuing to operate in a free-enterprise system. Ramelson warns that we must face up to

'the considerable limitations to a full flowering of industrial democracy – falling far short of what can be described as workers' control if words are to have any meaning at all – within the framework of a capitalist society.'

INDUSTRIAL DEMOCRACY – WORKERS' CONTROL?

With Ramelson, I recognise that there are limitations to industrial democracy within the framework of a capitalist society. But the aim of workers' control is to replace the capitalist framework with a socialist one. A capitalist society will inevitably impose limitations on the development of the workers' struggle, but that is no reason for giving up the struggle. Socialism doesn't simply 'appear' the day after the revolution, and workers' control does not spring up overnight. Workers' control in a capitalist economy will be quantitively and qualitatively different from workers' control in a socialist economy; the latter will develop out of the former, and will find its limitations a challenge. Ken Coates expresses the same point of view in his *Essays on Industrial Democracy*, although he chooses to use different names for the capitalist and socialist forms of struggle:

'. . . the Yugoslavs use the term "self-management" to describe the government of their socialised sector. Following this usage, it seems sensible for us to speak of "workers' control" to indicate the aggressive encroachment of Trade Unions on management powers in a capitalist framework, and "workers' self-management" to indicate attempts to administer a socialised economy democratically . . . Between the two, however it may be accomplished, lies the political transformation of the social structure.'

The struggle for workers' control is a continual struggle, and it will continue even under socialism. Giving the struggle a different name will not alter that fact. At the present time, capitalist control and workers' control are out of balance, with the scales heavily weighted in favour of capitalism. But previous struggle has ensured that some measure of control exists even at this stage, and every gain made by the workers, every battle won, encroaches upon the power of the employers, and will eventually increase the workers' power to the stage where they can make an open challenge to the capitalists. At this crisis point, one more victory for the working class would 'tip the scales'. Of course, the nearer the working class get to the achievement of complete power, the fiercer will the capitalist class fight, but still every gain by the workers contributes towards the eroding of what Ramelson calls 'the framework of capitalism'.

It is possible that we will pass through Ramelson's ideal of industrial democracy on the way to workers' control. But the workers, having achieved so much, will not then stop short of *complete* democracy – that is, workers' control. While Ramelson sees industrial democracy as an end in itself, the workers' control movement sees it as a means to an end.

In the early days of trade unionism, activity was mainly 'limited to wage determination, later extended to the length of the working day', and after this came demands for 'the extension of workers' rights to determining the whole process of production'. But this, he continues, had its foundations in syndicalism, and it was the 1917 revolution which first led workers to realise that industrial action alone was not the answer, that 'political action is the means to achieve' power over the whole process of production.

SYNDICALISM – WORKERS' CONTROL?

Control by industrial struggle only is 'utopian', rooted in syndicalism, and bearing no relation to today's problems, says Ramelson. Will Paynter carries the 'syndicalist' tag further: 'The term "workers' control" is used . . . loosely and appears to me as a throw-back to the earlier and less mature days of the socialist movement in Britain when "syndicalism" appeared to mean the same thing.'

Yet the workers' control movement has never claimed to be syndicalist, and its early supporters recognised that 'political action' was the means to achieve their aims. Precisely because it is impossible to encapsulate workers' control within a single company or an individual factory (which is the idea behind syndicalism), it is impossible to achieve workers' control without political action. Companies interact with each other, and with governments. It is therefore necessary to replace the succession of capitalist-supported and capitalist-supporting governments with a socialist one, and how else can this be achieved but by political action? Industrial action for political ends is part of that struggle – for example, the experience of the strikes against the Industrial Relations Bill. The type of struggle which is taking place today – against redundancy, victimisation, changes in work conditions, etc. – is only the embryo. Political action comes with increased political understanding. Ramelson, however, seizes on the fact that the struggle is taking place around practical, everyday issues of working life, as 'evidence' that circumstances and not 'agitation' are giving rise to the demand for industrial democracy:

'The considerable struggles against redundancy, victimisation of militants, against changes in work practices . . . are evidence that it is these real objective circumstances rather than the agitational activities of this or that group that have given birth to this movement.' (The movement = the expansion of industrial democracy.)

Yet such circumstances existed for a good many years without leading to any substantial demand for an extension of industrial democracy, and Lenin himself rejected the idea of spontaneity as the means through which the workers would achieve socialism.

It is the agitational activities which give impetus to the general discontent, and the combination of agitation, organisation and struggle which gives rise to general action being taken against the objective circumstances of capitalism. And what could be more natural than workers' actions being centred upon those things which affect them most immediately, rather than on the abstract idea of political action?

Democracy is always 'in the process of becoming'. The present struggle has developed out of demands for increased industrial democracy (that is, more control), because those demands centre upon and bring to light the many areas where such control does not exist. It is the most glaring of these areas which are being tackled first. Once these points have been won, the struggle will develop, and more and more aspects of life will come under the control of the workers. But there will be no clean dividing line between workers' control and the system which exists today. The practical demands mentioned by Ramelson – victimisation, changes in work practice, and so on – are simply part of the process of becoming, and not the workers' practical fight for improved democracy 'within the framework of capitalism' versus the pie-in-the-sky agitation of the workers' control movement.

SOCIALISM – WORKERS' CONTROL?

One of the Tory arguments against socialism is that we can't have it, because it doesn't exist. Ramelson argues against workers' control in the same way:

'I do not wish to belittle the efforts of those who have devoted considerable effort to explain and further this movement. But unless we see its real roots, we will fail to understand its great potentialities for the movement, as well as its limitations. It is necessary to see both sides if we are not to add to the confusion and the furthering of illusions.'

Is workers' control an illusion? Ramelson goes so far as to admit the 'potentialities' of workers' control; in fact, the only illusions are the 'limitations' which he insists on seeing. His list of limitations includes 'a clear distinction between what is possible before the working class take power and after'.

He talks about 'before and after', as though workers had only to climb a wall and find Control on the other side, 'with limitations', of course. Ken Coates (*Essays on Industrial Democracy*) makes the same distinction: he says that 'workers' control' is a term used to describe complete control over production, on the one hand, and the present attempts to encroach upon the employers' power, on the other. He goes on:

'It is misleading to use the same term to speak of two such different conditions. To do so implies that an unbroken continuity of democratic advance stretches between the imposition of a Trade Union veto on dismissals and the ultimate overcoming of capitalist property relations. This is a naïve view . . .'

It is even more naïve to imply that, come the Revolution, all the workers' problems will be solved! The working class 'taking power' is the point at which they tip the scales in their favour. The method by which this is done depends wholly on the workers and the problems they are trying to solve, but there can certainly be no clearcut before-and-after dividing line. There will be an uphill struggle both before and after the balance of power changes. Tamara Deutscher, in a short account of Trotsky's life (*The Sunday Times*, 19 September 1971), describes the theory of permanent revolution as follows:

'He [Trotsky] viewed the transition from capitalism to socialism not as one final act, but as a series of interdependent and interconnected social upheavals occurring in countries of diverse social structures and on various levels of civilisation. No single phase of this process was self-contained or self-sufficient; it was a chain reaction in which every new impulse set others in motion.'

'What is possible' at any stage in the struggle (that is, the amount of control which is possible) depends on the nature and extent of the struggle, and this will be decided by all the workers. This, of course, was at the root of the Cultural Revolution in China – a recognition that a single revolution does not suddenly transform society, wipe out the ingrained bourgeois ideas, and make everything in the garden lovely and every worker a socialist; on the contrary – it is vital to be constantly alert, and ready to halt the backsliding which inevitably takes place if we allow ourselves to settle down into an apathetic acceptance of that which exists. No system is so perfect that it does not need many improvements.

Democracy is a relative concept, not an absolute one. Compared with a hundred years ago, industrial democracy has made great strides, yet it is still only in its infancy. The fight for democracy does not stop at the crisis point of 'taking power' – in fact, it should *never* stop, although Ramelson insists that it must, since there are certain aspects of life which are apparently beyond the capabilities of the workers:

'Nevertheless it would be wrong to assume that . . . "workers' control" or "self-management" exists or is theoretically possible, that is if by these phrases, is meant control over all aspects of production, e.g. including what to produce, pricing, investment, etc.'

So workers' control is not even theoretically possible! Why not? Ramelson does not offer an explanation.

The benefits which he attributes to socialism – control over hiring and firing, redundancy, disciplinary questions, welfare and safety, training and education programmes in industry – are not the prerogatives of a socialist state. These things are being demanded, and to an extent obtained, in this country. It is just this kind of demand which will begin to erode the power of management. But it is the *other* kind of demand – over pricing, investment, production programmes and so on – which will be the hallmark of workers' control.

CAPITALISM – WORKERS' CONTROL?

As Ken Coates says (*Essays on Industrial Democracy*), workers' control is not limited in its demands to control over machines, but over management, too:

'The workers wish to limit the scope of the action of other *persons*, of managers or owners, and not merely, as is often implied, to "control" inanimate objects such as their machines, asd raw materials. Inanimate objects appear to be at stake, because reification is at work; what the machines do is not the result of any will of their own, but the outcome of a tussle of wills between people, whose relationships have been refracted through things and camouflaged in the process. Whether at the level of shop control of hire-and-fire, and agreements on 100 per cent Trade Union membership, or at the level of detailed Union inspection of a firm's account books and workers' veto on investment decisions and the distribution of profits, workers' control in this sense involves a balance of hostile forces, a division of authority between rival contenders.'

This can be achieved even within the capitalist framework, says Coates, and 'once property and its taboos are overcome', the new problem is 'democratic self-regulation'. The fight between 'them' and 'us' is superseded.

Ramelson insists, however, that although there is 'no fundamental clash of interests' between workers and management in a socialist state, the conflict between the state or management and workers' interests does not disappear. This is hardly surprising when the 'state has responsibility for appointing top management':

'While the State has the responsibility for appointing top management, it is as a rule done with the approval of the workers' elected representatives. Where the men through their organisation (the trade union) demand the dismissal of management, management will in general be replaced.'

Even if the workers can 'in general' make changes, this kind of elitism is hardly conducive to reducing the conflict between state and workers. This is not workers' control. It is not even industrial democracy.

Moreover, continues Ramelson, although there is no 'fundamental' clash of interests in a socialist state, management 'will tend to show greater concern for output and unit costs' which could 'very well encroach on the workers' rights and interests'. Why should this be, when worker and consumer are the same person? There may be an attempt to continue the conflict, but under a genuine workers' control system, such a conflict would always be resolved in the interests of the workers.

Ramelson's argument presupposes that differences between State/management and workers will always be such that 'a vigilant trade union will be indispensable', and he cites the 'conflicting interests' of the various power industries as an example.

The role of trade unions in our present society is to protect workers against the management's zeal for profit and to convince members of management that they too are workers whose real interests lie with the working class in its efforts to gain control of society, by protecting their members' wages and conditions of work, and attempting to extend the amount of control a worker has over his own life. Will Paynter describes their function as follows:

'The capitalist system is a "free for all" system using any means to get for those who own property in one form or another, the maximum "rent, interests and profit", in a competitive economy. The trade unions are therefore justified in using any and every means available in the prosecution of their aim for justice and freedom.'

Once they have achieved control, workers will no longer have to fight state and management, for both these functions will be carried out by workers. Hence the need for trade unions will be superseded by the democratic control by workers over their own lives. 'Sectional differences' will become minor problems, since the political understanding of the workers will either remove differences or rationalise them, and so the kind of protection afforded by trade unions under today's conditions will no longer be necessary. This is not to argue the abolition of trade unions, but to observe that their functions will change as the workers take more and more responsibility for their own lives.

The example of conflicting interests in the power industries would not be tenable in a socialist society, for the simple reason that profitability would no longer be a criterion, and the interests of society as a whole would be paramount. The choice between coal, oil, gas, electricity, etc. would be made on the basis of national need ('the nation' = the workers), and should pit-closures or other contractions of an industry become necessary, adequate provision would be made for fresh employment and retraining before the change took place, so that there would be minimum disruption. Moreover, if the miners and other power workers are not to take these decisions *themselves* in a socialist society, who is? In Ramelson's society, there is a superior breed of man, an elite, ready to take all the decisions. No wonder he foresees 'conflicting interests', since his ideas of industrial democracy appear to reproduce the drawbacks of capitalism!

THE SOVIET UNION – WORKERS' CONTROL?

It is interesting to compare his point of view with that of Zinoviev. Ramelson insists that

'only in the sense that the workers as citizens have a political say in determining the economic and social policies of the state, in determining the main lines and indicators of the overall plan and in contributing towards the plant plan, can it be argued that workers' control becomes feasible under socialism. Pricing, allocation of investment funds, decisions on whether a particular plant or industry should expand or contract, I think must remain a function of the state during the first stage of communism – Socialism.'

Zinoviev, in a Statement of the Communist International to the Industrial Workers of the World, in 1920, saw no such limitations:

'Now is no time to talk of "building the new society within the shell of the old". The old society is cracking its shell. The

c

workers must establish the Dictatorship of the Proletariat, which alone can build the new society . . .

'We understand, and share with you, your disgust for the principles and tactics of the "yellow" Socialist politicians, who, all over the world, have discredited the very name of Socialism. Our aim is the same as yours – a commonwealth without State, without Government, without classes, in which the workers shall administer the means of production and distribution for the common benefit of all . . .'

It would appear from what Ramelson says that later developments in the Soviet Union have not brought to fruition the ideals of Zinoviev. Yet even Ramelson admits that workers' control was not only possible but actually existed in the Soviet Union, before the State took control from the workers:

'Workers' control in the full sense, historically existed in the Soviet Union only in the immediate post-revolutionary period before all means of production were taken into public ownership. Its function was to give the workers full powers, that is control to prevent the private capitalist from sabotaging his plant before it was taken over by the state.'

What went wrong? The answer to that question lies in the phrase 'taken over by the state'. 'Taken over by the state' means much the same thing as 'nationalisation' does in this country. Policy decisions are taken out of the hands of capitalists, and given to the state, and the state is always above the workers, a thing apart. This is not industrial democracy, even when the majority of the product of the workers' labour is redistributed to them in one form or another.

Yet Ramelson does sometimes appear to equate industrial democracy with redistribution of wealth:

'. . . it is the incompatibility between the maximisation of profit and the workers' tireless struggle to achieve the greatest possible share of the product of their labour which lies at the root of the eternal conflict, the basis of the incessant class struggle at the place of work.'

It is superficial to see the class struggle simply as one of wages; class struggle is also about *control*. The problem is one of power, and who wields that power. According to Ramelson. it is sufficient for power to be in the hands of a 'revolutionary political party'; in my estimation, there is no substitute for political action *decided by the working class*, which will ensure power for the workers. Political elitism is anti-democratic, and its dangers were pinpointed by Trotsky:

'The party organisation would . . . substitute itself for the party as a whole; then the Central Committee would substitute itself for the organisation; and finally a single dictator would substitute himself for the Central Committee.'

Ramelson puts the answer to the dictatorship of an individual in a nutshell: 'For only when the working class have power can the workers . . . exercise control of their total environment . . .'

Hear, hear! Workers' power over their total environment = workers' control. But it must be understood that 'total environment' includes pricing, marketing, expansion and all the other factors which Ramelson reserves to the State.

WORKERS' DIRECTORS – WORKERS' CONTROL?

What methods have been used successfully by workers to increase industrial democracy? Consultation is not one of them, says Ramelson, although he qualifies this a little by saying that 'where the workers . . . have not seen it as a substitute for using their organised strength, such consultations have proved useful'.

In my opinion, the consultation with workers and the election of workers' directors are important developments in the struggle, partly for his reasons – that the experience of management techniques is useful to workers – but also because the workers, if given an inch, may one day feel disposed to take a yard!

Will Paynter (*British Trade Unions and the Problem of Change*) regards 'accountability' as an important principle in the extension of industrial democracy, but goes on to say:

'The other existing method of involving workers and unions in decision making in nationalised industries is by the inclusion of union men on the Boards, either as full-time or part-time members. The weakness of this form of involvement is that the person so appointed ceases to have any organised connection with the trade unions and is not accountable to them.'

It is easy to say that, because the workers' directors in, for example, the steel industry, have been totally divorced from those they claim to represent, this method of extending democracy has proved to be a failure. This does not mean that all forms of representation must be rejected out of hand.

It is important to realise first exactly why previous attempts have failed. So far, there has been no effort to enforce the principle of accountability on union representatives, or to apply the principle of recall. This has led to the creation of a new elite, of workers translated into the boardroom, severing all ties with the shopfloor.

But the danger foreseen by both Ramelson and Paynter, of representatives being 'committed' to board policies and absorbed into the capitalist machine, need not arise. The accountability of the representatives to the workers must be of prime importance. The representatives, knowing the wishes and needs of their electors, should contract out of anti-working-class policies, and fight against them. They are not honour-bound by board decisions which they have openly opposed, and the workers have not given up the right to strike against any decision which goes against their interests.

The situation of workers not knowing whether their representative has supported their cause or not should never be permitted to arise. The decisions and discussions of the board should be made available to the workers, who should always have the right to recall any representative who is found to be neglecting the workers' interests.

Whereas Ramelson considers 50 per cent worker-representation is acceptable, I can see no reason why 40 per cent or even less should not be acceptable as a starting point, bearing in mind that whatever the initial percentage, struggle can win more.

Furthermore, whatever the percentage, I agree with Ramelson that 'under no circumstances should the workers feel themselves committed by board decisions accepted by their elected members – any more than they feel themselves bound by decisions of a Labour Government that are contrary to their interests.'

I would, however, go a step further than this, and say that they are no more bound by anti-working-class decisions taken by their trade unions or their political parties, than they are bound by those taken by nationalised industries or a Labour Government. In fact, workers' control over their elected representatives in any sphere must be absolute.

Whether or not he sees workers' representation as a useful form of struggle, Ramelson is convinced of one very sound principle – that the problems of redundancy, manning, training, etc. are problems 'which the workers dare not allow to be resolved unilaterally by management – whether in private or nationalised sectors'. He goes on:

'The nature of the problem is how – as complimentary to and not a substitute for, the political revolutionary struggle to transform society – to extend the workers' rights to have a say in policy-making on the growing range of problems in industry vitally affecting his interests.'

Radek, however, in his contribution to the Second Congress of the Communist International, describes the political and industrial struggles as one and the same thing: 'Every economic struggle is at the same time a political struggle . . . The theory and practice of splitting the class struggle of the workers into two independent parts is . . . extremely harmful.'

Political and industrial struggle only appear to be different when the political understanding of the people is low, and the sooner the workers begin to see that every industrial victory is a political victory also, the higher the level at which the struggle will progress.

Ramelson rightly speaks of the changes which have taken place in industry, as a result of actions 'which compelled management to yield in what had hitherto been the sole preserve of management'. These advances have been achieved 'as a result of struggle using the traditional methods', and 'whatever other methods are advocated . . . they must be seen as supplementary and subsidiary to the traditional method'.

OCCUPATION – WORKERS' CONTROL?

The traditional methods include strikes, work-to-rule and bans on overtime. All methods other than the tried and tested ones are clearly suspect to Ramelson, who considers 'the right to strike is the be all and end all of industrial trade union struggle'. How, then, can we struggle against closures? A strike only closes a plant quicker! Through the struggles at Plesseys and Upper Clyde Shipbuilders, it is becoming clear that occupation can be an alternative way of dealing with industrial closures.

The chief drawback of the UCS 'occupation' was the determination of the leaders to be strictly non-political. Non-political means non-productive. It means fighting a battle with one hand tied behind your back. Perhaps it would seem an honourable course of action if the employers were also non-political, but this is patently not the case. Take, for example, the proposition of Stenhouse Holdings to take over two of the yards, creating largescale redundancies in the others. How could this be 'non-political' when the bulk of the money would be provided by a Tory Government? Moreover, according to *The Sunday Times* (26 September 1971): 'Last year Stenhouse Holdings contributed £30,000 to Tory funds and Stenhouse . . . was the extremely successful national treasurer of the Scottish Conservatives.'

Ramelson talks about employers' policies which 'masquerade as those of the state'; but the employers and their allies *are* the State, and for that reason every strike, every occupation, every action taken to extend industrial democracy *must* be political. Not only that, but it must be seen to be political, and it must be understood by the workers to be political.

Strikes have indeed proved valuable in the fight for trade union recognition, as Ramelson says (witness the well-publicised struggles at Roberts-Arundel, and Caterpillar Tractor Co.), and in addition to strikes he mentions other important aspects of the fight – such as strengthening the status of shop stewards, impressing the need for solidarity on the workers ('Any gain made by any section of workers as a result of struggle is a springboard for other sections'). the possibility of action by workers' representatives on nationalised industry boards, given suitable machinery for accountability to the electors, and 'opening the books'.

The slogan of 'Open the Books', instituted by the workers' control movement, has been taken up by both the Labour Party and the TUC, but the detailed information which Michael Barratt Brown sees to be necessary in his pamphlet *Opening the Books* is, says Ramelson, 'utopian' and 'frightening'. Utopian, because the workers will never have sufficient power over marketing and production to need that amount of information; frightening, presumably because the workers are not capable of understanding so much. Neither of these 'reasons' is really tenable.

Workers should have access to the most detailed information available, not because they will need to use it in every negotiation, but because it is their *right*, and they should be able to draw on it freely as and when it is required. 'Opening the Books' has an additional importance: not only does it help 'to win public support by the dissemination of the real facts and circumstances of the struggle as a counter to the distortions in the press aimed to alienate public support' (Ramelson), which I think is extremely important, but it also helps to convince the workers themselves that the employers can pay!

In conclusion, Ramelson mentions the Prices and Incomes Act, the Donovan Report, and trade union participation in the Neddies, as efforts to convert the trade unions into 'passive Establishment institutions'. The Donovan Report has now been followed by the Industrial Relations Act; the Prices and Incomes Act has been reinforced by a clamp-down on wages in the public sector. These will be superseded by new attempts to muzzle the unions and repress the workers. The accounts of industrial legislation contained in Appendix A illustrate that each new form of legislation (whether this represents a gain for the workers or for the employers), each new effort to cut down the workers' bargaining power, has been only an *armistice* in the fight, and a new point from which to resume the struggle for workers' control and to develop sufficient strength to win the major battle.

Chapter 3

Public Ownership and Workers' Control

To secure for the workers by hand and by brain the full fruits of their industry and the most equitable distribution thereof that may be possible, upon the basis of the common ownership of the means of production, distribution and exchange, and the best obtainable system of popular administration and control of each industry or service.

Constitution of the Labour Party, Clause 4.

At the present stage of the battle, as a direct result of the efforts of the common people, certain industries and services have been brought under the control of the state apparatus of local and national government, for example, roads and sewers, water, street lighting, libraries, parks, art galleries, postal and telephone services, education, railways, gas, coal, steel and electricity.

But the industries and services which are now under government control were not *socialised* by the Labour Governments of the past, and workers' control is not operated within them. In fact, the present varying degrees of control or participation in these industries are grossly unsatisfactory. The Labour movement has been persuaded to accept the idea of Herbert Morrison and Ernie Bevin, Sir Stafford Cripps and the right wing, the idea known as 'joint consultation'; and this idea has also been accepted by the right wing of the trade union movement.

The excuse offered by the leaderships of the Parliamentary Labour Party, the National Executive of the Labour Party, and right-wing trade union leaders for this watered-down version of public ownership, was that the movement had no prepared, clearly defined principles for the control and management of the industries and services after they had been nationalised.

This is not true. The annual conferences of the Labour Party held between 1931 and 1937, after serious debate, laid down some basic principles upon which publicly owned industries should be operated and controlled. These principles were:

1. The previous owners of those industries to be nationalised shall have no further control or say in the running of these industries. (This was not carried out.)
2. The first charge upon the industry or service nationalised shall be the wages and conditions of the employees. (This is not so – the first charge is the interest to be paid on compensation to the former owners.)
3. That the workers should be given the right, acknowledged by law, to participate by representation in the running and control of their industries and services at all levels, with the right to participate in the day-to-day management of the place in which they work. (This has not taken place – the name has been changed at the company entrance, but it's 'business as usual' within.)

The above principles decided at Party conferences have been ignored by the anti-socialists in the Labour Party and the trade unions, although many trade unions, including my own, have in their constitutions demands for the public ownership and control of the industries and services in which their members work. The Transport and General Workers' Union, Rule 2a, states that one of the objects of the workers 'is to endeavour by all the means in their power to control the industries in which their members are engaged'.

The National Union of Railwaymen, having achieved its own nationalisation, goes even further: Rule 1.4.(a) claims that the union is to work for 'the supercession of the capitalist system by a socialistic order of society'.

Yet there has been, and still is, a struggle inside the Labour Party and trade unions about the need for nationalisation, which industries should be nationalised, and the form nationalisation should take.

NATIONALISATION = SOCIALISM?

In 1944–5, the left-wing socialist forces of the trade unions and Labour Party, in keeping with the mood of the workers and the 1939–45 anti-fascist war, pressed upon the right-wing National Executive of the Party at the 1945 Conference a policy for nationalising a number of industries and services. These proposals were contained in the policy statement *Let Us Face the Future*, which called for:

'1. *Public ownership of the fuel and power industries*

The coal industry has been floundering chaotically for a quarter of a century, with many hundreds of independent companies.

Amalgamation under public ownership will bring economies in operation, make modernisation of production methods possible, and the raising of safety standards.

Public ownership of gas and electricity will lower charges, prevent competitive waste, open the way for co-ordinated research and development, and lead to the reforming of uneconomic areas of distribution.

Other industries will benefit.

2. *Public ownership of inland transport*

Co-ordination of transport services by rail, road, air and canal, requires unification. This, without public ownership, means a struggle with sectional interests or the enthronement of a private monopoly which would be a menace to the rest of industry.

3. *Public ownership of iron and steel*

Private monopoly has maintained high prices and kept inefficient high-cost plants in existence. Only if public ownership replaces private monopoly can the industry become efficient.

These socialised industries are to be taken over on the basis of fair compensation, and to be conducted efficiently in the interests of consumers, coupled with proper status and conditions for workers employed in them.

4. *Public supervision of monopolies and cartels*

With the aim of advancing industrial efficiency. Prohibition of anti-social and restrictive practices.

5. *Firm and clear programme for the export trade*

State help in any necessary form to help get the export trade on its feet and enable it to pay for essential food and raw materials. But state help on condition that industry is efficient.'

The Bank of England Act was the first nationalisation measure to be introduced. D. N. Pritt, in his book *The Labour Government 1945–1951*, describes the effects of the Act:

'. . . after nationalisation, the Treasury was unchanged and the "Court" of the Bank consisted, not just immediately but for the whole period of the Labour Government, of the same Governor (Chairman) as before, of a group of orthodox bankers and "high-ups" from big industry and commerce, and – the solitary exception – one right-wing trade unionist.

. . . compensation was dealt with by giving the stockholders enough government stock to assure them the same income as they had been receiving for a good many years from the Bank, namely 12 per cent per annum on the Bank's capital. Thus, one group of owners of capital was guaranteed against any lessening of their wealth or power by the new Labour Government.

The real importance of the nationalisation, from a socialist point of view, can be gathered from the comments of the capitalist press and politicians at the time. *The Economist* said on the 1st October 1945: "It would take a very nervous heart to register a flutter at what is contained in the Bill. Nothing could well be more moderate." And on the 13th October 1945, the same journal wrote: ". . . the stockholder certainly has no legitimate ground for complaint . . . It is plain that the present government does not contemplate revolutionary changes in personnel, and is certainly not intending to recommend 'political' appointments to the Court".'

So while the right wing had to accept defeat on the principle of nationalisation itself, they made certain that the industries and services nationalised did not fall into the hands of the workers, and that compensation was – in the words of Herbert Morrison – 'full and fair'. As Pritt comments:

'That socialism "cannot come overnight" was perfectly true, but to many that was no reason for not making a quicker and bolder start on the journey. Nationalisation, to many people, is socialist; but in truth the value of any measure depends on its character and conditions, and nationalisation itself is not either socialism or a guarantee of socialist advance.'

The battle for a measure of workers' control in the nationalised industries was fought by the AEU and a minority of other unions in the Labour Party. The fight broke to the surface at the 1947 Labour Party Conference. The AEU President, R. Openshaw, moved a resolution on behalf of the AEU delegation, declaring that

'. . . this Conference is gravely disturbed at the system of administration which has been adopted in these industries. Determined to convert nationalisation into socialisation,
1. Conference urges that, in all nationalised industries: administrators and technicians should be chosen from (a) persons of proved ability possessing a sound practical knowledge of the industries, and (b) the organised workers by hand and brain who do the useful work in society.
2. The principle of workers' participation through their trade unions in the direction and management of nationalised industries *at all levels* should be firmly adopted in practice . . .'

Ever since 1945 there have been criticisms by the left-wing minority of the lack of workers' rights in the nationalised industries and services, and of their organisational form and anti-democratic content. But the trade unions and the Labour Party majorities have not supported any radical changes towards workers' control.

CRIPPLING COMPENSATION

The crippling effect of exorbitant financial compensation given to the previous shareholders of these industries, which in some cases were bankrupt and rundown (e.g. coalmines and railways), was sharply attacked by socialist workers, but this has nevertheless continued.

An argument developed between the left wing, led by Nye Bevan up to 1953, and Herbert Morrison, spokesman for the right wing, about whether there should be any extension of nationalisation. Bevan argued for public control of the commanding heights of the economy, and Morrison demanded no more nationalisation until we had consolidated control over the existing public sector. Morrison was supported by the majority of trade union leaders. This argument was reflected in a contribution I made at the 1953 Labour Party Conference, in which I challenged those right-wing trade union leaders who were opposed to nationalisation:

'I am certain that the miners, the railway workers, the agricultural workers and all those that take part in the productive processes in industry understand the need for increased technological efficiency, with the introduction of a greater amount of up-to-date machine tools. We understand this in the various sections of our own engineering industry.

I would like to remind Will Lawther, Ernest Jones, Arthur Deakin, and the railwaymen's leaders, that they have from this rostrum over the years asked for the support of the engineers and all their other trade union brothers and comrades in the socialist movement, to support them in their fight for nationalisation and public control of their industries. We gave them our support; nationalisation is essential to their industries, and where they have been denationalised, we are going to fight with them to renationalise them.

We ask them to understand our point of view. We know that nationalisation is equally as important to our industry as it is to theirs. Our jobs, our standard of living, depend just as much on the nation's taking control of our industry as it does in the case of their industries. Nationalisation in the mining and transport industries is not only a good thing for you, it is a good thing for us too.

We ask you who are already enjoying the benefits of nationalised industries to stand with us, to give us your vote, to give us your support, so that the workers of this country may see that nationalisation is something which is going to be supported by all sections of the Labour Movement for every worker in every industry.'

Arthur Deakin, Transport & General Workers' General Secretary, said in reply that eight hundred delegates in their union

Conference – representing 100,000 members in the engineering industry – opposed the Confederation of Engineering Trade Unions' plan for nationalising the main sections of the engineering industry. He said: 'This so-called plan is a mumbo-jumbo of meaningless words and phrases, and it is the worst abortion ever conceived in the mind of man.' The fight is still going on to compel the Labour Party and a Labour Government to implement the plan to publicly own sectors of the engineering industry.

One of the major basic industries of Britain is agriculture. The nationalisation of land has been a policy of the Labour Party since its early days. In 1932 a report was produced on the nationalisation of land, but its recommendations have yet to be carried out. A motion debated at the 1953 Labour Party Conference declared that the Party should 're-affirm the acceptance of the principle of land nationalisation, and that the Party will place a plan for carrying this out before the electorate at the next General Election'.

E. G. Gooch MP, right-wing general secretary of the Agricultural Workers' Union, opposing the motion, said that 'this would mean nationalising 59 million acres, of which 48 million acres was agricultural land' and furthermore 'the agricultural workers, through their union, are opposed to the nationalisation of agricultural land'. Conference rejected the motion to bring land under public ownership.

THE COMMANDING HEIGHTS

It is evident that there is still much explaining to do, to convince workers of the need to take control over our nation's industries and services. In 1963, with the 1964 General Election in sight, I contributed the following article to the rank-and-file paper *Union Voice*, under the heading *Public Ownership of the Commanding Heights*:

'The Labour Party says, let the people control the means of production, distribution and exchange, and they will control their own lives.

Mr James Callaghan, at the Labour Party Conference in

1962, said, "The British people are ENTITLED TO KNOW before a Labour Party becomes the government what industries we intend to take into public ownership." '

In reply, I put the following propositions in the *Voice* article:

'STEEL

The British people's prosperity depends upon a nationally planned and expanding steel industry.

"The Labour Party stands four-square and resolved behind the proposition that the steel industry must be re-nationalised," said Harold Wilson, House of Commons, 23 March 1961. Why not include: Colvilles, John Summers, Dorman Longs (Steel), Consett Iron, Steel Co. of Wales, Hadfields, Stewart and Lloyds, South Durham Iron and Steel, United Steel, Firth Brown.

We must bring Steel under public ownership.

AIRCRAFT INDUSTRY

"I do not believe we can get a proper build-up in the aircraft industry until it is publicly owned" – Fred Lee, Shadow Minister of Aviation, in 1962, at Labour Party Conference. The plague of unemployment is spreading throughout this important British industry.

It is time we included: The British Aircraft Corporation, Hawker Siddeley Group, Rolls-Royce, Handley Page and Westland Aircraft Co.

It is time to publicly own the Aircraft Industry.

EQUIPMENT

for Coal, Gas, Electricity and Railway Industries should be manufactured by publicly-owned companies. Harold Wilson has said: "Why should not the Coal Board be free to manufacture its own mining machinery, or the Electricity Generating Authority to have a go at the tight ring of generating equipment manufacturing?"

Why not include: Associated Electrical Industries, English Electric, General Electric, Westinghouse Brake & Signal Co.

We must bring Equipment Manufacture under public ownership.

DRUGS and the National Health Service

"We propose that the health service meets its needs increasingly from public enterprise, either through new publicly-owned undertakings, or by acquisition of existing ones" – Harold Wilson.

Why should profit be made out of ill-health? Let's include: British Drug Houses, Burroughs Wellcome, CIBA Laboratories, Boots Pure Drug Co., Beecham Group, Glaxo Group.

Why not public ownership of these companies?

INTEGRATED TRANSPORT

"We intend, as has been made clear in Signpost for the Sixties, to bring back into public ownership road haulage" – Mr James Callaghan, Brighton, 4th October 1962.

Every sensible citizen knows that we need a nationally planned and integrated transport system. Dr Beeching's butchery will not accomplish this.

Considerable wasteful overlapping takes place between thousands of road haulage companies and traders who run independent services.

Why not include many of these when re-nationalising road transport?

We need an integrated National Transport system.

INSURANCE

controls finance, the lifeblood of our British economy. Why permit private bloodsuckers?

In 1961 Annual Conference, the policy was adopted that the Labour Party's "National Plan" would be carried out by a "greater control over the investment policies of pension funds and private insurance companies".

Why not include: Prudential, Legal & General, London Assurance, Sun Life, Liverpool, Victoria, Pearl, Royal Exchange, Eagle Star, Equity & Law, Guardian, etc.

Public ownership of these financial companies is vital to the control of our economy.

PRIVATE MONOPOLIES

conflict with public interests. The well-being of the workers and security of employment can be assured only through public ownership and control.

Harold Wilson has said: "Labour's social and economic

objectives can be achieved only through an expansion of common ownership, substantial enough to give the community power over the commanding heights of the economy. What are the commanding heights?"

I suggest that he includes in his list: ICI, Unilever, Shell, Dunlops, Esso, BMC, Ford, Vauxhall, British Oxygen, Imperial Tobacco Co., Bowaters Paper Co., Tube Investments, London Brick Co., Associated Portland Cement.

In the public interest!

WATER
flows freely; but it is very expensive to buy when privately owned.

The next Labour Government should nationalise water undertakings. Why not include: Bristol Waterworks Co., Lee Valley Water Co., Sunderland & South Shields Water Co., etc.

LAND
was created by no man. Yet some men make a fortune by owning it. To reduce the cost of house, school and hospital building, Harold Wilson has stated: "We propose that a Land Commission shall be established to come in and purchase the freehold of land where development or redevelopment takes place."

PUBLIC OWNERSHIP
Harold Wilson sums up: "So, with Steel, Road Transport, Water, the creation of new publicly-owned industries, with State-owned factories in backward or declining industries, with control of state money that is put in . . . you have there a substantial expansion of public ownership" – Blackpool, 3rd October 1961.

FORWARD TO THE NEXT LABOUR GOVERNMENT AND AN EXTENSION OF PUBLIC OWNERSHIP'

At about the time of publication of this article, I was invited to speak on the same platform as Harold Wilson in the Wrekin constituency, prior to the 1964 General Election, and I took the opportunity of giving him a copy of this issue of *Union Voice*, asking him to consider it when he became Prime Minister.

D

The 1964 and 1966 Labour Governments of which he was Prime Minister have come and gone; the only piece of nationalisation has been the steel industry, with the Tory Lord Melchett placed in control.

STEEL NATIONALISATION – 'BUSINESS AS USUAL'

D. N. Pritt's account (in *The Labour Government 1945–1951*) of the first nationalisation of steel seems equally applicable to its re-nationalisation by the last Labour Government. There was, says Pritt, great opposition from the owners, the House of Lords, parts of the Cabinet, and the Americans. He goes on:

'The opposition of the owners, and of the Tory party, was natural enough. Iron and Steel was not as "sick" an industry as, say, coal . . . It was on the contrary a highly profitable stronghold of monopoly, with many ramifications. There was also the feature, as Anthony Eden described it in the Commons Debates, that "there is no point after this at which the advance towards the extinction of private capital in British industry could be halted".

The case in favour of nationalising iron and steel, apart from any arguments based on socialist principles, was a strong one. Steel was basic to our economy; almost every industry depended on an adequate supply of good quality steel at a reasonable price. It was moreover a restrictive private monopoly; half the productive capacity was in the hands of six concerns, who were linked to one another by interlocking directorships; and the same directors controlled most of the smaller concerns. All the concerns were further associated in monopolistic trade associations catering for different sections of the industry.'

The Tory argument about private competition keeping prices down is blown sky-high by Pritt, who says that the British Iron and Steel Federation

'maintained high prices through the exercise of cartel controls; its general principle was to fix prices enabling the least efficient of its members to make a profit, leaving all the more efficient to make vast profits. Competition was eliminated, so far as foreign producers were concerned, by an agreement with the International Steel Cartel, and at home by preventing new concerns from entering the industry. Such a set-up provided little incentive to eliminate obsolete plant or methods, and the industry was in truth very backward.'

The companies taken over by the Labour Government retained their original names, with the ostensible object of 'keeping intact the identity of individual concerns'. Though, as Pritt says, 'In the matter of ownership and control, the Government seemed anxious to make its omelet in such a way that the eggs *could* be put back in the shells – which the Tories later did!' The steel industry was handed back to private profiteers by the Tories, and the 1966–70 Labour Government set about retrieving it for the public sector yet again.

This was not done on the basis of 'confiscation', however. On the contrary, 'full and fair' compensation was paid, and *The Financial Times* on May Day 1965 declared that 'they [the terms of reference] were far more generous than the market was looking for'. But Tory Edward du Cann MP knew better – he had previously prophesied: 'I believe that nationalisation will go ahead eventually and on reasonably generous terms.'

The extent of Labour's generosity was disclosed on the day that the White Paper outlining the nationalisation proposals, including compensation terms, was published – steel prices jumped by £160,000,000! The table of comparative prices shows Labour's magnanimity towards the capitalist steel shareholders.

	Price on 29 April 1966		Compensation price		Denationalisation price	
	s.	d.	s.	d.	s.	d.
Colvilles	28	0	47	6	34	7
Consett	15	6	19	10	25	6
Dorman Long	23	9	29	10	15	0
Lancashire	21	4½	34	3	11	0
South Durham	19	9	26	3	27	6
Steel of Wales	19	9	32	5	20	0
Stewarts & Lloyds	29	9	32	5	18	0
United Steel	27	6	38	3	14	7
John Summers	29	3	36	0	10	3

In all cases except those of Consett and South Durham, the Government paid out considerably more than the denationalisation share price. We paid £660 million compensation for the steel industry when it was taken over again in 1967, and an annual burden of £45 million in interest payments was put on the backs of the steelworkers.

COMPENSATION OR CONFISCATION?

It is about time the nonsense of 'confiscation' was exposed; it is not possible for the workers to confiscate wealth – they can only take back what has been stolen from them by the capitalists. They can 'expropriate the expropriators', as Marx put it.

Industries exist because workers have worked. All the wealth of an industry is the product of the workers' endeavours. It is iniquitous, then, to take an industry into public ownership on the basis of 'compensation' for the 'owners', since this means in effect that the workers are paying twice for the privilege of owning their own industry. Nationalisation must be carried out without compensation.

Since the re-nationalisation of the steel industry in 1967, the former owners have absorbed many millions of pounds in compensation. Not content with this, the Tories have set about dismantling the *profitable* areas of public ownership and handing them back to their friends to exploit privately.

These Tory plans for denationalisation include the Sheffield Special Steels plant, which makes a profit of £250 million. The President of the Sheffield Trades and Labour Council, Councillor Bill Owen, has declared that plants threatened with closure or denationalisation should be occupied. Under the Tory proposals, 4,500 workers in Sheffield alone would lose their jobs.

But steel is not the only sufferer under the denationalisation policy. There was the breaking away of some of the most profitable routes from BOAC, which were presented for the asking to a private airline.

There is the proposed sale of state-owned breweries in Carlisle, about which a local councillor said: 'It is disgusting treatment. The State sells the best and cheapest beer in Britain, and they are just about to announce the highest-ever profit of £269,000 for last year.' The private brewers have made generous donations to the Tory Party in the past. So what?

The present Government is considering hiving off some of the most profitable parts of the postal services; £4 million worth of state farms are to be sold; £11 million profits are made by subsidiary undertakings of the Coal Board and North Sea Gas, and these too must go to private enterprise.

But what action will be taken by the Labour Party when it is next returned to power, to redress the balance of this massive Tory handout of public concerns? The National Executive of the Labour Party has decided that if the Tory Government hives off subsidiaries of the publicly-owned industries, they should be taken back by the next Labour Government without compensation, and a resolution to this effect was carried by the 1971 Labour Party Conference. Indeed, there was some support in the Conference for an absolute non-compensation policy, both for renationalisation and for newly nationalised industries, as the following extract from the debate indicates. Mr T. Bradley MP (North-East Leicester) said:

'Let us remember too, it is normal for us to compensate former owners of companies in private industry which are brought into the public sector. (Interruptions)

Conference must learn to draw a distinction between re-acquiring public assets which have been hived off and entering into new fields of public ownership. Because in that respect – (Interruptions) – we have not yet become a confiscatory Party. (Interruptions)

I am only recording the fact. (Interruptions) But this forms an addition – '

At this point, the Chairman intervened to request a 'fair hearing' for Mr Bradley, whose point of view was coming under strong attack from the Floor.

Those of us who are struggling for workers' control, industrial democracy, and socialism, must quite clearly state our point of view on 'compensation', and make a stand against it. We must decide which parts of our national economy should be brought (or brought back) into public ownership, and the kind of democratic control we want in those industries, and fight for these things.

'The public' consists of workers and their families, totalling 52 million people, and rich owners and their families, totalling 3 million. Therefore true 'public' ownership *must* mean workers' control. Under genuine workers' control, there would be no opportunity for any government to play financial games with an industry, to the detriment of the workers and the national interest.

Unfortunately, the workers' livelihoods and the 'national interest' are not always to the forefront in the plans of the Labour Party leadership, either. It is patently obvious that the obstruction of the Prime Minister and Cabinet members, and sometimes of members of the Parliamentary Labour Party, has led to a repeated failure by Labour to implement socialist policies once power has been achieved in Parliament.

CONFERENCE DECISIONS AND PARLIAMENTARY ACCOUNTABILITY

In fact, the 1970 Conference found it necessary to pass a resolution demanding that the Parliamentary Labour Party leaders should respect Conference decisions, whether they were made while in government or in opposition. At the 1971 Conference, however, the leaders of the Party made it plain once again that Conference decisions are considered only as 'advice' to the Parliamentary Party; and 'advice' is seldom taken.

The 'Socialist Charter' group, with the help of *Tribune*, has produced a policy around which it wants the left wing to organise and fight, in order to combat such tendencies. The Charter states that the members of the group

'see no alternative in Britain to working through the Labour and trade union movement so painfully built up by our working people. Thus we hope to reawaken a spirit of audacity within the Labour Party, to encourage young people in particular to contribute their devoted energies to the cause of Socialism . . . The central principles of a Socialist Charter of our time must be that those who take decisions affecting the welfare and happiness of the people must be made *accountable* to the people.'

For this to be so, the new Chartists continue,

'the Government must govern – not the Treasury, or the City, or organised business, or the International Monetary Fund, or the State Department – but *our government* must govern. Events have proved that it cannot do so unless it encroaches upon the irresponsible power of the private controllers.'

The Socialist Charter consists of eight demands, among which is a call for

'PUBLIC OWNERSHIP AS A REAL WEAPON FOR SOCIALISM. Develop and extend public ownership until the private sector is brought under the control of the public sector in the interests of Socialist plans, giving full scope to various forms of public enterprise and industrial democracy. We should take over the biggest companies which account for the greater part of production and exports.'

The fifth point of the Charter demands

'FULL PUBLIC ACCOUNTABILITY of private and public institutions and growing democratic control by workers and employees over the decisions which determine their working lives.'

The whole range of industries and services must be subject to

'SOCIALIST PLANNING based on the essential interests and requirements of the British people and not on the profit-making decisions of industry and finance. This requires a National Plan which takes fully into account the needs and contribution of the different regions of the country and allows them full participation in the planning process.'

The eighth and final point of the Charter concerns the organisation through which all the other points will be integrated, that is

'A SOCIALIST AND DEMOCRATIC LABOUR PARTY committed to challenging for power through its transformation into an instrument of popular control responsive to the members and their Conference.'

The left wing of the trade unions and Labour Party have been concerned about the domination of the Labour movement by the right wing, many of whom are petty-bourgeois, middle-class professionals, so-called intellectuals, and professional politicians.

These are still the kind of people who are being chosen as Labour Party parliamentary candidates by constituency selection conferences composed of a majority of working-class people. (See page 233ff for a discussion of this.)

Yet for all its faults – and the selection of such candidates is a major one – the Labour Party is still the political expression of the mass of trade unionists, social democrat organisations, and the co-operators. To oppose its existence would be futile. What we must do as socialist-minded trade unionists is to build up the strength of the rank and file to exercise real workers' control over this political federal organisation, and change it to suit the needs of the working class.

The development of genuine inner party democracy is fundamental to the attainment of democracy in Britain as a whole, and to the attainment of a 'Socialist and Democratic Labour Party' of the kind envisaged by the Chartist Movement.

For this reason, among others, the workers' control movement was founded by those of us who believe that the working class organisations, as well as the industries and the wealth of the nation, were created by the workers, and therefore should be controlled by them collectively.

The operation of workers' control in society means, to me, a society in which all those who perform socially necessary labour have the decisive control over their activities and over the distribution of the products of their activities.

This is obviously not to be attained by 'nationalisation' as it operates at present. It must mean a complete change from the established order which controls the lives of the working class today.

Ian Mikardo MP, in the Chairman's Address to the 1971 Labour Party Conference, put a similar point of view:

'I don't see much point either . . . in pretending that the only thing that divides us from our opponents has something to do with managerial efficiency, or tinkering with the economy, as though we were merely some rather superior firm of efficiency consultants. According to some people, all you need is a bit more interference here, a bit more pressure there, and a new board of control for something else, and everything will be all right in the mixed economy . . . I am not one of those – and I think I have made it plain – who believe we can overcome the forces of modern industrialism and of the capitalist system by minor adjustments or accommodation . . . We have got to persuade the people of this country by open argument and democratic persuasion that the ultimate frame of reference is not to powerful economic or intellectual elites but to the people and community at large.'

CONTROL OF STATE POWER

This means that the superstructure of society must be built upon the foundations of the interests and needs of the majority of the working class. The superstructure must reflect the aims and aspirations and class relationships of the workers.

The State apparatus – that is, parliament, judiciary, armed forces, police, education, communications (e.g. mass media), local government and all social services – must be composed of workers by hand and brain, must be controlled by them.

In this way, we would have a real democratic society, in which the majority, the working class, would decide and control as the government of their country.

This was the aspiration of the workers a hundred years ago, in 1871, when the Paris Commune was established in France with the cry of 'Liberty, Equality, Fraternity'.

This was the ambition which fired the Russian workers in 1917, and also the Czechs, Hungarians, Poles, Romanians and Yugoslavs.

In 1949, seven hundred million Chinese people established their power, and since then have been building, under a workers' and peasants' government, a society which puts their needs and aspirations first, a society in which there is considerable control over industry by the workers, and over the land by the peasants.

The Vietnamese have been engaged in a long and bloody struggle in order to have the same right to create a life which is free in a society in which they themselves control their own way of life.

In none of these countries has the struggle been conducted in precisely the same way. The struggle for workers' control varies from country to country, according to history and the circumstances prevailing at the time, and the fight takes on many forms, depending on the strength and political understanding of the working class.

To reduce the demand for 'workers' control' to mean 'syndicalism', as certain of our critics do, is to distort and misrepresent the aims of the workers' control movement, which is a political movement. The movement for workers' control in Britain has roots which can be traced back to the Industrial Revolution, and exists as a tradition which is inextricably bound up with the workers' ideas of Socialism.

IWC ADVANCES WORKERS' CONTROL

The Institute for Workers' Control states that its aim is to help the movement of the working people to develop by communicating and exchanging experiences from basic organisms, providing studies in the field of political and economic theory, such as will help the new forces find a greater confidence and sense of unity and purpose.

The Constitution of the Institute for Workers' Control pledges the Institute to assist in 'the unification of workers' control groups into a national force in the Socialist movement. These aims are based on the conviction expressed in the Declaration [of the Sixth National Conference on Workers' Control] that

'. . . democratic controls can only be defended if they are systematically extended throughout the unions, the political movement of Labour, and national and local governments, as well as into education and every form of industry and work. These controls will be built in the day-to-day struggle of workers in their organisation and at their places of work . . .'

The Institute has held a number of annual conferences to promote discussion and the exchange of ideas, and successive years have brought increasing numbers of delegates together at these conferences – 500 at Nottingham in 1968, 1,000 at Sheffield in 1969, 1,300 at Birmingham in 1970 – consisting of representatives from all working-class parties, trade unions, student bodies, etc. These conferences have been the means of bringing workers in a variety of industries together in trade and industry groups, to consider the immediate demands for workers' control at all levels, and to discuss the extension of whatever successes have already been won.

In addition, the Institute has produced and distributed thousands of copies of books and pamphlets dealing with the aims and demands in specific industries – for example, in mineworking, docks, transport, aircraft, and agriculture.

The value to the workers in these activities is in the encouragement and promotion of the demands which the workers are making in the various industries in preparation for complete control.

However, it is primarily through *their own practical everyday experiences* that the workers will learn about the nature of the capitalist state, and how to consolidate and extend their control over various aspects of their working lives. As a result of their experiences, they will evolve a theory and practice which will lead to the complete overthrow of the existing order and its substitution by a worker-controlled state.

Chapter 4

Governments as Employers: The Role of Workers' Control

*In our own day the tyranny of vast, machine-like organi-
sations, governed from above by men who know and
care little for the lives of those whom they control, is
killing individuality and freedom of mind, and forcing
men more and more to conform to a uniform pattern.*
Bertrand Russell

The Central Government is the biggest employer of labour in
this country. It employs approximately 6,000,000 persons, for
example, engineers, transport workers, teachers, civil servants,
professional and manual workers.

With this in mind, I wrote to Harold Wilson MP, just prior
to the 1964 General Election, and pointed out to him that,
should he become Prime Minister with a Labour Government,
he would become Britain's biggest employer. Therefore he and
the Labour Party should state quite clearly what they, as
employers, would do for their employees. The Tory Party,
I pointed out, had an 'Industrial Charter' printed as a booklet
for over ten years, although they had never given effect to its
main proposals. It was time the Labour Party had an 'Industrial
Charter' to put before the electorate, and I set out some of the
matters which should be included in such a Charter:

An Industrial Charter for Labour
1. A Labour Government, as the biggest employer in Britain,
should give a lead to the rest of the employers on wages; it
should set a good example to other employers by raising the
wages of its employees, particularly those whose incomes fall
below those on similar jobs in private industry. It should introduce equal pay for equal work for all women in government
employment. There must be no talk of wage-freeze.

2. The 40-hour week ought to be introduced for all those workers who have not yet achieved it, and steps should be taken as soon as possible towards the 35-hour week, which is now the aim of millions of workers in this country.

3. Training must be given to all young people in government employment. There must be no dead-end youth on dead-end jobs. Wages of young people should be increased so that the gap between adults' wages and theirs is not so great.

4. Many workers in local and central government employment have not yet been given three weeks' holiday with pay. This should be conceded by a Labour Government, thereby assisting the unions in their efforts to achieve a three-week minimum in private industry.

5. Adequate non-contributory pensions should be conceded by the government to all its employees. Sick-pay should be granted for all their workers.

6. Furthermore, the Labour Government should be a model for private industry through workers' participation in the control and direction of all local and central government industries and services.

7. It is time that real democracy was introduced in all government employment. There should be no victimisation of shop stewards. There should be no political, religious or cold-war prejudice in their employment policies. Employees should be consulted through their trade unions on all matters concerning their jobs, safety and welfare. All these matters should be dealt with in an industrial charter which the Labour Party should put before the 24 million workers in Britain.

In reply, Harold Wilson wrote that this was

'an interesting idea, but one that does, I think, have two serious weaknesses: first, it is limited in scope to the public sector; second, many of its provisions would require detailed wide-ranging discussions with the unions concerned, discussions which could not easily be undertaken by the Party in Opposition.'

He went on to say that some of these proposals were already Party policy, and 'given the relatively short time before the General Election, I think we should do better to reiterate our major proposals in this field rather than to embark upon new policy discussions'.

I also put the proposals to the General Secretary of the Labour Party, who replied that 'the National Executive Committee has already put forward proposals affecting conditions of work in its various policy statements' and 'there may be a case for bringing all these together and presenting them in some such form as an Industrial Charter – but not, I think, for making new proposals on such matters as hours of work, and length of holidays, which are very much the concern of the trade unions'.

Nothing on industrial democracy was put before the 1964 electors. Indeed the general attitude of the 'employing classes' of the Labour Party seemed to be that it was the trade unions' business to promote such ideas, and it was nothing to do with them as employers. But it should and must be the responsibility of a Labour Government to set the standard of employment in the country, and to move significantly towards greater control by the workers on the job.

THE LABOUR PARTY AND WORKERS' RIGHTS

The NEC set up a sub-committee to go into the matter of industrial democracy and workers' rights on the job, and they produced a pamphlet on the subject which they put before the 1968 Labour Party Conference, and in which was stated the following:

'1. That the growth of industrial democracy must be firmly based on the general and effective recognition of the *right* of workers to organisation, representation and participation in major matters affecting their working lives.

2. That the development of industrial democracy should be pursued through the creation of a *single channel* of communication between workers' representatives and management. The scope and subject matter of collective bargaining should be extended so that all the elements of management (dismissals, discipline, introduction of new machinery, forward planning of manpower, nationalisation and so forth) are within the sphere of *negotiations* at plant level.

3. That workers' representatives should have the *right* to adequate information covering all aspects of their company's affairs, providing only that this does not seriously jeopardise the firm's commercial interests.

THE LEGISLATIVE FRAMEWORK

In order to achieve for workers an effective voice in the control of policy and administration, the Government will be required to act in a number of ways. First and foremost, the Government must accept the right of workers to representation. This will lead to the acceptance of a wider subject matter for collective bargaining. Second, the Government must improve by law the availability to workers of information on their firm and its prospects, which is essential to make bargaining effective. Disclosure of information on the part of the company should cover:

(*a*) *Manpower and remuneration questions*
For example, labour turnover; manpower forecasts, labour costs per unit of output; management salaries and fees, etc., etc.

(*b*) *Control questions*
Such as details of associated companies, directors' shareholdings and internal management structure.

(*c*) *Development, production and investment data*
Including the rate of orders being received, research plans, and purchasing policy.

(*d*) *Cost, profit and pricing policy*
Making a meaningful discussion of financial structure and policy possible.
The right to information should be ensured in a reform of company law.

(*e*) Furthermore there is a need to increase the protection afforded to workers, to shield them from the consequences of mergers and rationalisation, going far beyond the right to compensation for redundancy under the Redundancy Payments Act.'

I believe that, while these proposals do not give workers' control, they would if won take us a few steps along the road towards it. But the Labour Party must set out a real workers' charter, which will give genuine control to government employees and all other workers.

The following extract from an article by Anthony Wedgwood Benn (*Labour Weekly*, 8 October 1971) discusses the 'democratisation of public enterprise', indicating that the pressure for such democratisation must start with the workers – freedom has been won from employers, but never volunteered by them:

'Although there have been some modest attempts in nationalised industries to improve consultation and broaden the range of people eligible for Board appointments, their inner power structure still reflects the power structure of private industry.

Private industry claims that because it is privately owned the Government has no right to interfere with its business; and the workers being employed 'by courtesy' of the owners, have no right to interfere either. This doctrine is politically unacceptable, and explains why private ownership has already been hedged around by statutory limitations on the crude exercise of its power.

But we have made practically no progress in achieving accountability within public enterprise in spelling out the area of power which properly belongs to those who work in the industry as a whole.

The central question that remains to be settled is therefore the democratisation of public enterprise from the bottom up. We must find an answer by building upon the inalienable rights of those who work in nationalised concerns to shape those decisions that affect their lives ...

In the fight for industrial democracy, the shock troops must be the workpeople themselves.'

The suggestion from the NEC of the Labour Party that 'the development of industrial democracy should be pursued by the creation of a single channel of communication between workers' representatives and management' seems to be on the verge of being put into practice, on the union side at least.

A united campaign was planned by the leaders of three million workers in the public sector, to obtain better pay and conditions for rail, steel and mineworkers, post office workers, national airline employees, and workers in the gas and electricity industries. The policy of the Tory Government of holding back wage rises in the public sector caused a surge of anger among members of seventeen unions representing public employees, and there was a strong possibility that they would be joined by more unions representing a further three million workers in the teaching, public health and local government sectors, although this plan did not come to fruition.

The idea of all the unions putting forward their own individual wage-claims simultaneously, and taking united action to back up these claims, was one of the ideas put forward to beat the Tory 'incomes policy' which operated only in the public sector.

There is no reason why this unity should stop at pay claims. Why not extend it to cover the hiving-off of nationalised concerns, the question of workers' representation in all levels of negotiations and decision-making in public enterprise, etc? The resolution on re-nationalisation without compensation at the 1971 Labour Party Conference was moved and seconded by the Railwaymen's and Mineworkers' unions respectively – both unions representing members working in publicly owned enterprises, and both standing to lose by the policy of the Tories towards nationalisation. The resolution was plain enongh:

'This Conference opposes and strongly condemns the hiving-off by the Government of parts of the public sector and declares that Labour Party policy towards any assets denationalised is complete renationalisation without compensation, immediately upon the return of the next Labour Government.'

But how much it would be strengthened by the united voices of six million workers in nationalised concerns, supported by their united action! The united demands and action of six million workers could have far-reaching effects, especially if equally strong action were continued during the period of a Labour Government, and not simply as a last resort under the Tories.

CENTRAL AND LOCAL GOVERNMENT CONTROL

A Tory Government looks after Big Business. The present Tory Government has 168 MPs, who share 531 directorships in

E

business. They certainly look after their class interests. (The Tory Party 1970 Election Policy statement was called 'A Better Tomorrow'; from the workers' point of view. 'A Bitter Tomorrow' would have been a more apt choice of title!)

It's time a Labour Government looked after the interests of the working class only.

Parliamentary by-elections and local government elections in 1971 prove that the Tory Government has lost the support of the majority of the electorate, and 1972 results reinforce this. They have been given notice to quit. The Labour Party made a total of 2,804 gains in the 1971 local elections in England, Wales and Scotland, and a further 1,053 in 1972. Labour has control of a considerable number of the boroughs and district councils in the country.

Here and now is the opportunity for Labour to introduce measures for workers' control in municipal affairs, in the many aspects of local government in which the principle of workers' control can operate.

First, of course, there are the local Labour councillors, who are themselves working-class men and women. The people have given them power to control. We should not allow the local government chief officers to exert so much influence on committees that they virtually control the council.

Labour councillors become the employers of a considerable number of local government workers – 20,000 or more in some areas. Why should councillors not share the power with those who do the work in local government services – for example, teachers, transport and building trade workers, engineers, clerical and administrative workers? Why not give them representation on sub-committees? Why not joint committees of councillors and workers to manage the various departments and activities of the council?

Local councils can take control over many local industries and services, and bring about municipalisation with workers' control.

Why not do what we Coventry councillors pressed the Tory Minister of the time for permission to do – set up a municipal dairy to supply all the local authority's needs, and thereby cut out some of the profiteers?

The Government controls milk through the Milk Marketing Board. They could supply local authorities in bulk. There are some comparatively cheap machines for packaging milk, and it is easy to distribute in waxed cartons. Milk could then be supplied to both young and old.

Instead, the Tories have stopped the supply of free milk to schoolchildren, and arguments are proceeding about whether it is 'legal' to levy a local rate so that children can continue to receive milk at school. Merthyr Tydfil was the first council to defy the Government on this issue, and many other councils have followed suit, including all the Labour-controlled London Boroughs.

The *Morning Star* wrote on this issue in an editorial:

'So determined, however, are the Tories to prevent any child over seven getting even a teaspoonful of free milk that their Bill will make it illegal for local authorities to supply it out of the rates.

Thus individual councillors could be charged with the cost, and sent to jail if they refused to pay . . .'

'Legal advice' insists that it is against the law to supply free milk to schoolchildren. But when the law is against the majority of the people, it is our duty to refuse to accept that law, and to actively oppose it. What is important? The law or the health of children?

Here is a clear case where workers' control can operate at a local level, to benefit society.

Why not, as we did in Coventry, breed your own cattle, on your own municipally owned farm, take the cattle to your own abattoir, build your own butchery, and distribute the meat directly to all your institutions and schools? Meat 'from the Grass to the Class'. With the private profit margins cut out. The workers on the job will show you how to do it.

Local transport and fares are a continual problem for local councils. Tories on the Greater London Council have decided to charge full fares for schoolchildren, and arrangements are proposed whereby private companies, and even private cars, will be encouraged to supplement poor rural bus-services, at an economic price no doubt. Why not do the most sensible and economical thing – run a free transport service?

If there is any loss, or any subsidy needed, under the present system, the local ratepayers have to find it. So why not run the whole undertaking on the rates? It would be cheaper and more efficient in the end for both bus-users and ratepayers. Here again, the transport employees could help to control and organise such a municipal enterprise.

Why not take over complete control of all building for the council, and do all necessary building work by 'direct labour'? The workers on the job could help in such a scheme, and the ratepayers would not have to subsidise private profiteers.

Joint discussions held between the local unions, Trades Councils, and the delegates to the local Labour Party could produce many such schemes for taking control of the local industries and services, as a step towards complete national public ownership and Socialism.

Chapter 5

What Measure of Workers' Control Has Already Been Achieved?

Large streams from little fountains flow,
Tall oaks from little acorns grow.
David Everett: *Lines Written for a School Declamation*

The working class, since the time of the Tolpuddle Martyrs, has, through its struggles with both employers, Tory, Liberal and Labour Governments, developed and strengthened the trade unions and working-class political organisations. They have won the right to vote in local and national elections, and have won this right for women as well as for men, and reduced the voting age to eighteen years. They have also won some direct victories against capitalism: women and children no longer work in coal mines, children no longer work, eat and sleep in textile mills; boys no longer go up chimneys; governments have been compelled to introduce Factories Acts; trade unions have forced governments to recognise them, and are no longer illegal organisations; the anti-Combination Acts have been defeated; laws have been passed giving trade unionists certain rights to strike and picket, and the right for trade unions to function freely on behalf of their members; trade unions have forced agreements on employers about restriction of working hours, training, safety and holidays.

The struggles in the engineering industry over the years show clearly the opposition of the employers to the workers' efforts to win some control over their industrial life, and they also show the progress that has been made.

In 1851, the engineering employers locked out the members of the Amalgamated Society of Engineers. Whilst the main issue was wages, there was also a fight for shopfloor bargaining, which meant a certain amount of workers' control through the

(a) 'TERMS OF SETTLEMENT', 1898

GENERAL PRINCIPLE OF FREEDOM TO EMPLOYERS IN THE MANAGEMENT OF THEIR WORKS

The Federated Employers, while disavowing any intention of interfering with the proper functions of trade unions, will admit no interference with the management of their business and reserve to themselves the right to introduce into any Federated Workshop, at the option of the Employer concerned, any condition of labour under which any members of the Trade Unions here represented were working at the commencement of the dispute in any of the workshops of the Federated Employers.'

1. FREEDOM OF EMPLOYMENT

'Every workman shall be free to belong to a Trade Union or not as he may think fit.

(b) PROVISIONAL AGREEMENT OF 1901 REJECTED BY THE UNIONS

GENERAL PRINCIPLE OF FREEDOM OF MANAGEMENT

The Employers shall not interfere with the proper functions of the Trade Unions, and the Trade Unions shall not interfere with the Employers in the management of their business.

Employers shall have the right to introduce into any Federated Workshop, at the option of the Employer concerned any condition of labour under which members of the Trade Unions were working prior to the date of this agreement in any of the workshops of the Federated Employers.

FREEDOM OF EMPLOYMENT

Every workman may belong to a Trade Union or not as he may think fit. Every Employer may

(c) AGREEMENT OF 1 OCTOBER 1907

THE FEDERATION ON THE ONE HAND AND THE TRADE UNIONS ON THE OTHER, BEING CONVINCED THAT THE INTERESTS OF EACH WILL BE BEST SERVED, AND THE RIGHTS OF EACH BEST MAINTAINED BY A MUTUAL AGREEMENT, HEREBY, WITH A VIEW TO AVOID FRICTION AND STOPPAGE OF WORK, AGREE AS FOLLOWS:

1. GENERAL PRINCIPLES OF EMPLOYMENT

The Federated Employers shall not interfere with the proper functions of the Trade Unions, and the Trade Unions shall not interfere with the Employers in the management of their business.

2. EMPLOYMENT OF WORKMEN

Every Employer may belong to the Federation and every workman may belong to a Trade Union or not, as either of them may think fit.

'Every Employer shall be free to employ any man whether he belong or not to a trade union.

'Every workman who elects to work in a Federated workshop shall work peaceably and harmoniously with all fellow employees, whether he or they belong to a Trade Union or not. He shall also be free to leave such employment, but no collective action shall be taken until the matter has been dealt with under the provisions for avoiding disputes.

'The Federation do not advise their members to object to union workmen or give preference to non-union workmen.'

NOTE: The right of a man to join a Trade Union if he pleases involves the right of a man to abstain from joining a Trade Union if he pleases. This clause merely protects rights.

employ any man whether he belong or not to a Trade Union.

With the desire to secure peaceful and harmonious working in Federated Workshops, the Trade Unions will not permit on the part of their members any interference with non-union workmen, nor countenance any objection to working with them.

The Federation will not permit of difference of treatment between union and non-union workmen in the course of their work and will not countenance their members objecting to employ union workmen.

Every Employer may employ any man, and every workman may take employment with any Employer, whether the workman or the Employer belong or not to a Trade Union or to the Federation respectively.

The Trade Unions recommend all their members not to object to work with non-union workmen, and the Federation recommend all their members not to object to employ union workmen on the ground that they are members of a Trade Union.

Source: *Thirty Years of Industrial Conciliation.* Engineering & Allied Employers' National Federation.

medium of shop stewards, whose organisation began to develop at that time. The employers, in response to this development, put the following statement in *The Times* of 17 January 1852:

'With every respect for noble and distinguished referees whose arbitration has been tendered to us . . . we must take leave to say that *we* alone are the competent judges of our own business; that we are respectively the masters of our own establishments; and that it is our firm intention to remain so.'

The same struggle has been carried on over the years around the issue of what the employers call 'managerial functions', and this struggle is described in a book produced by the Engineering and Allied Employers' Federation, called *Thirty Years of Industrial Conciliation*. The book describes the dispute from July 1897 to January 1898, which involved seven hundred federated firms, and quotes a Board of Trade statement which illustrates that the real cause of the dispute, 'managerial functions', was masquerading as 'demands for an eight-hour day':

'Though the immediate cause of the general dispute was the demand for an eight-hour day in London, the real question at issue between the parties had become of a much more far-reaching kind, and now involved the questions of *workshop control* and the limits of *trade union interference.*'

The growing incidence of disputes of this kind led to a series of agreements between the employers and the unions, and the excerpts reproduced here from the 1898, 1901 and 1907 terms of settlement illustrate the improvements which were being made (from the workers' point of view) in industrial agreements at that time, and the growing – if unwilling – tolerance by the employers of trade union activities.

But while undoubted improvements were being made, 'managerial functions' disputes have continued, and such functions continue to be, say the Engineering Employers' Federation, 'a cardinal principle of the present industrial system'.

YORK MEMORANDUM AND THE ALTERNATIVE

Following the gains made by the workers at the turn of the century, the 1922 dispute – in which the employers locked out all members of engineering trade unions, resulted in the unions being forced to accept the 1922 Procedure for Avoidance of Disputes – the York Memorandum.

This procedure for manual workers stated among its principles of 'managerial function' that

(a) The Employers have the right to manage their establishments and the trade unions have the right to exercise their functions.

(b) In the process of evolution, provision for changes in shop conditions is necessary but it is not the intention to create any specially-favoured class of workpeople.

(c) The Employers and the Trade Union, without departing in any way from the principles embodied in Clause (a) above, emphasise the value of consultation, not only in the successful operation of the Procedure set out in Section 11 but in the initial avoidance of disputes.

The Memorandum then sets out the procedure shown over leaf. Trade unionists in the engineering industry have been negotiating with the Engineering Employers' Federation since 2 April 1969 for a more satisfactory procedure agreement to replace the infamous York Memorandum which was forced upon them by the 1922 lock-out. For over two years, talks have gone on without settlement.

Opening the discussion in 1969, Mr Martin Jukes, Director-General of the Employers' Federation, said:

'We do this against a background of considerable criticism of our present arrangements. Quite apart from the unsolicited advice of the ill-informed (which we can ignore) we have in recent months been taken to task by the Donovan Commission, by the National Board for Prices and Incomes, and by the Government in its White Paper "In Place of Strife".'

He went on to say that the present procedure is sometimes criticised in that 'because the employer claims "managerial functions", acts of management are carried out without prior negotiation and thus lead to disputes which could be avoided if the status quo principle were observed'.

He further stated that the Federation was 'not prepared to

Until these stages of procedure have been carried out
there shall be no stoppage of a partial or general character

FUNCTIONS AND PROCEDURE

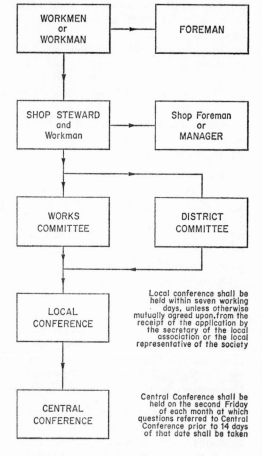

(a) A worker or workers desiring to raise any question in which they are directly concerned shall in the first instance discuss the same with their foreman

(b) Failing settlement, the question shall be taken up with the shop manager and/or head shop foreman by the appropriate Shop Steward and one of the workers directly concerned

(c) If no settlement is arrived at the question may, at the request of either party, be further considered at a meeting of the Works Committee. At this meeting the Divisional Organiser may be present, in which event a representative of the Employers' Association shall also be present

In the event of either party desiring to raise any question a local conference for this purpose may be arranged by application to the secretary of the local association or to the local representative of the society

Failing settlement at a local conference of any question brought before it, it shall be competent for either party to refer the matter to a Central Conference, which, if thought desirable, may make a joint recommendation to the constituent bodies

WORKMEN or WORKMAN → FOREMAN

SHOP STEWARD and Workman → Shop Foreman or MANAGER

WORKS COMMITTEE — DISTRICT COMMITTEE

LOCAL CONFERENCE

Local conference shall be held within seven working days, unless otherwise mutually agreed upon, from the receipt of the application by the secretary of the local association or the local representative of the society

CENTRAL CONFERENCE

Central Conference shall be held on the second Friday of each month at which questions referred to Central Conference prior to 14 days of that date shall be taken say that there is no room for change', and, referring to the provisions regarding the appointment and functions of shop stewards, submitted the following proposals on behalf of the employers:

'1. There should be basic age and service qualifications for shop stewards.
2. Employers should provide mutually acceptable balloting facilities for the election of shop stewards where this is required or requested by the workpeople.
3. Provision should be allowed, by arrangement with the employer and unions concerned, for a shop steward to represent all the workpeople in his shop or department regardless of the union or unions to which these workpeople might belong.
4. Provision should be made, by agreement between the employer and shop stewards, for the recognition of a chief shop steward from each principal union in the factory, or for the appointment of a chief shop steward representative of all the unions in the factory. This would again be subject to a service qualification.'

(The employers, in their magnanimity, make proposals for the appointment and functions of shop stewards; when will the unions be permitted – or take the right – to determine the appointment and functions of management?)

Also included in the employers' case are suggestions for the setting up of works' councils:

'If, as we have suggested, there is to be, in the larger establishments, a negotiating body comprising representatives of management and shop stewards, it would be necessary to lay down principles as to how the shop stewards should be appointed to the negotiating body. Let us call it, for the moment, the works council.

One possible approach would be that each factory would be divided into a number of "constituencies", and that from each "constituency" the shop stewards would have the right to appoint one of their number as a member of the works council. Any individual or departmental claims which had not been settled either by discussions between lower management and the individuals concerned or by higher echelons of management and the shop steward concerned, would have to be processed through the "constituency" steward before such an issue could be competently referred for consideration at the final stage of the domestic procedure, namely the works council.'

(The employers reserve the right to specify the method of election of shop stewards to the works council, but no mention is made of the appointment of management representatives. Presumably their appointment is no business of the trade unions.)

On the question of payment to shop stewards, the employers said:

'You have from time to time raised with us the question of shop stewards being paid for time spent in carrying out their duties as shop stewards. We have hitherto resisted this concession and one of the considerations we have had in mind is the unordered way in which much domestic negotiation is carried out. Provided we could agree with you a more orderly basis of shop stewards' representation, and provided we could agree principles with you regarding a more orderly method of discussing factory problems, we would then be much more agreeable to discussing and agreeing with you some provision for an appropriate payment to shop stewards when engaged in meetings with management in ordinary working hours.'

In summary, the employers' proposals for replacing the York Memorandum were:

'(a) A national industrial relations council for the engineering industry should be established.
(b) There should be established agreed principles for subsequent incorporation through factory negotiations, in all domestic procedure agreements. These procedure agreements would include a provision that, for factories of a specified size, the final stage of domestic discussion should be through the medium of a works council comprising senior representatives of management and shop stewards. All grievances and claims would have to be processed through this council before the external stages of the procedure could be invoked.

(c) There should be agreed provisions relating to the qualifications, appointment and functions of shop stewards, including provision for (a) the recognition, by mutual agreement, of chief shop stewards and (b) the election of shop stewards to works councils on a "constituency" or other mutually agreed basis.

(d) Arrangements should be made under which, subject to a limited provision for discussions at executive level, domestic wage claims would not be eligible for reference beyond the stage of local conference.

(e) Provision should be made for works conferences to be held within seven working days of receipt of application, unless otherwise mutually agreed.

(f) A review of the procedure adopted for considering questions in central conference should be carried out with a view to deciding whether any changes are required.'

(See Appendix C).

BREAKDOWN—STATUS QUO

Speaking to the National Committee of the AUEW (Engineering Section) on 19 April 1971, Brother Hugh Scanlon, President, reported that

'we have a basic agreement for a shortened procedure, for legal non-enforceability, for the role of works committees, and for the establishment of a National Council. All these things, in principle, have been agreed, but not necessarily however, the phraseology attached to them. As usual, the overall problem is the issue of *status quo* . . .'

The employers have said that their interpretation of *status quo* is stated clearly in the following clause:

'Where an employer seeks to change –

(a) an existing system of wage payment or a condition of employment, which is either agreed or is customarily applicable to employees in an establishment or part thereof, or

(b) an individual workers' conditions of employment (unless the change required is in accordance with agreed or established practice in the establishment or part thereof) the existing term or condition shall be maintained until agreement has been reached or the procedure laid down . . . has been exhausted.

Nothing in the foregoing shall require management to invoke the procedure when carrying out its responsibilities within the framework of agreed or established conditions. In such circumstances the decisions of management shall be implemented immediately without prejudice to the right of the workpeople concerned to raise such issues in the procedure thereafter.'

This, say the employers, 'does not seem to be so very different' from the draft proposal put forward by the unions:

'It is accepted by the trade unions that managements have the right to manage and to expect all normal management decisions concerning the efficient operation of the establishment to be implemented by the workers immediately, except that any decisions which alter the established wages, working conditions, practices, manning, dismissals (except for gross industrial misconduct), or redundancy, to which the workpeople concerned object, shall not be implemented until the Local Conference procedure has been exhausted.'

Speaking on behalf of the engineering unions, Bro. Scanlon said that the *status quo* position throughout its existence has envisaged that the act of management will prevail through the whole of the operation of the Agreement, and that the workers must carry out the act of management while discussions are taking place.

Any future procedure agreement, he said,

'must fundamentally change the real issues which are the cause of the present dispute. That is, the length of time, and the fact that *at all stages we are the appellants and you sit in judgement.* We are trying to envisage an agreement which will be short and effective, and which will place in the position of being the appellant that party which desires the change.'

The employers' proposals do not, he told the AUEW National Committee, alter the present position:

'There is no fundamental change and, therefore, the Joint Working Party and the Confederation Executive Council have come to the conclusion that, in their present form, the employers' proposals on "status quo" do not constitute a basis for continued negotiation.'

These few pages represent a very much shortened account of the negotiations to date – more than two years of argument. The old York Memorandum, however, is nearly half a century old, and the infamous provisions which it forced upon unions during a lock-out are a surviving reminder that our rights, once lost, are difficult to regain.

SHOP STEWARDS—REAL WORKERS' CONTROL

One part of the struggle for workers' control which has been fought for over a hundred years and is not yet completely won, is the struggle over the recognition of, and provision of facilities for, shop stewards.

Shop stewards came into existence in the engineering industry around the 1850s in the most militant areas. They were the early industrial commandos who organised the non-trade unionists into the unions and encouraged the members of unions to keep up their membership. In the Amalgamated Society of Engineers, the shop stewards took over the role of showing up the members' grievances, and trying to negotiate with the employers about them. They wanted some say in the control of the workers' lives in industry.

This the employers refused to concede. The early struggles of the shop steward with the employer were on the improvement of wages and conditions; there was also the fight for the recognition of shop stewards. There were many strikes, and other industrial action was taken in order to force recognition, with the support of the district committees of the Union.

It was not until 1917 that the employers were forced to agree to the recognition of shop stewards and their official rights to negotiate on the job on behalf of members of the union. The issue was brought to a head in November 1917, when the firm of White and Poppes of Coventry refused to recognise the right of shop stewards to negotiate with them in a dispute with their toolmakers. Coventry had one of the strongest shop stewards' movements in the country, and they brought out 50,000 workers. The united strength of the workers and the war situation with Germany compelled the Government and the employers to concede recognition to the first real representatives of workers' control, and finally in 1919 an official agreement was signed regarding shop stewards.

The employers came back on the attack during the economic depression of the 1920s and wiped out the shop stewards' organisation in many places. Workers risked their livelihood by continuing to act as shop stewards, and had to hold the trade union organisation together under cover. It was during that period that the York Memorandum was imposed, but in spite of that, the shop stewards still remained the directly elected democratic representatives of workers on the job.

Throughout the years, the number of shop stewards has increased, and today there are over 200,000 in various industries. There has been and still is a continuous fight by rank and file members and shop stewards to obtain stewards' recognition and rights to represent the members: the fight to establish shop stewards' committees in factories, and the recognition of convenors of shop stewards; the right to represent women workers, youths and apprentices, the growth of women shop stewards and youth shop stewards – all these things have been won by hard struggle on the part of the workers.

With the spread of big firms all over the country, shop stewards have fought for the right to establish joint shop stewards' combine committees, which bring together the shop stewards of one company from all parts of the country, and representing different unions, in order to establish and exercise some measure of control over the company's operations. This has been done in spite of the opposition of employers and the national trade union leadership. Recently, the National Committee of the AEU gave encouragement to the formation of Shop Stewards' Combine Committees.

Shop stewards still bear the brunt of attacks by employers. They continue to be attacked and victimised in many ways. (I speak from personal experience as a shop steward on twenty-five different jobs, in as many years, never having left a job voluntarily in my life.) Shop stewards do need protection both by the membership and by the official trade union organisation. The shop stewards are the most trade-union-conscious and vigilant members of their union, democratically elected, and in constant touch with, and responsive to, those who elected them.

There is an irreconcilable conflict between workers and management, on wages versus profit. Shop stewards exist to protect the workers. Management exists to defend and extend the profits of employers.

So the capitalist press and right-wing labour leaders try to blame shop stewards for the deficiencies in industry. When workers are compelled to strike against the actions of employers, shop stewards are accused of promoting industrial strife and creating great losses in production. The real loss in production arises largely from the operation of private enterprise and capitalist economic anarchy, as these figures show:

In 1970:

Production lost through *unemployment*	= 200 million days
	= £800,000,000
Production lost through *sickness*	= 300 million days
	= £1,100,000,000
Production lost through *accidents*	= 24 million days
	= £300,000,000
Production lost through *strikes*	= 10 million days
	= £40,000,000

It is clear that if the Government were really concerned about loss of production, they would first tackle the problems of unemployment, industrial injuries and sickness. Instead of which they batten on to the 'unpatriotic anarchy' of the workers' struggle, which is personified in the form of the shop steward!

The strike record is more important to the Government and to the employers because of the strikes which *don't* happen, rather than the ones that *do*. The reason for this is that the threat of a strike can always be used by workers in their struggle with the employers, as an ultimate sanction in the event of not being satisfied in their demands. So the strike is an important weapon, even when it is not used, and the shop steward is 'dangerous' because he is a representative of the workers' organised strength, which makes such a threat possible.

F

FOR EVERY 11½d LOST THROUGH STRIKES

19/10½d IS LOST THROUGH ACCIDENTS & ILLNESS

BRITISH SAFETY COUNCIL, 163/173 PRAED STREET, LONDON W2 SF.452

Reproduced by permission of the British Safety Council

The shop stewards' right to function freely is therefore closely linked with workers' control. There are continual attempts by the Government and employers to bring shop stewards more and more under the control of the establishment, to integrate them into management's functions, and to use them to discipline the working class. The workers' control movement must fight within the unions to see that they do not succeed in turning shop stewards into eunuchs. Shop stewards must fight for the right to function fully as the shopfloor representatives of the union members, and facilities must be provided for them to do this adequately.

DEMANDS FOR MORE SHOP STEWARDS' CONTROL

The TUC recently prepared a report on shop stewards' facilities which was intended for the CIR. After the decision on 18 March 1971 not to co-operate with any body connected with anti-union legislation, the TUC published their report independently. They stated that the minimum facilities for shop stewards should be:

1. Right to contact all employees, especially newcomers, collect subscriptions, and receive notice from management of all new employees hired.
2. Right to distribute union literature.
3. Right to negotiate over work rules, individual and group grievances, bonus schemes, shift work, manning, work load, overtime, safety, grade structures, lay-offs, redundancy, all aspects of work-study and job evaluation, and the interpretation of agreements including national agreements.
4. A desk, telephone and filing cabinet, and a room to interview members.
5. Time off at full pay to attend union conferences and training courses.
6. Union notice boards and use of internal post system.
7. Right to consult with other shop stewards in working hours without loss of earnings.
8. Right to conduct shop steward elections during working hours without loss of earnings.

9. Right of trade unions to jointly supervise management's shop stewards' training courses and other training which might affect industrial relations.

10. Right to hold meetings with members on the job without loss of pay.

11. Use of firm's clerical, typing, duplicating and photocopying facilities.

While being in broad agreement with most of these proposals, it is important to reject the principles involved in two of the points.

Number 5 calls for 'time off *at full pay* to attend union conferences and training courses'. It is quite correct that the employer should make up a shop steward's loss of earnings while he is carrying out his job as a shop steward on the shop-floor (points 8 and 10 cover this). However, the employer should have no say, financial or otherwise, in the unions' provisions for the training of shop stewards. This is, and must continue to be, an entirely independent issue, and the union must be responsible for the training, and the expense involved in training, its own shop stewards.

Point number 9 is linked with this: the TUC, in claiming the right for trade unions to 'jointly supervise management's shop stewards' training courses', is conceding that employers should have a say in how shop stewards' training is carried out, and what education is given to them. This is completely wrong. Shop stewards are employed not because they are shop stewards, but because they produce goods for the employer to sell; a shop stewards' responsibility is to the union members he represents, and his stewardship and training are the responsibility of his union, not of his employer.

When managements volunteer to 'train' their shop stewards, the red warning light should go on immediately!

Barbara Castle, when Minister of Employment and Productivity, instructed the Commission on Industrial Relations to investigate shop stewards' facilities, and it was this investigation which prompted the TUC Report. A sixty-page report was subsequently presented to Parliament by the CIR, dealing with 'Facilities Afforded to Shop Stewards'. This shows a wide gap between different places of work in the amount of control already won by shop stewards on the job. An indication of the progress already made by shop stewards is shown by the CIR's recommendations. Some of the most important ones are:

'Paragraph 110: We recommend:

(a) As a general principle the shop steward should be given leave from the job to perform his agreed functions. This requires prior agreement on the role of the shop steward at the establishment.

(b) Permission to leave the job should be sought from the appropriate management representative. Such permission should not unreasonably be refused.

Recommendation 129:

(a) The TUC should draw up a guide on election arrangements with regard to such matters as voting by the work group, selecton by ballot, defined periods of office, qualifications for candidates and methods of nomination for candidates.

(b) Trade unions should review their existing election and appointment arrangements, and give a clear indication of these procedures in their rule-books.

(c) Trade unions should ensure that their membership at the workplace is aware of the unions' procedures for the election of stewards.

(d) Managements should be prepared to provide and unions to accept where appropriate the following facilities:

  (i) elections for stewards to be conducted in works time;

  (ii) provisions of ballot boxes, forms and allied typing services, use of notice boards for nominations and election results;

  (iii) provision of polling areas within the factory/office area.

Recommendation 141:

(a) Management and trade unions should seek agreements on constituencies for an establishment and on the appropriate number of stewards, including senior stewards and convenors and deputies where necessary.

(b) Trade unions should notify management or the appropriate employers' association, in writing, of all stewards' appointments and resignations, within the shortest possible period of time.

(*c*) Each steward should receive a written credential from his union setting out his union rights and obligations.

(*d*) Managements and unions should seek agreement on the issue of joint credentials. These should be in a written form and state the rights and obligations of both management and steward arising out of the appropriate establishment, company or industry-wide agreements.

Recommendation 146:

(*a*) Trade unions should be given, as part of the procedure arrangements of the establishment, facilities to collect dues in works time.

(*b*) Managements and unions should where possible encourage the deduction of dues from the payroll.

(*c*) Stewards should be provided with lists of new entrants in an establishment and should be given facilities to talk to them as part of the company's induction process.

Recommendation 155:

(*a*) Management should make accommodation available for meetings of stewards with other stewards, with constituents, and with full-time officials. Prior agreement should determine the types of meeting to be allowed during works time and on works premises, and the accommodation which should be provided.

(*b*) Management should make every effort to provide appropriate office accommodation where the size of the establishment and volume of the stewards' work justifies it. In the majority of cases the provision of this facility will be limited to senior stewards and convenors in larger establishments.

(*c*) There should be access where appropriate to both external and internal telephones, and due regard given to the need for privacy.

(*d*) Notice boards should be made available. We consider that the best way of doing this is to set aside one or more notice boards specifically for union use within the terms of a jointly agreed policy.

(*e*) Typing and duplicating facilities should be provided, where the need has been established. In the case of the senior steward and convenor in larger establishments this is likely to be a necessity.

(*f*) The steward should be given storage facilities, where appropriate, for various documents which need to be kept private.

Recommendation 161:

(*a*) Management and Unions should individually and jointly review the type of training considered most appropriate for the steward's needs.

(*b*) The steward should be given leave from the job, with compensation for loss of earnings, when attending acceptable training courses.'

(Recommendation 161 (*a*) and (*b*) I would reject on the same grounds that I mentioned earlier: that *the unions alone* must be responsible for shop stewards' training.)

MORE POWER FOR SHOP STEWARDS

Some time before the publication of the CIR proposals, I had publicly advocated the following demands which, if implemented, would give shop stewards far greater rights than either the CIR or the TUC recommendations:

1. Election of shop stewards to be the prerogative of the trade unions, with no interference whatsoever from the employer.
2. The employer to provide all necessary facilities for the election of shop stewards.
3. The shop stewards to represent all workpeople in the department.
4. Recognition of convenors.
5. Facilities for convenors: office, office services, telephone, duplicating machinery, etc.
6. Payment by management to shop stewards for all time lost on trade union business within the company.
7. The right of trade unions to choose their own side when discussions are taking place at plant level.
8. The setting-up of shop stewards' committees.
9. Facilities for reporting-back by delegates the proceedings of any discussions concerning the plant.
10. The setting-up of safety committees, with facilities for the election of trade union representatives on to such committees.
11. Shop stewards' representation on apprentice committees.

12. Facilities for shop stewards to interview all employees prior to engagement.

13. No worker to be dismissed without his shop steward being consulted.

14. No shop steward to be dismissed or suspended without discussion with the trade union.

15. The *status quo* to apply while a dispute is going through procedure.

16. The right of shop stewards to examine all books and records of the firm and to be given all information about the company.

But these rights must be fought for within the factories. The 200,000 shop stewards and workers' representatives on the job in British industries have enough strength to win adequate facilities to function in their place of work, and to progress towards real industrial democracy and workers' control in the everyday life of the workers.

Neither the Government nor the employers will introduce these recommendations of their own free will; they will have to be fought for on the shopfloor.

EMPLOYERS BREAK AGREEMENT!

It is not only necessary to fight for new victories on the shopfloor, but also to retain and if possible to extend those already won. An attack is at present being made against the wages of all engineering workers in the motor industry, particularly in Coventry, which has the highest rates for engineering workers in the country. This attack is centred on the Coventry Toolroom Agreement, which affects about 2,000 key toolmakers and in addition about 10,000 other skilled workers, such as experimental workers, machine tool workers and electricians, whose wages are also based on the district average for the toolmakers.

The Agreement came into existence in 1941. Previously, toolmakers' wages were based on a national agreement, reached in 1940, which was made in order to get the toolmakers producing the tools required for the war effort, because many had left the toolrooms (where they were paid on low day-rates) to work on piece-work production, where the wages were much higher. Under the national agreement of 1940, the toolmakers' rate in any given factory was the average of the skilled production workers' wages in that particular factory. But in the Coventry district, the centre of the arms industry, the national agreement did not solve the problem. because a number of workers, both on production and in the toolrooms, were already getting much higher wages than some other factories in the district. Therefore the tendency was for toolmakers to gravitate towards the plants where the production earnings were highest.

As a result of meetings and threats of strike action, three toolmakers from the Coventry District Committee, of whom I was one, were mandated to meet the Executive Council of the AEU in London, with authority to say that the Coventry District Committee would declare a strike of all members in the district unless the Executive Council agreed to amend the national agreement, so that Coventry could have its own local agreement. For the first time, to my knowledge, the Executive Council agreed to meet the delegates on equal terms, in the Council Chamber, and also agreed to the negotiation of a district agreement.

The Coventry Toolroom Agreement was based on the weighted average of the skilled production workers' earnings in twenty-two firms in the area, and started at 3s 1d an hour in 1941. Thirty years later, the district average now stands at about £1 an hour.

These rates are provided monthly by the employers themselves, on the basis of their own calculations of the average wage of skilled production workers; the Coventry toolmakers' district average has therefore become a barometer for all workers in the engineering industry in their demand for parity of earnings.

For this reason, with encouragement from the Tory Government, Coventry engineering employers decided to scrap the Agreement. This is a prelude to an attack on the rest of the skilled workers in the car industry, and ultimately on the standard of living of all workers in the engineering industry, on the principle of 'divide and conquer'. Not only would many workers' wages be reduced, if the Agreement were scrapped, but also the present unity between workers in different plants would be lost.

The fight then is not only for the retention of the Toolroom Agreement, which has proved to be of considerable value over the years, but ultimately for the maintenance of production workers' wages throughout the country. It must be seen in that light by the hundred thousand workers in the engineering industry in Coventry, and they must stand united with the toolmakers in their fight to retain the district toolroom agreement. At mass meetings, workers showed overwhelming support for the ban on overtime and the one-day strikes held to demonstrate the general dissatisfaction with this unilateral act on the part of the employers, but because of the engineers' divided struggle, the employers succeeded in ending the Coventry Toolroom Agreement.

The new procedure agreement to replace the York Memorandum, and the struggle for more rights for shop stewards, are indicative of the action being taken to extend the control the workers have over their own jobs. But while we are busy looking ahead to new forms of control, we must not allow the employers to attack us in the rear, and steal the gains we have already made, as they are attempting to do with the Coventry Toolroom Agreement.

SHOP STEWARDS—PROTECTORS OR TROUBLEMAKERS?

The part played by shop stewards in assisting workers to protect wages and conditions, as well as in improving them, has led the national press, radio and television to do what they can to make the words 'shop steward' into dirty words: shop stewards have been labelled wild-cat strikers, werewolves, and 'irresponsible unofficial troublemakers'.

The AEU Executive Council, in its written evidence to the Donovan Commission, however, made the following points:

'We do not feel that there is any need for us to defend the existence of shop stewards. Indeed, we believe that, "If they were not in existence then we would have to invent them."
The functions of the shop steward, as formally laid down in the Shop Stewards' Manual of the AEU are (1) securing and

maintaining strong Union membership and (2) maintenance of the best possible wages and working conditions of their members. But of course in practice the scope of shop stewards' activities are as varied as those of any other group of people whose role is that of dealing with human problems . . .

It is our experience that employers generally get the type of shop steward their outlook reflects: a moderate employer will get moderate shop stewards and the hard employer will get hard shop stewards. In fact, shop stewards will be belligerent or co-operative in proportion to the respect and conditions under which they operate.'

The Donovan Report picks up these points in its account of the role of shop stewards in industry. Paragraph 98 states that:

'Without shop stewards, trade unions would lack for members, for money, and for means of keeping in touch with their members. Even so none of them is the most important of the British shop steward's tasks. That is the service which he performs by helping to regulate workers' pay and working conditions and by representing them in dealings with management.

99. Until a few years ago little was known for certain about this part of the steward's work, but several studies have now appeared and are summarised in our first research paper. Their findings have now been generally confirmed by the inquiry conducted for us by the Social Survey (Research Paper No. 10, W. E. J. McCarthy and S. R. Parker, *Shop Stewards and Workshop Relations*, HMSO 1968). First of all it must be emphasised that there is no uniformity. A minority of stewards do not negotiate with managers at all, whereas some of them negotiate over a wide range of issues. But over half of them regularly deal with managers over some aspect of pay, and about half of them deal regularly with some question relating to hours of work, the most common being the level and distribution of overtime. About a third of them regularly handle disciplinary issues on behalf of their members, and other matters which some of them settle include the distribution of work, the pace of work, the manning of machines, transfers from one job to another, the introduction of new machinery and new jobs, taking on new labour and redundancy. Since there are probably about 175,000

stewards in the country, compared with perhaps 3,000 full-time trade union officers, this suggests that shop stewards must be handling many times the volume of business conducted by their full-time officers.

100. From where does the shop steward derive his authority to deal with all these items? Where union rule books mention shop stewards, and many of them do not, they generally say something about the method of appointment, and the body to whom the steward is nominally responsible. They may mention the duties of recruiting and retaining members, and collecting subscriptions. If the business of representing members is touched upon, little is said about it. Most major unions now have *Shop Stewards Handbooks*, which set out some of these tasks at greater length. But when it comes to telling the steward what issues he is competent to handle and how he should go about raising them, most handbooks refer the steward to the industry-wide agreement in force in his industry. These in their turn are rarely comprehensive.'

The Commission refers to the mistrust which shop stewards show towards consultative discussion with management, and their preference for proper negotiating machinery, which gives certain rights to him and the workers he represents. The Commission reported that:

'In dealing with pay or overtime or discipline the steward could be dealing with the application of industry-wide agreements, a responsibility mentioned in most of the handbooks. In fact this rarely happens, for two reasons. In the first place most industry-wide agreements on pay lay down minimum rates or minimum levels of piecework earnings which are very generally exceeded. In dealing with such issues, therefore, the steward must be concerned with obtaining or retaining a concession in excess of the terms in the agreement. In the second place most industry-wide agreements say nothing at all about many of the issues with which the steward deals, such as discipline, the pace of work, the introduction of new machinery and the distribution of overtime.

102. In dealing with this second class of issue, the steward might merely be entering into consultation at the discretion of manage-

ment on matters outside the industry-wide agreement but nevertheless of interest to the workers. However, case studies show
that this is not so. When a decision is reached it is regarded as
an agreement even though it may not be recorded. Managers
would not normally alter it without further negotiation, and if
they did sanctions might be applied. These are not the procedures of joint consultation. Joint consultation, moreover, has
never been as popular with shop stewards as with managers.
A wealth of evidence supports the conclusions reached by
Dr McCarthy that shop stewards regard "any committee on
which they serve which cannot reach decisions . . . as essentially an inferior or inadequate substitute for proper negotiating
machinery", and that joint consultative committees in the strict
sense "cannot survive the development of effective shop floor
organisation. Either they must change their character and
become essentially negotiating committees carrying out functions which are indistinguishable from the processes of shop
floor bargaining, or they are boycotted by shop stewards, and
as the influence of the latter grows, fall into disuse" (Research
Paper No. 1, W. E. J. McCarthy, *The Role of Shop Stewards
in Industrial Relations*, p. 33).
103. In any case there are many shop floor decisions on these
issues in which managers take no part at all. "Ceilings" on
piecework earnings and limits imposed by road haulage drivers
on the scheduling of their vehicles are examples of the regula-
tion of work by workers themselves. The distribution of overtime is another matter which may be left to the stewards.'

Paragraphs 104–106 refer to 'custom and practice' – these are
the *de facto* issues in which the workers frequently establish a
measure of workers' control. The shop steward

'could not of his own volition impose a limit on output or a
ban on non-unionists. This can only be done by decision of the
group of workers which he represents. "Custom and practice",
which settles so much in British industrial relations, consists of
the customs and practices observed by work groups. If workers
did not keep to them, the customs would cease to exist.
105. The work group does not derive its power from the union.
The printing chapel with its chapel father, the best-organised

of all work groups, existed before the printing unions, and was subsequently incorporated into their branch structure. Work groups can exert considerable control over their members even when there are no trade unions, or where unions refuse them recognition. Until recently there were no shop stewards in most British docks. Accordingly the "ganger" or "hatchboss" negotiated for the members of the gang in any dispute with management, although he was paid to be the gang's supervisor and all negotiations were supposed to be reserved for full-time officers. In coalmining "chargemen" performed the same service for facework gangs, although they too were supervisors.

106. Full employment would in any case have increased the influence of the work group, but British managers have augmented it by their preference for keeping many matters out of agreements, by the inadequacy of their methods of control over systems of payments, by their preference for informality and by their tolerance of custom and practice.'

SHOPFLOOR SPOKESMEN

So the work group exercises control over its shop steward, and, according to the Donovan Commission (paragraph 108), management generally prefers to deal with shop stewards in preference to full-time officers; 75 per cent of managers, when they have the choice, prefer to deal with shop stewards – and this, in my opinion, is because management realises where real power and control operates. The Commission declares that the managers' chief reason for the preference is 'the intimate knowledge of the circumstances of the case possessed by shop stewards, but this is as much a consequence of their preference as a cause of it'.

A further survey conducted by Dr McCarthy (Research Paper No. 1, W. E. J. McCarthy, *The Role of Shop Stewards in British Industrial Relations*, pp. 26–9), made a study of managers' reasons for preferring 'informal and unwritten arrangements', and the Donovan Report quotes the four reasons given, in paragraph 108:

'If agreements were formalised they would become established *de jure* rights which could not be withdrawn; even if existing

stewards would not abuse formal confirmation the next generation might, and managers like to believe that they can vary
privileges according to the response they get; once the process
of formalising began it would extend indefinitely; and finally,
"some *de facto* concessions could not be written down because
management, particularly at board level, would not be prepared
to admit publicly that they had been forced to accept such
modifications in their managerial prerogatives and formal chains
of command". The more concessions are made the stronger
become all these reasons for preferring informality.

109. It does not follow however that shop stewards and work
groups exercise effective control where industry-wide agreements and managers fail to do so. In systems of payment by
results with no effective work study, each man may settle his
own times with the rate-fixer, and this may lead to a wide spread
of earnings with an uncontrolled upward drift. In other instances,
the control of shop stewards over the distribution of overtime
may be undermined by workers "greedy" for overtime earnings.
In such circumstances industrial relations can border on anarchy.

110. Consequently it is often wide of the mark to describe shop
stewards as "trouble makers". Trouble is thrust upon them.'

How true this is! Trouble is forced upon shop stewards
because they have to directly represent the demands of the
workers. Failing this, the workers will take steps to replace
them as their representatives. This is workers' control in action.

The 200,000 shop stewards themselves are the best example
of the growth of workers' control in Britain, and this example
is being copied by trade unionists in other countries.

Chapter 6

Attacks on Workers' Control Through the Use of Law

Laws grind the poor, and rich men rule the law.
Oliver Goldsmith

The working class have for centuries struggled to achieve some control over their conditions of life at work. The struggles of workers have taken on various forms dependent upon the development of tools and techniques used by them in their efforts to gain mastery over the rest of nature. One of their forms of struggle has been the organisation of workers into trade unions.

Trade unions have not always existed, in spite of the example of the Hebrew brickmakers' revolt in 1490 BC, against being forced by the Egyptians to make bricks without straw. The Webbs, in their classic book on the history of trade unions (*The Origins of Trade Unionism*: Sidney and Beatrice Webb), chart the development of workers' organisations in this country from the earliest available records. They say:

'It is clear that there were at times, alongside of the independent master craftsmen, a number of hired journeymen and labourers, who are known to have occasionally combined against their rulers and governors. These combinations are stated to have lasted several months and even for years. As early as 1383 we find the Corporation of the City of London prohibiting all "congregations, covins, and conspiracies of workmen".'

So we find the law being used, even in these early days, against developing workers' organisations. The Webbs refer to another incident two centuries later:

'In 1538 the Bishop of Ely reports to Cromwell that twenty-one journeymen shoemakers of Wisbech have assembled on a hill without the town, and sent three of their number to summon all the master shoemakers to meet them, in order to insist upon an advance in their wages, threatening that "there shall none come into the town to serve for that wages within a twelve month and a day, but we woll have an harme or a legge of hym, except they woll take an othe as we have doon".'

The law was used in 1563 to control wages by means of justices of the peace.

Acts were passed in the seventeenth and eighteenth centuries against combinations of workmen as restraints upon trade.

Forces of the State, i.e. *troops and police* have been used against the efforts of trade unions to develop their strength – for example, in the Peterloo massacre of 1819, and the South Wales miners' strike of 1911.

The *Law Courts* of the State have been used in attempts to crush or restrict the growth of workers' control through trade union organisation, as in the case of the Tolpuddle Martyrs, and also the £20,000 fine imposed on the Railwaymen's Union in 1903, known as the Taff Vale Judgement. The fine of £55,000 on the Transport & General Workers' Union in 1972 is another glaring example, as are the fines of £60,000 on AUEW.

Parliamentary power has been used on numerous occasions over the centuries, either to outlaw or cripple the unions, and to win back the control the workers had gained.

(For further details of these and similar events, see Appendix A.)

All the Acts of Parliament concerning trade unions and industrial relations have only been 'armistice agreements' at particular stages of the long battle by the workers for their emancipation from exploitation.

History shows that whenever the capitalist system is in crisis, the Government attempts to cut back the power of the trade unions. The power of the workers to exercise any control over industrial activities is attacked by Parliament and by employers.

G

THE LAW V. THE TRADE UNIONS

In the economic crisis which has been developing in the past few years in Britain, the Wilson Government acted against the trade unions in the same brutal way as the previous and present Tory Governments. The Wilson Government, with *In Place of Strife*, endeavoured to shackle the unions with legal restraints and penalties. The trade unions used their power within the Labour Party to force the Labour Government to withdraw their proposals. However, the present Tory Government has carried through its own plans to try and control industrial relations by force, through Parliament and the Law.

The Tory Industrial Relations Act is a bare-faced attempt to destroy whatever measure of workers' control has been won by the working class. Its undeclared intentions are:

1. To destroy the power of the shop steward.
2. To impose rigorous discipline on the workers.
3. To destroy the negotiating strength of those trade union officials who are willing to fight.
4. To break up trade union organisation.
5. To cripple the unions financially.
6. To fine and imprison those who do not accept the law. Then, having weakened the strength of the unions.
7. To attack the living standards of the working class in an attempt to solve their own economic problems.

They will impose redundancies on a greater scale and create a massive number of unemployed. They will continue to attack the social services and generally depress the lives of workers. These are the actions of the capitalist class in crisis.

We must either struggle or go down. There is no alternative. We must continue the fight against these anti-working-class measures, even though they are now made law. We shall suffer if we fight – but we shall suffer even more if we don't!

The will of the people is the highest law: this is a maxim which we must enforce.

During the period of the 1939–45 war, strikes were made illegal through Defence Regulations 1305 and 1AA, but in spite of these regulations, we took strike action in the engineering industry against the employers' attempts to worsen wages and conditions during that period. They could not afford to take legal action against so many thousands of striking workers, just as in the following case of coal miners who went on strike illegally. Sir Harold Emmerson GCB, KCVO, in his written evidence to the Donovan Commission, reported that 'The prosecution of 4,000 men seemed a tall order, but as the dispute had started with 1,000 underground workers we decided to concentrate on them.'

Thirty-five miners were fined £3 or one month's imprisonment, and nearly a thousand were fined £1 or fourteen days' imprisonment. Only nine miners paid their fines. The county jail could only accommodate a few at a time, and it would have taken years to work through the list, so the Court was advised not to enforce the unpaid fines.

We are now faced with the Industrial Relations Act, the operation of which could be made equally embarrassing to the Government. It is the most savage attack for a hundred years to curb and finally remove the workers' gains which have been made since 1872. Already, at every stage in its development, this legislation has been attacked by workers throughout the country.

WORKERS ACT TO "KILL THE BILL"

The Eighth Workers' Control Conference, held in October 1970 and attended by 1,300 delegates, issued a call supporting the demand that a one-day strike take place on 8 December 1970, and that the National Council of Labour and the TUC should organise a massive demonstration of trade unionists as a start to the fight against the Industrial Relations Bill. The Liaison Committee for the Defence of Trade Unions, at another rank and file conference in November 1970, attended by 1,800 delegates, urged an all-out response to their call for a general strike on 8 December, and that the 12 January TUC Rally at the Albert Hall should be converted into a massive day of protest, during working hours. Six thousand trade unionists at the TUC Rally witnessed the promise of Harold Wilson of unremitting opposition to the Industrial Relations Bill.

The TUC called for a national demonstration in Hyde Park on 21 February 1971, with a march to Trafalgar Square for a meeting to be addressed by members of the TUC General Council. 140,000 trade unionists came from all parts of Britain, representing millions of trade unionists in the country, and demanded strong action by the TUC and other trade union leaders to 'Kill the Bill'.

The policy conference of the AUEW on 4 February 1971 issued the following instruction to its 1,400,000 members:

'It has now been decided that all members, in whichever industry they work, shall cease work for their full normal shift following 6 a.m. on Monday 1 March 1971, and for their full normal shift following 6 a.m. on Thursday 18 March 1971.

This instruction included apprentices, staff members and foremen . . .

District Committees are, therefore, requested to ensure maximum unity with all unions, with a view to ensuring united opposition and demonstration against this Bill.

In addition, Executive Council are requesting that all full-time officials donate two days' pay to the funds of the Union.'

These decisions and the pressure of trade union representatives, e.g. Hugh Scanlon, Jack Jones, on the TUC General Council caused the General Council to stiffen its attitude to the Industrial Relations Bill and the Tory Government.

The decision of the EC of the Transport and General Workers' Union to press for industrial action through the TUC, and the encouragement to its members to support the strike on 18 March, raised the fight to a new level, but on the other hand, the national leadership of such unions as the General and Municipal Workers, the EETU/PTU, the Mineworkers, and certain others, had a retarding effect on their members by not supporting the industrial action. Nevertheless, the call by the AUEW for a one-day stoppage on 1 March resulted in over two million workers striking for the day.

The demonstration at which I spoke in Liverpool on 1 March was representative of all engineering trade unionists – 15,000 marched through the centre of Liverpool, including 10,000

Merseyside dockers who stopped work too, showing their traditional working-class militancy.

Throughout the length and breadth of Britain, meetings, marches and rallies of workers were held on that day. The local and national press, TV and radio, in loud-mouthed anti-trade union alliance, tried their damnedest to throw doubt and disruption on the growing unity of the workers in action, but they did not succeed. They are becoming discredited as real news agencies, and are being treated as organs of the Establishment, supporters of the Government and employers.

The refusal of the Tory national press to print an AUEW advertisement calling on its members to strike on 1 March, is an example of how 'free' the press is. (Compare this with the anti-strike advertisements, paid for by large companies, which appear in the press from time to time.) Despite mass media opposition, however, millions of trade unionists flexed their muscles. 1 March 1971 is a Red Letter Day in our history, indicating a growth in stature and understanding by the working class. Howls of rage and fear are expressed by the reactionary forces in the country against workers who are learning how to use their united strength in order to attain their aims and defend their trade union rights.

Prior to the second strike on 18 March, there were threats of closures, lock-outs and dismissals by employers, attempted intimidation of strikers through their wives, and moans from the employers about their estimated loss of £70 million in production (although they conveniently continue to overlook the thousands of millions of pounds lost in production due to over 900,000 unemployed!).

In spite of the Government's and employers' opposition to the preparation of the 18 March strike, the organisation was excellent. Approximately three million took strike action. This coincided with the Special TUC Congress in Croydon, where strikers lobbied trade union leaders and delegates and insisted on the whole of the trade union movement taking action to 'Kill the Bill'.

During the course of the battle against the Bill, the printing workers produced a leaflet, *Spies at Work*, which read as follows:

'1. A few years ago Complete Security Services Ltd circulated to employers the details of one of their services, which is produced below for the information of Trade Unionists.

From: Complete Security Services Ltd

Dear Sir,

Most business concerns, however scrupulously managed, lose an appreciable amount of money each year through pilferage. This pilferage takes the form, not only of petty larcenies from stock but also misuse and wastage of time by employees, mismanagement or laxity of discipline on workshop or stockroom floors, and falsely entered figures on time sheets and vehicle schedule sheets.

In some form or other, this is taking place in your Company at this moment. We specialise in preventing this unwarranted sharing of your profits. Our services include:

1. The supplying of undercover agents – a man planted among your employees to provide you with a complete appraisal of any unauthorised happenings.

2. The following of vehicles used by employees during the course of their work.

3. The investigating of thefts, frauds and embezzlement.

4. Reporting on any person who may be suspected of causing dissension or inciting employees to defection.

5. The screening of prospective employees – a search into their antecedents and background.

Our agents are carefully selected and thoroughly vetted and their methods of approach, discretion and loyalty are of the highest standard. Our consultant will be pleased to call to advise you, without obligation or cost, as to the most practical method of dealing with your particular problem.

Yours faithfully,
signed . . . L. DAVENPORT
Manager, Complete Security Services Ltd.

2. No wonder the Trade Union Movement thinks that the Industrial Relations Bill is a Charter for Spies, Narks and Blacklegs, because one of the Directors of Complete Security Services Ltd was no other than Mr L. Robert Carr.'

'MORE LITIGATION, LESS NEGOTIATION'

All the action taken against the Bill, however, did not succeed in smashing it, or in bringing down the Tory Government, impressive though that action was as a demonstration of the trade unionists' attitude to the proposed legislation. Now that the Bill has become law, the TUC says 'there can be no legal or moral obligation on the TUC or on the unions to do anything to facilitate the implementation of an Act to which they are fundamentally opposed, and to the repeal of which they are unconditionally committed'.

The TUC's demands to the unions are:

1. Don't register.
2. Don't sit on new courts.
3. Don't work with the CIR.
4. Don't use Agency shops.
5. Don't sign legal deals.

The 'legally enforceable agreements' referred to in the last of these TUC instructions is the subject of an article by Dr Paul O'Higgins, a Lecturer in Law at Christs's College, Cambridge. Dr O'Higgins, writing in the *Industrial Relations Review and Report*, discusses legally enforceable agreements from every angle – and in doing so, reveals the complexities which will lead to what the TUC describes as 'More litigation. less negotiation'. Dr O'Higgins writes:

'It is important to note that it is not provided that collective agreements shall be contracts. The method chosen of making agreements legally enforceable between the parties is to provide for a presumption that they are to be legally enforceable contracts. This would make sense if the real reason for all collective agreements not being contracts is that the parties tacitly intend them not to be contracts. But if this is not the case then Clause 34 will not have the effect of making all collective agreements into contracts.'

The article continues at some length in this vein, and it is not difficult to see how the operation of the Industrial Relations Act could become a lawyer's bonanza – if we allow it to do so.

But, as I have said before, 'The will of the people is the highest law', and if a majority of the people refuse to accept the law, it will not – cannot – operate.

UNIONS REJECT THE LAW

Not content with their attempts to crush the trade unions with the Industrial Relations Act, Carr and company are considering how the Monopolies Commission can be extended to include trade unions, so that unions can be summoned before the Commission, their size and structure examined, and instructions given to them to give up some of their members. The big unions like the AUEW and the T&GWU could be the first under attack. But the plan to use the Monopolies Commission against the organised workers will meet with the same determined opposition.

In an attempt to 'sugar the pill', the Government's *Code of Unfair Practices*, which is being based on the Conservative Party booklet *Fair Deal at Work*, will include many spurious contentions in an endeavour to persuade workers to accept the Industrial Relations Act, to which the Code is to be a supplement. Workers must not be fooled by these proposals nor by the *Code of Industrial Relations Practice*, put forward in June 1971 as a consultative document, by Robert Carr, 'Secretary of State for Unemployment'. Brother Vic Feather, General Secretary of the TUC, said that 'No trade unionist or progressive should have any truck with it. The code, like the Industrial Relations Bill it is intended to reinforce, should be totally rejected'.

The Code contains the principle of the 'employer's right to manage' (a stop to this workers' control danger!). There is also a demand for the trade unions to keep the shop stewards disciplined, and for the shop stewards to discipline the workers. The Code also advocates work measurement and job evaluation.

All attempts to sugar the pill, and to kid the working class that the Tories are only concerned for their good and do not really represent the employers' interests, have been tried before; the workers have had a hundred years of anti-trade union experience, and now that the unions are again threatened by the law, they must demand that the unions refuse to co-operate in any way with the legislation. The AUEW at its conference in June 1971 decided on behalf of its 1,400,000 members to refuse to register under the Industrial Relations Act. The Conference carried the following resolution, which, if its proposals were repeated throughout the trade union movement, could cripple the Act at the outset:

'This Conference records its implacable opposition to the pro-posed legislation on Industrial Relations, and any law which requires any agreements to be in the form of a legal contract. We instruct the NEC to use all the resources of our union to develop a mass campaign at district and national level, including if necessary strike action supported by the TUC to defeat this proposed legislation.

In the event of the proposals becoming law, we further instruct National Executive Council not to register this Union as required by the Act and to press through the TUC that all Trade Unions advise their members that they must in no way assist in carrying out the provisions of this Act and will initiate immediate industrial action in the event of any member being penalised as a result of this legislation.

All Trade Unions must pledge not to co-operate in Industrial Tribunals or any other Government sponsored body connected with the Act and to call upon the Parliamentary Labour Party to pledge that all anti-Trade Union legislation will be repealed upon the return of a Labour Government.'

The first President of the National Industrial Relations Court is Sir John Donaldson, a High Court Judge. Mr Justice Donaldson is little known in Labour law circles, but practised at the commercial bar. He was educated at Charterhouse and Cambridge, and was Chairman of the Federation of University Conservative Associations in 1940.

Will he be the first President to receive the concerted non-co-operation of the working class?

When a law is against the desires of the majority of the working class, that law is not operable. The law must receive the consent of the majority. Here is an area where workers' control must operate. Workers are not made to serve the law – the law must be made to serve the workers. The present Tory Government must be removed, with its industrial relations law, and a truly democratic one elected – a government representing the interests of the working class.

Chapter 7

International Monopolies –
International Workers' Control

The greater the power, the more dangerous the abuse.
Edmund Burke, 1771

The trade unions on an international scale are already deeply
involved with the problems arising from international finance,
international and multinational companies – problems which
arise from the worldwide merger boom, which is threatening the
lives of the world's working class, and causing untold misery
through the creation of massive unemployment in various parts
of the world.

Stan Newens, a left-wing Labour MP and a member of the
Institute for Workers' Control, introduced a resolution in the
House of Commons in 1969, in an effort to extend workers'
control over the economy, and to demand a legal code for
mergers:

'This House, deeply conscious of the rapidly accelerating trend
towards the formation of huge national and international companies as the result of mergers, takeovers and closures, with
the consequent concentration of enormous powers over employment, the location of industry, investment and other vital issues
of public concern in the hands of small minorities, sometimes
not even domiciled in this country, notes that this process presents a serious long-term threat to democratic government in so
far as the policies of elected authorities are increasingly undermined by decisions taken by those minorities who are not
responsible to the public; and considers that it is an urgent
necessity to provide a comprehensive code of conduct for takeovers as an interim measure to safeguard workers, consumers,
and the community in general and to bring companies in a
dominant position in the British economy into public owner-

ship at the earliest possible date with full provisions for democratic control in their respective spheres by workers and the representatives of the workers as a whole.'

In his speech to the House of Commons on this resolution, Stan Newens said:

'I say quite clearly that I do not think that privately-owned industry is at all able to consider these three aspects, namely, the workers' interests, the consumers' interests, and the interests of the community in general. Profit is supreme, and therefore the only question which is considered is the efficiency of the use of capital, and that consideration is not by any means adequate for the safeguards of the workers.'

Replying, a Tory member said:

'I congratulate the Hon. Member for Epping [Mr Newens] upon the way he has stated his case. It is a long time since I have heard the authentic voice of Socialism in this House or elsewhere . . . it is quite refreshing to recognise the mind of Socialism that I was brought up to try to combat.'

An Irishman is reputed to have said to a motorist who asked him the way to Dublin: 'Sure, if I wanted to go there, I wouldn't be starting from here.' Like the Irishman, I would prefer not to be 'starting from here' on the journey towards workers' control. But the growth of multinational companies – those whose production operations are carried out in two or more countries – cannot be ignored, and must be tackled by the international trade union movement.

As Mr G. H. Doughty, General Secretary of the Technical and Supervisory Section of the AUEW, said in his speech to an AUEW Summer School (1971):

'The fact that capitalism is an international system should surprise no-one; the logic of competition in the market with the elimination of the less efficient producers through a combination of bankruptcy, mergers, takeovers and the continuous drive to increase monopoly power in fewer and fewer hands is in no way restricted by national boundaries.'

The dominant force in the world of multinational companies

is the USA. The USA owns 60 per cent of the world's wealth, but has only 6 per cent of the world's population. Some of the US international companies control wealth equal to, and sometimes greater than, that of some national government budgets. Charles Levinson, in his book *Capital, Inflation and the Multinationals*, states that:

'On the basis of output, among the top 100 countries and enterprises with a volume exceeding $2 billion annually, 54 are business enterprises and only 46 are countries. General Motors' turnover of $24 billion makes it the fifteenth economic power in the world, slightly under Spain, Sweden and Holland, but ahead of Belgium, Argentina and Switzerland. Standard Oil of New Jersey and Ford produce more in monetary terms than Pakistan, Denmark and Austria.'

It is scarcely surprising then that (in Levinson's words) 'the ability of the nation state to control its own economic system is being put into question'.

A paper presented to the 1970 TUC Conference on International Companies declared that the international company was rapidly replacing the nation state as the 'basic operating and accounting unit in the international economy'. It is easy to see this diagrammatically in the comparison in the figure of the ten largest American firms with the gold and dollar reserves of selected countries for 1966.

Levinson draws the conclusion that 'by 1975, nearly 35 per cent of the Western world's non-US production will be accounted for by American subsidiaries or American-associated firms'. Of course, the motive for this high rate of expansion is not philanthropic, since much of their vast profit is made overseas. In the United Kingdom, for example, 10 per cent of our total manufacturing and nearly 20 per cent of our exports come from US-controlled companies.

INTERNATIONAL COMPANIES – CONTROL IN BRITAIN

When other countries' investment is taken into account, it is clear that some of our major industries are dominated by foreign capital.

Industrial Sectors directed by Foreign-owned Companies

Sector	Approximate per cent Foreign Controlled	Major Companies	
Motors	58	Ford	USA
		Vauxhall – General Motors	USA
		Chrysler	USA
Electronics	50	IBM	USA
		Philips	Neths
		Honeywell	USA
		Texas Instruments	USA
Pharmaceuticals	65	Brown Polson	USA
		CIBA	Switz.
		Geigy	Switz.
Office machinery	80	IBM	USA
		Imperial	USA
		Olivetti	Italy

Source: TUC Report 'International Companies'.

Approximately 15 per cent of all our manufacturing industries are foreign-owned, with a work-force of over 1,000,000. We provide not only the labour, however, but also the bulk of the finance. For example, IBM (UK)'s original assets of £271,000 in 1950 had grown to £76,593,000 by 1968, and the profits to be made are high – according to *The Sunday Times* (10 October 1971), the rate of profit is 'nearly 50 per cent on capital employed, three times the national average', and 'one thousand pounds invested in 1930 would now be worth more than £9 million'.

Other foreign-owned subsidiaries – for example, General Motors and Fords – have also taken out of Britain far more than they invested originally. 'Buy British' is the slogan used by such big businesses; they play the role of vociferous national patriots. But, as Oscar Wilde said, 'patriotism is the last refuge of a scoundrel'.

The 1966–70 Labour Government made a mistake in not

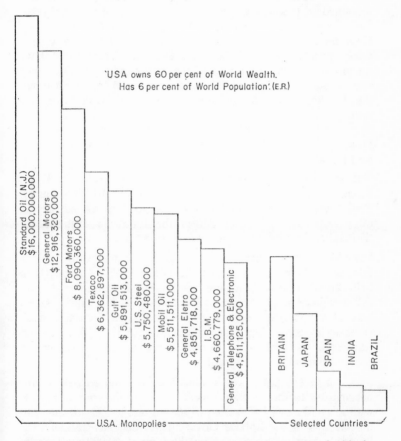

'USA owns 60 per cent of World Wealth.
Has 6 per cent of World Population'. (E.R.)

Standard Oil (N.J.)
$16,000,000,000

General Motors
$12,916,320,000

Ford Motors
$8,090,360,000

Texaco
$6,362,897,000

Gulf Oil
$5,891,513,000

U.S. Steel
$5,750,480,000

Mobil Oil
$5,511,511,000

General Eletro
$4,851,718,000

I.B.M.
$4,660,779,000

General Telephone & Electronic
$4,511,125,000

BRITAIN

JAPAN

SPAIN

INDIA

BRAZIL

——————— U.S.A. Monopolies ——————— / ⌣—Selected Countries—⌣

Dollar assets of the ten largest American companies compared with the gold and dollar reserves of selected countries for 1966. (Source: *Monopoly Capital: An Essay on the American Economic and Social Order.* Monthly Review, 1966) taking over the motor industry of this country, and bringing it under public ownership with workers' control at all levels. If this had been done, many millions of pounds would have remained in this country, and the power of multinational companies to threaten the industry would not exist. The Labour Government had the opportunity to do what has already been done successfully in France and Belgium. They could have taken over an important part of the motor industry, which they were urged to do by Rootes workers, instead of letting it fall into the hands of a foreign investor – Chrysler Motor Corporation.

INTERNATIONAL COMPANIES – CONTROL BY BRITAIN

But the foreign investment traffic is not all one-way. While foreign companies take over large parts of British industry, British capitalists own and control big sections of industry in other countries. Levinson quotes the following examples of 'British' companies whose interests lie overseas:

'ICI's nearly two dozen branches are under the control of its ICI-Europe holding company in Brussels. Shell, Unilever (both half-Dutch), Fisons, Beechams, Glaxo, Reed, Bowater, etc., are full members of the Common Market. As tariffs, border taxes, and other non-tariff barriers are only negligible factors in decisions to invest and produce abroad, these large firms would transfer investment to the Continent regardless of whether the UK is a political member or not.'

A single company which illustrates the dangers of multinationalism to the working people is GEC. Following its merger with AEI and English Electric in 1968 – a merger carried out with the blessing of the Labour Government – GEC has 'rationalised' its production in this country to the tune of 60,000 workers by 1972 (40,000 redundancies, the remainder in 'natural wastage'). Yet GEC has thirty-five subsidiaries in Europe, eleven in South Africa, and large numbers in Rhodesia, Zambia, Nigeria, the Americas, Asia and Australasia (see Appendix B for details).

A further example is the Dunlop-Pirelli merger, which made the Dunlop company half-Italian. In 1971, I was involved in negotiations with the Dunlop management about the closure of their plant in Leicester, in which about 1,200 were employed. I urged them to keep this old-established factory going – a factory which had helped to lay the foundation in the past for Dunlop's present prosperity. But the company representatives were adamant, although I pointed out that Dunlop's profits had been increasing by several millions each year, and in 1970 stood at £59,292,000. Total profits for the five years up to 1970 were £243,527,000.

In addition to the £940 million merger with Pirelli, new factories were being opened in South Africa, France and Malaysia, and the company was planning further capital expenditure of £21 million on overseas development. But in spite of all this, the company refused to keep the Leicester plant open. It is obviously more profitable to supply their markets from factories in foreign countries. After all, they must consider the interests of their shareholders!

Trade unions have also had other bad experiences of international companies: Kodak, for example, has its own 'company union' and has refused to recognise genuine trade unions; Caterpillar Tractor refused recognition to the AUEW members in a Scottish factory, which led to a thirteen-week strike. Recognition was eventually granted when the union withdrew members from another factory of the same company. Probably the most notorious example to date has been that of Roberts Arundel, where trade union members were made redundant and replaced by non-union staff. A twelve-month strike led to the reinstatement of the trade unionists, but shortly afterwards the company closed down the plant and withdrew its capital to the United States.

Foreign-owned companies are even stiffer in their attitudes to staff unions than to manual workers' unions – but they are fearful of *any* measure of trade union organisation, not to speak of workers' control!

LABOUR GOVERNMENT ASSISTS MERGERS

Anthony Wedgwood Benn, as Minister of Technology, claimed credit for the 1964–70 Labour Government in creating mergers,

H

although these have been the cause of considerable redundancies. When speaking to West German businessmen in Hamburg in 1968, he said:

'Already, as you know, the new Rolls Royce has won its first order for the immensely powerful, and quieter advanced technology engines for the Lockheed Airbus – the RB11 – This order followed by the demand for replacements and spares could be worth over £100m. over the next ten years. There is little doubt that without the merger, Rolls Royce would never have achieved this order.'

(The subsequent history of Rolls Royce, its collapse and take-over by a *Tory* Government, shows how inadequate a safeguard mergers are for the jobs and well-being of the workers.)

Mr Wedgwood Benn went on to quote the effects of mergers in shipbuilding, computers, and so on, as making it possible for British-based firms to compete with their rivals on the international front.

The implications of this kind of reasoning are tremendous. With the possibility of Common Market tariff barriers being removed, virtually every industry will be in direct competition with a vast range of continental competitors. Sheer size will be a prime factor in determining who survives and who goes to the wall. *The Sunday Times* examined the problem in an article (17 October 1971) on the £80 million Chloride/Oldham battery merger. The new company would then have more than 40 per cent of the British domestic car battery market, and 70 per cent of the industrial battery market. The Monopolies Commission investigates all mergers involving assets of more than £5 million, or a control of more than one third of the market, but Chloride argued that their merger should not be referred to the Commission, on the grounds that a merger will 'help it compete in the Common Market countries, while European producers with similar ideas for expanding here will keep the UK market competitive'.

So the race for international industrial surpremacy is on. The efforts of Benn and the last Labour Government assisted British capitalism to strengthen its position in the field of international competition. It is the task of British trade unionists to strengthen the ties of international trade unions for the purpose of unitedly defending and extending workers' living standards on an international scale. Unity must be the keynote, and this means mutual aid and solidarity.

In 1970, trade union members at the International Nickel Company's works near Swansea were being made to accept two penal clauses:

1. That trade union members engaging in a sympathetic strike with fellow trade unionists would be fined by reducing their wages to the basic rate – a fine of £6 a week.
2. That where the company considered a worker was not operating to the requirements of the management, his pay would be reduced to the basic – again a fine of £6 a week.

At about this time, workers in the International Nickel Company's plant in Canada went on strike for four and a half months over a wage demand, and as a consequence of this strike, supplies of raw materials to this country began to dry up. The Swansea management took advantage of this situation to have a battle with the Swansea employees, saying that the penal clauses would become operative immediately. The company underestimated the workers, however, and after a strike in Swansea lasting four months, they were compelled to withdraw the clauses.

Bro. J. Bullard (Transport & General Workers' Union), reporting this case, made the point that if the Swansea workers had been advised of the likelihood of a strike in Canada, they could have picked their own battleground for the removal of the penal clauses, rather than have the company attempt to impose them at a time convenient to itself.

There is still a lot to be done by trade unionists to combat the growing threat of international combines. That growth has been taking place gradually over the past twenty years, but trade unions have only comparatively recently begun to operate on an international scale, and even now their meetings are generally limited to 'top level' officers, and rarely involve shop-floor workers.

It is essential that workers at all levels should take part in discussions about this problem, and there should be effective channels of contact between workers in all branches of a multi-national company. But in order to understand the dangers of multinationalism, and develop ways of overcoming them, it is first necessary for trade unionists to understand the reasons for the existence of worldwide companies.

THE PATRIOTISM OF CAPITAL

The simple answer is, of course, 'higher profitability'. But then the question arises: why is it more profitable for American and European companies to base part of their production in Britain, while at the same time it is more profitable for British companies to open plants in America and Europe? The TUC listed some of the answers to these questions in its report on international companies, a report which arose out of a conference held in October 1970:

'The principal reasons for this development are:
1. Faster growing markets abroad;
2. The need to circumvent tariff barriers;
3. Differential labour and material costs;
4. Cheaper transport costs;
5. Differential taxation systems;
6. More flexible exchange controls.'

Numbers (2) and (5) are closely linked. The use of 'transfer pricing', for example, offers rich tax gains to multinational companies, ignores tariff barriers completely, and leaves workers and their country the possibility of a reduced standard of living and a balance of payments problem. Bro. Doughty (Gen. Sec. TASS) describes the system:

'Transfer pricing is a device whereby goods are moved intra-company, which means across national boundaries, and the prices charged are not the real cost. This means a hidden transfer of resources from one country to another.

Multinational companies may do this for a number of reasons. A major reason might be the level of corporate taxation within a given country. If the subsidiary in a country where corporate taxation is high sells at artificially low prices to a holding company, possibly based in Switzerland, where corporate taxation is low, and the holding company then sells at a much higher price, the profit is declared where taxation and the cost to the company is lowest.

This not only represents a transfer of resources from one country to another but a loss of revenue to the central government; since such a loss may limit the effectiveness of government action in the area of social policy this represents a potential reduction in the standard of living of our members.'

Is Bro. Doughty making a mountain out of a molehill? Not at all. *Sovereignty and Multinational Companies* (Fabian Tract, No. 409) quotes the examples of British Petroleum and Rio Tinto Zinc. Rio Tinto Zinc pays only 2 per cent of its tax bill to the British Exchequer. BP pays none at all, although 37 per cent of its employees are in Britain.

Among the countries offering such tax advantages to multinational enterprises are Switzerland (with 6,700 holding companies), Luxemburg and Holland.

CAPITAL IGNORES POLITICAL BOUNDARIES

Labour costs are another incentive to multinationalism. The obvious centres for low-cost labour are countries like Spain and Portugal, but there is another less obvious area which needs to be examined – Eastern Europe. An example of West–East collaboration is that of an Austrian company joining forces with a Polish enterprise to build a sugar factory in Greece. Again, an American financier invests in a new tyre plant in Eastern Europe, basing the Western half of the company in Switzerland, thus benefiting from low labour costs and low tax rates.

Charles Levinson remarks that 'even the commercial relations between Spain and the communist countries have been quietly extended', citing the example of Polish coal being sent to Spain during a strike of Spanish miners in 1970.

The action needed to prevent multinational companies from riding rough-shod over workers in the pursuit of profit can therefore not be confined to 'capitalist' countries, since it is evident that multinational enterprises are truly global in extent. Unfortunately the ties between workers in Western and Eastern European countries are more tenuous than those between capitalist enterprises and communist management.

It is becoming more and more difficult for workers in one plant, or from various plants in the same country, to substantiate their claims without reference to their company's workers in other countries. The TUC Report on International Companies puts its finger on the reasons for this:

'The disclosure of information required of international companies by national governments relates only to its operations within the national economy;

The incompatibility of disclosure requirements of the company law of the nations concerned;

The blurring of internal financial mechanisms.'

BANKERS' CONTROL

The 'financial mechanisms' represented by the big names in banking, in this country have worldwide ramifications, with a total of 5,300 branches overseas – the most extensive range in the world – to cope with the business generated by transactions which cross national boundaries. There are about 13,000 people employed in the London branches of foreign banks.

The tendency towards internationalism in banking has not been ignored by Eastern European countries, which successfully operate branches in London and elsewhere on capitalist lines. Various bank groups have emerged, consisting of partners from both East and West Europe, with the ostensible aim of 'furthering international trade'.

Banks, being privately owned, operate on the basis of profitability. They are engaged in the transfer of financial resources from country to country, for the purpose of producing and paying for goods. They add nothing to the value of the goods, but take a percentage of the profits for 'services rendered'. The increasing complexity of the banking system in response to the multinational growth of private enterprise illustrates the difficulties involved in bringing about the nationalisation of banking.

Banking must be considered as important a branch of multi-national development as the giant companies whose names are household names throughout the world.

'The greater the power, the more dangerous the abuse.' Private companies have combined into colossal concentrations of power. Their economic power is undisputed. But they also wield political power, since they are largely free from government control and entirely free from accountability to the public. Our task is to bring these giants under workers' control, both nationally and internationally.

While there has been a massive concentration of capital on an international scale, the slow development of international trade union organisations has also been taking place. The International Metalworkers' Federation, which is the largest international federation and probably has the most international companies in its field, has made several moves towards co-ordination among its affiliates for defence against international companies, particularly in the motor and electrical engineering spheres. In 1964, for example, the IMF held the Second World Autoworkers' Conference, from which stemmed the World Autoworkers' Councils for multinational firms: in 1966 – Ford, General Motors, Chrysler, Volkswagen, Fiat–Citroen; in 1968 – Nissan–Toyota, BLMC–Renault–Volvo.

These Councils meet only once every four years, to discuss developments within these firms, to exchange information and decide on bargaining tactics. The 1968 World Autoworkers' Conference in Turin agreed that one of their objectives should be the establishment of common termination dates for collective agreements. Under this plan, no agreement would be signed anywhere until the basic trade union demands put before the individual subsidiaries of the global corporation had been met.

IMF GUIDELINES

The International Metalworkers' Federation, representing some eleven million trade unionists in the capitalist world, was founded seventy-five years ago, including among its guiding principles equal rights and opportunities for all, improvement of working conditions, freedom of collective bargaining, and the right to strike. In reaction to the growth of multinational corporations, the IMF published the following appraisal of the situation:

'The Federation

1. points out that the growing concentration of capital and production is causing far-reaching structural change in the world economy;

2. draws attention to the fact that in the metal sector, especially in the automobile and electrical industries, gigantic power groups are growing up;

3. is aware that these large corporations in their efforts to make profits by ruthlessly exploiting every political economic and social weakness of a country, seek to play the workers of different countries one against the other;

4. notes that these corporations, wherever they settle, strive to avoid the trade unions, exclude them, or strangle them at birth;

5. knows from experience that the arbitrary decisions of these corporations to transfer production facilities and research centres from one country to another can have serious consequences for the workers and the economic, social and scientific position of a country ...

6. is determined to oppose the united front of capital with the united strength of the trade unions and will continue to resist everywhere the efforts of multinational corporations to exploit their workers;

7. is resolved to strengthen the co-ordination of its activities and to further intensify the work of the various IMF World Company Councils and committees covering various multinational companies.'

Here is a basis on which the various national union organisations and the rank-and-file workers in individual multinational companies should come together, stretching out their hands to each other over the heads of national governments and other national bodies. There is a need to take these decisions of the IMF forward to the highest degree of workers' control on an international basis.

Yet in spite of the potential power of the millions of trade unionists throughout the world, the employers are still using one group of workers in one country against workers in another country, and the growth in trade union solidarity has not kept pace with the employers' expanding power.

As the IMF said, international companies 'seek to play the workers of different countries one against another'. Not the least important of their manoeuvres is that of siting their new plant in countries where the labour costs are lowest. Charles Levinson, in *Capital, Inflation and the Multinationals*, cites the following examples:

'For some years West European companies have been making co-production deals with communist enterprises . . . An even more elusive form of East-West business link is being established with the purpose of penetrating markets in third countries. Austria's Simmering–Graz–Pauker, for example, is collaborating with a Polish enterprise in building a sugar factory in Greece. The Poles will supply equipment, and the Austrians will put up the plant. Swedish furniture is made in Poland, finished at home, then exported.'

INTERNATIONAL TRADE UNIONS

Clearly it is not enough for links to be established with trade unions in Europe, in the United States, and the capitalist world in general. Links already exist between Western companies and the companies of Eastern Europe; it is time that stronger links were forged between the workers of Western and Eastern Europe. The social democratic, communist and catholic union members *must* unite, certainly at the base. More workers' control from the rank and file must be exercised over the two mighty trade union internationals, the ICFTU and the WFTU.

The International Confederation of Free Trade Unions (ICFTU) has 123 affiliated organisations in 95 countries, with a total membership of *63 million*, including the American AFL–CIO unions, the British TUC, and the West German DGB unions, which together account for over half the ICFTU membership.

The World Federation of Trade Unions has an affiliated membership of approximately *160 million* workers, the majority of whom live in communist countries. At its Sixth Congress in 1965, it was reported that workers were represented from Europe, Africa, Asia, the Middle East and America.

The World Confederation of Labour is an organisation of the Christian national trade union centres, and has a membership of *16 million*.

Unless the 239,000,000 workers in these international groups compel their leaders to come together in order to combat the fast-growing world power of the international capitalists and their monopolies, we shall see the establishment of fascism in many countries, including Britain.

In spite of the scepticism voiced by their more pessimistic critics, meetings, discussions and solidarity between the three major groups of trade unionists are not only possible, but are actually taking place – though not yet on a sufficiently large scale.

In October 1971, for example, a conference was held to discuss tourism, and its effects on hotel, café and restaurant workers. The delegates 'unanimously adopted a platform of demands which condemns the stranglehold of the monopolies, multinational companies and banks on tourism', and the conference approved a programme of demands for workers in the industry. Twenty-one countries were represented at the conference, from four continents, and including both WFTU and ICFTU representatives.

The United Conference of Italian Metalworkers in 1971 declared that

'As far as the socialist countries are concerned, FIM, FIOM and UILM believe it useful to retain relationships with the trade unions of these countries. These relationships must take the form of exchanges and frank discussions on the conditions of the workers, the uses of technology and technological advances, and also on the autonomous role of the trade union, its right to control its own affairs, and the workers' control of the socialist economy . . . To this end Conference calls upon FIM, FIOM and UILM to undertake initiatives to construct new forms of co-ordination, which, by creating the conditions of a new trade union organisation at European level, satisfy the basic conditions for an effective answer to the international monopoly system.'

INTERNATIONAL TRADE UNION UNITY

In Britain, The 1971 National Committee of the AUEW (Engineering Section) passed the following resolution for the TUC Agenda:

'This National Committee instructs Executive Council to do all it can to encourage fraternal relations between the ICFTU and World Federation of Trade Unions, and to raise this question with the TUC.'

These moves by ICFTU members have been met by a favourable response from the WFTU, both on specific issues and on the more general subject of 'coming together'.

On the question of the imprisonment of Spanish workers during 1970-1, for example, the Metalworkers' Trades Union International of the WFTU sent telegrams to both the IMF and the World Confederation of Labour:

'We have been approached by many organisations, and more especially by the Italian FIOM, FIM and UILM who desire that the three international organisations of metalworkers should jointly examine measures to be adopted for the development of the solidarity of metalworkers and their trade unions with their Spanish brothers.

As for us, we are ready to meet you as early as possible. We should also like the three international organisations to jointly write to the Spanish government and to demand that the lives of the Basque patriots be spared and amnesty be granted to all political prisoners and jailed trade unionists.'

At the twentieth session of the WFTU General Council, a message was approved, addressed 'to all workers, to trade union organisations everywhere no matter what outlook, and to international trade union organisations'. The message regretted the split in the world trade union movement, recognising that division means a reduction in power: 'But because of international division, this huge force is still wasting much of its energy which, if concentrated, could have an influence, possibly decisive, over developments in today's world.'

In order to remedy that division:

'We consider that the world's trade union organisations must discuss, must sit at the same table and try to unify their points of view.

It is in this spirit that the General Council of the World Federation of Trade Unions proposes that a meeting be held with the participation of the WFTU, the ICFTU, the WCL, independent regional organisations and non-national centres. A Round Table without prescriptions, without conditions, without preliminaries, in which each would put his own point of view, not to impose it but to exchange ideas and to seek the basis for agreement with the aim of finding the best ways of defending and achieving the economic and social demands and the international interests of the working class.'

It is time we realised that the objections to this kind of conference between the WFTU and the ICFTU do *not* come from the rank and file, but from some of their leaders. This is why more rank and file activity must take place, before such a conference can be usefully convened. The Transport & General Workers' Union, at its 1971 conference in Scarborough, called for its executive

'to campaign vigorously and urgently seek closer and more practical relations with all trade union organisations within the world trade union movement to reconcile divisions between the International Confederation of Free Trade Unions and the World Federation of Trade Unions to form one international organisation'.

Useful as this resolution could be, its purpose is defeated if the rank and file do not follow it up by attempting to create ties with the constituent unions of the WFTU at shopfloor level, and enforcing their resolution as far as possible, making sure that it does not simply lie dormant in the Conference Report. This also applies, of course, to every other effort by the rank and file to forge links with their trade union brothers overseas.

One of the 'objections' to WFTU/ICFTU unity is that of power, and who wields it. The same objection is at the root of the amalgamation difficulties between unions within one country, and it is also the reason for the large number of political splinter-groups, which differ from each other very little, but which steadfastly refuse to unite – even in the face of a common enemy, whether that enemy be the Tory Government, employers, or international monopoly.

Power struggles are always conducted at the expense of the rank and file. If workers really controlled their own unions, both nationally and internationally, unity between the workers of the world would follow.

RANK AND FILE UNITY

It is not enough for national trade union leaders simply to come together at intervals, to talk and carry resolutions. The international working class must strengthen their working-class organisations and come together in mutual support. There have already been some instances of unity proving successful against international companies. Rolls Royce and Concorde workers have been meeting to discuss problems arising from the production of Concorde. Trade unionists have held conferences in Geneva to discuss two international giants, the Bowater Group (British) and the Michelin Group (French), in order to coordinate their fight against these private monopolies. Ford shop stewards from Britain and Europe have been meeting on an international combine basis. About a hundred and fifty shop stewards and union representatives of Italian and some French unions held joint meetings, as a result of which they decided to establish links with car workers in West Germany, Belgium and the United States; a Belgian delegation visited London and met convenors from twenty-two Ford plants to discuss joint action, which resulted in Fords' settlement of a dispute to the unions' satisfaction.

The ultimate solution to the problem presented by international combines is for the working class to bring each part of these companies which operates in their country under public ownership with workers' control. The National Conference of the AUEW decided to 'instruct the National Executive to make available sufficient resources to complete research and submit a report to the 1972 Conference on a new plan for engineering, with special reference to the problems of international companies'. This will involve, in effect, proposals for the public ownership of major sections of the engineering industry.

The aim of British and European monopolists is to create a bigger and more economically dominated European Economic Community. The Common Market is their solution to their problems.

The capitalists of Europe are forced to unite in their struggle against socialism. So also must trade unionists come together if they are to fight successfully against the capitalist giants of Europe.

There have been numerous theories propounded on how this is best to be done. The Italian metalworkers' unions favour direct links between workers at all levels, not simply the leading trade unionists; they recommend:

'(a) Commencing bilateral contacts with the engineering unions of all European countries to open a full discussion of our respective policies, and to examine the possibilities of common initiatives.

(b) Direct links, along lines laid down by the national organisations, between the factory representatives in one country with the trade union factory representatives of the same international group in other countries, working towards the constitution of permanent liaison committees, at least at European level.

(c) United invitations to foreign trade unions to take part in our joint conference, or meetings of industrial sectors, so that they can come into direct contact with our experiences.

(d) United links with all trade union bodies willing to overcome the barriers created by different international affiliations.'

These suggestions bear some relation to workers at plant level, and involve the rank and file in international activities, instead of leaving it to national officers of their unions to establish contacts on their behalf. The TUC's proposals for developing contacts (contained in their Report on International Companies) place more stress on the unity of national bodies, and their possible effect on governments and multinational employers:

'International trade union contacts can be developed in the following three ways:

(*a*) bilateral and multilateral contacts between national unions and/or workplace representatives or workers in international companies plants in different countries;

(*b*) international trade union contact between affiliates of international trade secretariats to consider action in relation to particular industries and particular international companies;

(*c*) multilateral contact and action (through the ICFTU, for example, to which national trade union centres are affiliated) to bring pressure on Governments and international agencies.'

As we can see from the examples, there is no shortage of *words* to promote international unity; though, in spite of all the words, there is a surprising lack of any real move in the direction of ICFTU/WFTU rank-and-file unity. No progress can be made until more workers exercise power within their unions, and until this happens we shall continue to find that capitalists and bureaucrats can play off worker against worker, for there is more unity of action among capitalist concerns than there is among the world's trade unions.

Faced with this situation, trade unionists must develop connections internationally, particularly by forging links with branches of the same enterprise in other countries.

For this purpose, the national combine joint shop stewards' committees should endeavour to set up, in co-operation with the rank-and-file organisations in the enterprise overseas, an International Combine Joint Shop Stewards' Committee. In this way it will be possible to build trade union unity based on the rank-and-file members in action.

In the words of Karl Marx: 'The workers have nothing to lose in this but their chains. They have a world to gain. Workers of the world, unite.'

Chapter 8

Workers' Control
Over the Right to Work

Work, boys, work and be contented,
As long as you've enough to buy a meal;
For if you will but try, you'll be wealthy by and by,
If you'll only put your shoulders to the wheel.
Music-hall song, about 1910

'Oh, why don't you work like other men do?'
'How the hell can I work when there's no work to do?'
International Wobblies' Song, USA, 1930s

One of the disastrous results for the working class of the international concentration and centralisation of finance capital, is
growing unemployment due to mergers and closures of industries. Mass unemployment has fluctuated widely over the years.
The number of workers denied the right to work in 1920 was
691,103, but within a few months, by March 1921, this number
had increased to 2,171,288. The numbers of unemployed
workers varied during subsequent years, but by 1933 they had
reached dramatic proportions. *British Labour Statistics*, published by the Department of Employment and Productivity,
gives the registered numbers of unemployed workers in the
United Kingdom as follows:

January 1923	1,460,400
December 1928	1,565,300
December 1930	2,725,000
September 1931	2,897,000
January 1933	2,979,400

In 1966, the number of unemployed was 330,000, but after
the Labour Government's wage-freeze policy, the number went
up to 600,000, and remained at that level until 1970. Since then,
it has risen under the Tory Government, and it was correctly

forecast by many trade union leaders that the number of their members denied the right to work would reach a million by the end of 1971.

The number of workers declared redundant through mergers and closures totalled 80,000 from about two hundred companies in the first six months of 1971, under the Tories. In a single example of 'rationalisation', a company declaring profits of £36 million (20 per cent increase on the previous year) has made 33,572 workers redundant since 1968. The company? Weinstock's giant GEC–EE–AEI combine.

Not all redundancies are on such a large scale, but they are all equally hard-hitting to the workers concerned. A BBC Television programme, *Conflict in Industry* (18 November 1971), revealed that a redundancy agreement concerning 400 workers at Delta Metal, Birmingham, was signed by the district union

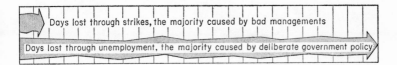

officials *two years* before the redundancies were due to take place. Yet the workers whose 'painless sacking' had been agreed upon so long before, were shocked when they were told of the decision *at the time of the closure.* Why were they not consulted in the first place? Does redundancy pay make such a predicament any easier to bear? Of course it does not, especially to workers who have given forty or more years of their life to producing wealth for their employer.

REDUNDANT MANAGERS

Some of the redundant employees who are finding themselves on the streets quite unexpectedly should take this opportunity of taking stock of themselves, and deciding where their interests lie. These are the executives and managers who, after years of allying themselves with the owner against the workers, suddenly find that their situation is no more secure than that of any other worker who barters his labour for cash. The Professional and Executive Register – a department of the employment exchange – is suddenly full of discarded executives looking for new jobs, whereas its main task until now has been in searching for better opportunities for executive climbers. Perhaps this boom in business is the reason why the Government is considering charging for the Professional and Executive service! Be that as it may, executives feeling the pinch of unemployment could do with bearing in mind that defending the owners' interests loyally carries little weight in the last analysis. The manager who works for a salary had much better throw in his lot with the wage-earner, since both are equally likely to suffer in the crisis of capitalism. The identity of interest which the executive is encouraged to recognise with his capitalist employer is largely illusory, and benefits no one but the employer.

REDUNDANT GRADUATES

Also turning to the P & E Register for jobs are the thousands of graduates who are unable to find work, six months or more after leaving university. Estimates of unemployed graduates at Christmas 1971 – those who had had no job at all since graduating in June – varied between five and ten thousand. Mr Neil Crichton-Miller, managing director of the Graduate Appointments Register, has made the point that, with 70,000 executives out of work, it is hardly to be expected that newcomers will walk straight into a job: 'In other words, when an employer is laying off the father, he doesn't recruit the son.'

A university degree is no longer a passport to the good things in life, and 'graduate today – tycoon tomorrow' no longer holds good. It must be recognised by both graduates and manual workers that their interests in and out of employment are the same, since both are mere pawns in the capitalist system. This becomes clear, when it is considered that:

1. the number of graduates in 1971 increased by 6 per cent over the previous year, while the demand for their services (according to the Confederation of British Industry) fell by 15 to 20 per cent.

2. unemployment throughout the country rose to about one million during 1971, while the Treasury boasted a 6¼ per cent rise in productivity in industry in the same period.

Productivity is increasing, but the number of workers required in the process of production is falling, and the workers who are surplus to requirements include 'workers by brain' as well as 'workers by hand'.

REDUNDANT APPRENTICES

Of course, the 'workers by brain' have nothing to worry about. They have at least been trained to work, and ought to be grateful to society for their education, even when there is no work to do when the training is finished. This 'training for unemployment', having succeeded in producing ten thousand unwanted graduates, is now being applied to prospective manual workers also.

The Engineering Industry Training Board, for example, finding that applications for off-the-job training courses fell by about 5,000 in 1971 (from 26,000 a year), has decided to offer a year's full-time course to 2,500 school-leavers who have been unable to get apprenticeships and are unemployed. This training course, which would normally be part of a young worker's apprenticeship to a company, will count towards the normal period of apprenticeship when a company can be found to employ a new apprentice; but no guarantee is offered by the EITB that entrants to the course will find jobs at the end of it – and indeed plans are under consideration for a further period of training if job opportunities are not forthcoming.

REDUNDANT EMPLOYMENT AGENCIES?

One area where the 'employment business' is booming is the area which provides secretarial and typing jobs – the employment agencies. The bosses of the agencies attribute their £4 million profit in 1970 to their sheer professionalism in finding the right job for the right person, and to the congenial surroundings and convenient siting of their branches. In short, a 'better service' than state employment exchanges can offer.

And where does the £4 million come from? The office workers get a 'free' service; the employer pays, on average, two weeks' pay when the agency fills a vacancy. And where does the employer get it from? Ultimately, of course, out of the pocket of his new recruit, who is happy in the thought that the agency charges her nothing.

As long ago as 1933 the International Labour Organisation called for these agencies to be banned, yet in recent years their business has rocketed. Clive Jenkins, speaking at the Labour Party Conference in 1971, quoted the 1969 profits of Brook Street Bureau alone as being £632,000; the Alfred Marks agency had expanded by 7,783 per cent in nine years, he said.

We already pay for a state service to provide job information for those who need it. Yet an increasing number of office workers go to a private bureau rather than the employment exchange. In this way, the workers pay twice for a service which ought to be provided solely by the state – and in doing so, they line the pockets of a few exploiters. Tempting advertisements encourage frequent changing of jobs, and the agencies presumably thrive on *dis*satisfied customers. And advertising costs are all in the price of the 'service', of course.

We can do without these employment sharks. They offer no service which cannot be provided more efficiently and economically by the state exchanges, although there is room for improvement both in the service and the environment in which it is offered. The conditions prevalent in employment exchanges are far from adequate; unemployment is depressing in itself, without the added misery of prison-like conditions and an almost complete lack of privacy. The 'Professional and Executive' departments boast a much higher degree of comfort, privacy and attention, and there is no reason why equally good service should not be offered universally.

SCHOOL-LEAVERS REDUNDANT!

A large number of school-leavers are now becoming acquainted with employment exchanges, gaining first-hand experience of unemployment before they have had the opportunity of working. Straight from school to unemployment. Every year, thousands of teenagers come on to the job-market, and swell the figures of registered unemployed, until they are absorbed into the system.

However much the Department of Employment try to disguise the fact, the process of absorption is taking longer each year. Two entries from a Government gazette illustrate how the job prospects for young people are worsening – and how the Government attempts to brush the facts under the carpet:

Employment and Productivity Gazette: October 1970
'Between August and September, the number of school-leavers registered as unemployed fell . . . to 20,696 . . .'

Department of Employment Gazette: October 1971
'Between August and September, the number of school-leavers registered as unemployed fell . . . to 34,733 . . .'

Fell? From 20,696 to 34,733? There is generally a month-by-month improvement in the figures of unemployed school-leavers, following the end-of-term bulge in the summer; but the figures issued by the Government indicate a 75 per cent worsening of the situation between 1970 and 1971.

'Hundreds of thousands of extra families suffering the hardship and insecurity of unemployment. Increasing problems of poverty and homelessness. Pensioners helpless as they watch the extra shillings eaten up by the fastest price rise for twenty years. Housewives struggling to make ends meet.'

So read the Tory Party Manifesto of 1970. And Ted Heath has made it all come true!

What is the Tory answer to unemployment? We must, apparently, count our blessings. The Newcastle-on-Tyne *Evening Chronicle* (17 September 1971) finds this advice a bit hard to swallow:

'Homilies such as that addressed to the unemployed of Wearside by the Under Secretary of State for Employment yesterday are more likely to anger than to inspire. At the very least they suggest a dangerous complacency.

An unemployment rate of 9 per cent, said Mr Dudley Smith, is "obviously too high". So obvious, one would have thought, as not to merit the breath wasted on saying it when what is needed is action.

But then, it appears, Mr Smith thinks we should remember that 90 per cent are *not* unemployed. Clearly we should be as grateful for that as for the fact that 50,000,000 people are neither killed on the roads every year, nor end up in jail.'

But let us not imagine that this is the full extent of the Government's concern for the unemployed. The Minister of Employment announced in September 1971 new measures for the re-training of Britain's unemployed workers, who at that time totalled nearly a million. Government training centres, said Mr Carr, already provide 10,600 training places, and he planned to increase this to 14,000 'as soon as possible'.

If each training course lasted six months, it would, at a generous estimate, take thirty-five years to train all the people who were unemployed when Mr Carr made his offer. Not that they could be guaranteed jobs after training, of course. And, to be honest, it would not be in the interests of the employers if jobs could be found. This was disclosed with undisguised honesty by the monthly publication of the banking world, *The Banker*, which declared that 'more demand, faster growth and *less unemployment* would surely intensify the militant union pressure for an ever-growing share of wages in the national income'.

UNEMPLOYMENT – A GOVERNMENT
RESPONSIBILITY

National governments after the 1939–45 war took the responsibility for creating conditions of 'full employment'. This was later changed in government statements to read 'a high and stable level of employment'. Now governments go back to pre-war days of mass joblessness, with 'control of the level of unemployment'.

D. N. Pritt, in his book *The Labour Government 1945–1951*, outlined the 'crisis' situation under Stafford Cripps in 1947;

the balance of payments problem, a high level of overseas expenditure, and the arms bill, brought the crisis to a head, and the Government attempted a wage-freeze. The General Council of the TUC was asked to 'consider the possibility of securing "greater stability" of wages, and it agreed to do so'.

Pritt continues:

'A few days later, on 23rd October, 1947, in the House of Commons, Cripps reviewed the whole economic position. He painted, correctly enough, a gloomy picture of our economic position, stating once again that the root of all our troubles lay in the overseas balance of payments, and in particular in the dollar balance. He made no mention of the true cause of the lack of balance, nor any suggestion for easing it by reducing our military expenditure either at home or abroad; and he preached the orthodox Tory remedy of curing the problem by importing less, consuming less, and exporting more.'

The problem about this solution was, in the words of Cripps, that 'there may well be a growing tendency for all nations to restrict imports and to attempt to force their exports'. Two of his measures for combating the crisis were:

1. Cutting capital construction and equipment by two hundred million pounds a year.
2. Reducing the purchasing power of the people by a wage-freeze, the removal of some subsidies, and more indirect taxation.

Write 'Harold Wilson' for 'Stafford Cripps', and '1967' for '1947', and the picture is still the old one of squeezing the workers to pay for the deficiencies of capitalism. The game's the same – only the names change!

Reducing the purchasing power of the people, cutting capital construction, wage-freezing, putting on the selective employment tax – every little helps in the battle to increase unemployment to the level where capitalism can refloat itself. Capitalism needs unemployment – but sometimes it is needed more than others.

Cripps obviously considered that his job was to make capitalism work more efficiently; this was Harold Wilson's plan, too, as it is clearly Edward Heath's. The fact that this must be done at the expense of the working class is a minor consideration – the balance of payments is infinitely more important.

This capitalist orthodoxy is apparently also the philosophy of Roy Jenkins, Deputy Leader of the Labour Party, whose speech on unemployment at the 1971 Conference was littered with references to the fine balance of payment surplus which the Labour Government built up during its 1966–70 period of office. This surplus was to have been used, he said, 'as a springboard for sustained and rapid growth', industrial expansion, and ultimately 'more jobs and greater prosperity'. In fact another great and glorious never-had-it-so-good capitalist boom.

Talking of future Labour Party policy, Roy Jenkins declared that, while nobody wanted a return to the past, we must have 'a solution freely agreed and compatible, of course, with collective bargaining which will not merely be a form of words to get us over the next General Election, but which will stand up to the pressures of office'.

This, coupled with a later comment that 'uncontrolled economies subject to no social disciplines have never succeeded in producing tolerable material standards for a whole nation', forewarns a return to prices-and-incomes policies under a new Labour Government, and no more effective handling of our economic situation than we have seen under previous Labour administrations. We cannot afford to permit the Labour Party to prop up capitalism any longer, at the expense of our livelihood. The Labour Party must be a socialist party, committed to socialist policies, and we must see that it becomes so, through the control of its rank-and-file members.

All the old 'policies' to deal with unemployment have failed; not once, but time and time again; not only under Labour Governments, but under Tory ones, too (and who could be expected to administer Tory remedies with better success than the Tories themselves?). What, then, can be done?

UNEMPLOYMENT – A POLITICAL EDUCATOR?

When I was a young unemployed worker in Coventry in the
1930s, there were about 17,000 unemployed in that so-called
prosperous city. I became a local organser of the National
Unemployed Workers' Movement, and spoke at meetings with
Tom Mann and Wal Hannington.

It was clear to me then, as now, that when a worker was
sacked, he ceased to have the strength of his union behind him.
He was on his own in savage competition with his fellow unemployed trade unionists for a job. He was fighting for his wife
and family. He was confused by the actions of employers, trade
unions, governments and political parties. He was led to believe
that unemployment is not the fault of any person, but rather
like the weather – bad sometimes, and another time a little
better, but quite beyond our control. He simply had to wait
until the economic climate improved.

We organised the unemployed separately from the trade
unions and political parties, thinking that they could exert
enough mass pressure through their own actions – after all, there
were millions of us out of work. But the mass of the unemployed
became demoralised, disenchanted with society and all its works.
Some turned to Sir Oswald Moseley's fascist movement. Some
joined the British Communist Party. The majority remained
apathetic. Hunger marches – yes; demonstrations and meetings
– yes; but only the minority. There were some instinctive blind
reactions by some of the unemployed who refused to starve in
silence.

I learned at that time that unemployment and suffering alone
did not bring revolution, or action to change the system that
was responsible for unemployment. No! Only when the working class understand politically why they are unemployed; who
stops them from using the means of production; who ejects
them from their jobs; who causes their suffering; who their
real enemy is; and the kind of organisation and action needed
to change it all; only then will they act to establish workers'
control over industry and society.

UCS FIGHTS BACK

With unemployment in parts of Scotland at 10 per cent, the Tory decision to withhold financial support from the four Upper Clyde shipyards was, as James Milne (Assistant General Secretary of the Scottish TUC) said, 'an act of criminal folly'.

The Government's refusal to put money into UCS put into jeopardy the jobs of 40,000 people, and caused the workers at UCS to put up a strong fight against the closures. This fight has led to a wider understanding of the political nature of unemployment, and of the system of society in which we live, both among the UCS victims and workers generally, and has also widened the belief that unemployment is not something to be accepted meekly, but to be fought tooth and nail.

The Tory leaders, while they anticipated and even actively connived at the bankruptcy of UCS, cannot have anticipated the firm stand taken by the workers against closure. A confidential report by Nicholas Ridley MP, dated December 1969, outlined his proposals for dealing with Upper Clyde's financial problems:

'I believe that we should do the following on assuming office:
(a) Give no more public money to UCS.
(b) Let Yarrow leave UCS if they still want to, and facilitate their joining Lower Clyde if they still wish to do so.
(c) This would lead to the bankruptcy of UCS . . .
We could put in a Government "Butcher" to cut up UCS and to sell (cheaply) to Lower Clyde, and others, the assets of UCS, to minimise upheaval and dislocation . . .
(d) After liquidation or reconstruction as above, we should sell the Government holding in UCS, even for a pittance.
22. At this stage we should confine ourselves to saying absolutely firmly that there will be no more money from the Tory Government . . .'

Here was the root of the Government's 'no help for lame ducks' policy. But they had not reckoned with the determination of the shipyard workers, who decided to occupy the yards rather than submit tamely to their closure. The local leaders say that this action was not intended to be occupation for ownership of the yards, but a 'work-in', with the demand for 'the right to work' and no redundancies.

The UCS shop stewards, recognising the need for support from workers throughout the country, published the following appeal:

'Brothers and Sisters,
No group of workers has ever had a better case than we in the UCS.

We have proof and evidence that if there was any decent or appropriate legal system in this country, Ridley would be in the process of being prosecuted for anti-social activity.

We believe that the more we make our case known through-out this country, and given the support of ordinary decent people, and the whole British Labour movement, such is the strength of our case that we can shake not only this Govern-ment but bring into action all decent-minded people.

No-one likes to see an injustice being done and this is an injustice that is happening right now to the UCS workers.

All this is being perpetuated by a Government who have not the slightest conception of what it means to stand in a dole queue – and who, for that matter, don't care.
WE ARE DEMANDING THE RIGHT TO WORK.'

Jimmy Reid, senior Clydebank shop steward, pledged that UCS workers would not be bought off by promises of some saving of jobs. 'We have always made it clear,' he said, 'that the price of our co-operation is the maintenance of all four yards and employment.'

The support given to the just demands of the shipyard workers was spontaneous in its class character. Trade union members and shop stewards over the length and breadth of Britain, as well as workers in other countries, have sent their moral and financial support. National trade unions have sent varying sums of money to help organise resistance to closure of the yards. An Executive Council member of the AUEW, Bro. Len Edmondson, was reported in the press as saying that the decision of the workers to occupy was fundamentally correct, a working-class policy, and should be supported, although, like Bro. McGarvey of the Boilermakers, he doubted the possibility of changing the Tory Government's mind on UCS. As Bro. McGarvey said, the Tory slogan 'Stand on your own two feet' should have four other words added to it: 'outside the Labour Exchange'.

Nevertheless, the Government must be fought. Bro. Garland, President of the AUEW Foundry Section, has called for a 'holding operation' until we can get this Government out, a Labour Government back, and nationalisation of the shipbuilding industry. In order to do this, the National Conference of the AUEW gave its support to whatever action the UCS workers might find necessary, in the following resolution:

'This AUEW National Conference condemns the attitude of the Government in refusing the request from UCS for liquid capital. It views as abhorrent the alternative proposed by the Board – of liquidation.

National Conference calls upon the Government to provide the necessary capital to maintain UCS as a shipbuilding unit of the Upper reaches of the Clyde with all the social and economic consequences in mind if this fails.

National Conference further sees this new injection of capital as a transitional stage to complete nationalisation.

National Conference fully supports the UCS workers in their determination to fight *by all means at their disposal* to maintain shipbuilding, and hence employment, on the Clyde upper reaches.'

Bro. D. McGarvey, at a conference of the Confederation of Shipbuilding and Engineering Unions, said that the labour force at UCS had been cut in the past by 25 per cent and yet production had increased by 87 per cent and the throughput of steel had risen to 1,400 tons in recent weeks, the highest level ever.

The crisis of the Upper Clyde Shipbuilders is not an isolated one, but a reflection of the crisis of the whole of British industry in which a growing proportion of workers and resources are unemployed. Nor is it only a national crisis, for in a number of capitalist countries shipbuilding is under stress, and government support is necessary for the sake of survival.

A pamphlet produced by the Institute for Workers' Control,

Whatever Happened at UCS?, gives the following account of the subsidies to shipbuilding by various governments:

'France pays a subsidy of 10 per cent on every order, plus further aid tied to the rate of inflation, while in Italy the rate of subsidy is 14 per cent. Apart from the advantage of low wages, and an undervalued yen, Japanese shipbuilders enjoy the protection of a 15 per cent tariff. The famous modernised shipyards of Sweden have been brought to the verge of collapse recently, and the Swedish Government have been forced to step in: the Gotaverken yard is facing losses of some £48 million and Uddervalla yard has lost money for each of the past five years. A similar situation is to be found in Germany, Denmark, Holland and Yugoslavia. The British Government itself has recently advanced a further £7 million to Harland & Wolff in Belfast in July this year, in addition to the £25 million advanced previously. [The Government had to pump a further £30 million into Harland & Wolff in 1972.] Of course this enterprise is crucial to the economy of Northern Ireland: but then, given the deteriorating state of the Scottish economy, UCS is of almost equal importance for Scotland.'

THE SOLUTION—NATIONALISATION AND WORKERS' CONTROL

In order to try and meet the competition in shipbuilding from countries where the industry is heavily subsidised, 'the Fairfield Experiment' was undertaken in 1965. The Fairfield shipyard was established with a share capital of £2 million, of which the Government provided 50 per cent, trade unions 10 per cent and private investors 40 per cent. (The Fairfield yard was incorporated into UCS in 1968.)

The unions, having played a financial part in setting up the Fairfield yard, were party to an agreement which said that there would be a prohibition on strikes, overtime bans and working to rule, unless the machinery for the settlement of disputes had first been exhausted. This agreement played a great part in increasing the production levels of the workers. This was done through breaking down craft differences and increasing flexibility of manning.

The AEU under Lord Carron contributed £50,000; the General and Municipal Workers, the Clerical and Administrative Workers, the Woodworkers, the ETU, all contributed various sums to the Fairfield experiment, and this led to some friction, because the Boilermakers' Union refused to contribute, and were at the same time fighting to win wage increases. This led to the strange situation of some of the members, in those unions which had contributed to the Fairfields company, requesting that the company should not pay these increases.

In total, the unions contributed about £180,000 to Fairfields. No dividends have ever been paid on the shares held by the unions, and because of the bankruptcy of Upper Clyde Shipbuilders, it is likely that no money will be returned to the unions. But more important than this is the fact that, in spite of the Fairfield workers contributing financially through their unions to the ownership of their company, they had no measure of shopfloor control to show for it.

In 1968, the AEF passed a resolution calling for the nationalisation of the shipbuilding industry, and sent a letter to the Minister of Technology, Anthony Wedgwood Benn, to inform him of the resolution. The Minister replied that he had noted our resolution, and then went on to explain how the increasing number of mergers were beginning to make the industry competitive again. In fact, his letter stated that 'competitiveness is the key to a secure future in the shipbuilding industry'.

Both Harold Wilson and Anthony Wedgwood Benn, who could have provided the only real solution when in the Labour Government, have been to commiserate with the UCS workers. Harold Wilson, addressing workers at the John Brown Yard, declared that he 'backed their fight to assert their right to work'. That right to work would not be in question if the 1964–70 Labour Government, under Wilson's leadership, had brought the industry under public ownership.

Anthony Wedgwood Benn suggested 'competition' to solve the industry's problems. Harold Wilson wanted the Tory Government to guarantee the continuation of work at UCS, with its pre-redundancy labour force, for a period of five years. The TUC economic committee called for a Clydeside Development Authority, to take over all UCS assets and liabilities and seek new orders, 'the financial basis to be an initial grant plus interest-free loans and the power to raise loans on the market'.

And so we are back to our capitalist solutions of a capitalist problem. Such proposals can at best be only a stop-gap effort. The only lasting answer is to carry on a struggle for a change of government and the return of a Socialist government which will set about the public ownership of all shipbuilding and repair, with workers' control at all levels.

The present position in the UCS of occupation of the yards has had an electrifying effect upon Government and political and trade union leaders. Occupation raises the political understanding of the workers, and has already had a significant effect in the case of UCS. But it is not realistic to view the UCS situation as an attempt by workers to take control of the yards. UCS shop steward Jimmy Reid was asked (in the BBC radio programme *It's Your Line*, on 7 December 1971) whether he foresaw 'a real takeover' of the yards, or a return to the old private-employer position. Reid replied that a pocket of workers' control in a sea of private enterprise was not a viable proposition; workers' control, to be successful, must be on a national scale, under a socialist government. The UCS workers, he said, have no illusions; the object of the occupation is primarily to save the jobs of all the workers, and to increase their area of control over their own jobs. In May 1972, a four-year production agreement was signed by the shop stewards, the trade unions and the Marathon Company of America for the Clydebank yard to be used for the building of oil rigs and small supply vessels. So victory was achieved in keeping all four yards open, as the Government provided finance for the other three yards.

UCS has aroused more interest than other occupations, but it has not been the only one. The five hundred workers of S. G. Brown Ltd, Watford, made similar plans to occupy their factory against the threat of closure about three years before. There were threats by workers to occupy the GEC plant in Liverpool two years ago.

But attempts at occupation have not up to now met with much sustained success, and an article in *The Sunday Times* on the GEC closures points a finger at the reason for this – lack of co-ordination and real unity, not only within the plant, but between plants in the same company. *The Sunday Times* put the facts plainly:

'One of the more puzzling features of the whole story is that opposition from the shop floor was so fragmented and incoherent. If everybody in GEC had come out in protest over, say, Woolwich, Weinstock's plans would have received a nasty setback. In practice it did not work like that. The factories are so geographically scattered that the shop floor leaders simply did not have the organisation to build a common front. The workers at Woolwich did try to raise company-wide support, but when they appealed to their fellow workers at Coventry all they got were expressions of sympathy. The attempted workers' takeover at Liverpool failed for much the same reason. There was admittedly a joint shop stewards' committee, but it never really became an effective body. After Woolwich and Liverpool there were isolated attempts to black the movement of some goods, but that was about as far as it went. "It is my impression," says Scamp, "that brotherly love does not extend far beyond the factory gate." '

A sad comment on our trade union organisation, and on our slogan 'United we stand, divided we fall', but unfortunately all too often it is true. How often workers know about a strike or a problem in another part of their own industry, and do – nothing. Then when the problems arise for them too, they expect universal support, and are genuinely surprised not to receive it. We must learn that an injury to one is an injury to all.

OCCUPATION – A NEW WEAPON

Experience shows that to be successful with the weapon of factory or shipyard occupation, serious preparations have to be made by the workers and their shop stewards, with assistance from their trade union officials, and with the understanding and concrete support of their fellow workers in the same combine or industry.

All the workers involved must take part in discussions on the meaning of the occupation and the methods to be used, and on the theory and practice of workers' control. A carefully planned and united occupation, backed up by strong support from

K

workers not directly involved, was successful in America in the 1930s, and can be successful again.

From 30 December 1936 to 11 February 1937, workers at two General Motors Fisher Body plants protested against low wage levels and production speed-ups – carried on in spite of massive profits being made by the workers for the company – by occupying the two factories.

In addition to taking precautions against attack, such as building barricades and preparing stockpiles of car-parts to use as weapons, the work-people elected committees to deal with the planning of the strike, defence of the plants, food, health, education and recreation; a shift-system ensured that the plant was manned at all times; a union paper began to be published, and union membership, which had fallen during the thirties when workers saw their interests being sold out by union leaders, began to grow again.

Outside the occupied plants, financial support was forthcoming from all over America, and physical support was organised in the form of the workers' wives, who formed an Emergency Brigade to protect their husbands against attack by the National Guard. In spite of increasing the National Guard, utilising the police force (fully armed with gas bombs, grenades and revolvers), and attempting to break the occupation by issuing an injunction in the law courts, the employers, the State Governor and the State administration failed to smash the unity of the General Motors workers. Armed attacks were met and repulsed, both by the workers within the plants and by the tens of thousands of their supporters who had come from other areas. The attack through the law courts was called off when it was disclosed that the judge had a financial interest in General Motors.

On 11 February 1937, the company signed an agreement recognising the United Auto Workers as sole bargaining agent for the workers, and this success snowballed as more occupations throughout the country brought wage increases and improvements in conditions for many thousands of employees.

In the same year, 1937, a Royal Navy torpedo factory was established at Alexandria, in Scotland. After many years of competition with private companies, the Alexandria plant was fitted out with costly machinery for the purpose of building a new type of torpedo. Unfortunately, after ten years and £50 million in research, the Navy decided that the torpedo did not work, and would take too long to redesign. It was the Labour Government, in 1969, which decided to make a clean sweep, start a new project – to be put entirely in the hands of private enterprise – and close the Alexandria plant, making 1,200 workers redundant.

It was a stroke of luck for the Government that Plesseys (who, coincidentally, were to manufacture the new torpedo for the Navy) showed an interest in buying the plant in Alexandria, although not, as they made clear, to make torpedoes. There were six hundred machines in the plant, all expensive precision instruments; one and a half million pounds had been spent on the building in 1968; there was £250,000 worth of steel in store. Plesseys bought the whole plant, lock, stock and barrel, for £650,000, and hinted that, instead of redundancies, there would be jobs for 2,000 in the manufacture of computer controls for machine tools.

The Labour Government defended the sale by professing to be anxious to prevent further unemployment in an area where the numbers unemployed were already far above average. But only a few months later, 440 of the workers at Alexandria were made redundant. The machine tool market had dropped, said Plesseys. In August 1971, Plesseys decided to close the factory completely, and the remaining workers there occupied the factory premises. *The Sunday Times* (10 October 1971) stated that Plessey 'has merely done what most companies would do in a time of stringency: close down its least profitable plant, which just happened to be in Scotland'.

The Plessey workers themselves could not be expected to be so complacent about the issue. They issued a statement outlining the causes of the occupation, and declaring their objectives in occupying the plant. Demonstrations, solidarity with UCS workers, were unsuccessful – their only defence was to occupy. The statement continued:

'. . . we have no illusions in protest. The Plessey issue is political. What we say is this. Here in the Vale of Leven and 20 miles away on the River Clyde workers have started something that they cannot finish alone. We need the support of an army and that army is the organised working class.

We ask you, brothers, to come to our aid, not out of charity but to guard your *own* class and for the future of your *own* children. Let us tell you about the Vale of Leven. Here in the thirties, like many other working-class areas of Britain, the employing class laid waste our community as the textile bosses closed mill after mill. Now it's happening again . . .

If you count ten men in the Vale, one will be unemployed. The dole queues have doubled in two years. If Plessey get their

---

THE PLESSEY Co. PLANT ALEXANDRIA – OCCUPATION

STATEMENT FROM THE WORKPEOPLE DATED OCTOBER 12, 1971:

❝ This occupation of the Plessey plant at Alexandria is now entering its seventh week and the workpeople are still as resolute in their actions as they were on the first day of the take-over.

The occupation of the Plessey plant has now been the subject of a discussion at the Plessey Sites' Co-ordinating Trade Union Committee, representing 40,000 trade union members employed in Plessey establishments throughout the United Kingdom, with the following results:—

✳ (A) Industrial Sphere:

1. That the Plessey workers' occupation of the Alexandria plant is unanimously endorsed by the representatives attending this meeting, being recognised as a fight to keep the Plessey plant at Alexandria as a viable concern.

2. That the representatives attending this meeting unanimously agree to 'black' all items of machinery, material etc. which may emanate from the Alexandria plant, or any other plant that may assist management in the processing of the jobs in question.

✳ (B) Political Sphere:

1. That this Joint Meeting of trade union representatives demand that a Public Enquiry should be held, in order that all the facts regarding the closure of the R.N.T.F. and its subsequent sale to the Plessey Co. should be made public.

2. Considering the fact that Tory ministers have shown little or no concern about the Plessey closure at Alexandria, or the high unemployment rate within the area, then this Joint Meeting of the trade union representatives demands the removal of the Tory Government and the election of an administration with a social conscience to rule in the interests of the working classes. **❞**

way well over 15 per cent of all male workers will have no job. In the past we migrated like dogs looking for work. We won't do this any more! ...

Now the offensive must start before the shadow of the 1930s falls across every working class family in the land. Workers at the Plessey factory in Ilford have already blacked machines the Alexandria management want to ship down there. Now we ask you to join in our struggle. It's Plessey, Alexandria, today. It will be your factory tomorrow.

- We ask you above all to call on your leaders at local and national level to start an offensive against the government by mass industrial action.
- We ask you to demand that TUC organise the unemployed now by affording them full trade union rights.
- We ask the Labour Party to pick up the Tory challenge now. Declare the socialist programme to take the property, without compensation, from the greedy few who control it.'

OCCUPATION DEVELOPS CONTROL

The last three points are of major importance: first of all, we must not suppose that 'somebody' is going to save our jobs, stop closures, reduce unemployment. We ourselves must accept responsibility for doing this. The success of the General Motors occupation in the thirties was due in a large measure to the concerted efforts of not only the workers directly concerned but also of many thousands of workers not even in the same industry.

Workers' control cannot be achieved overnight. Nor can it be achieved piecemeal. Even small victories are the result of unity. Disorganisation wins nothing. The Plessey workers demanded action from all trade unionists, asking them to spur their leaders to 'start an offensive against the government'. We must explode once and for all the idea that leaders lead, and workers simply follow. The workers must instruct their elected representatives, and make sure that they are leading in the right direction, which means action from the shopfloor upwards. We can't afford to wait for the employers to give us job security and satisfactory wage increases. We must press for these things ourselves – and that means lending full support to our trade union brothers in *their* actions, as well as expecting full support from them in *our* claims.

Secondly, there is the demand for 'full trade union rights' for the unemployed. The trade unions and working-class parties will be making a profound error if they continue to allow unemployed workers to drift about defenceless. They have a right to be protected; they are still trade union members, and we must show that 'the right to work' is not just a slogan. but also a basis for action by the employed on behalf of those without jobs.

In spite of mass unemployment and short time, the working of overtime still continues. We must support overtime bans in all industries hit by unemployment. The AUEW instructed its District Committees in November 1971 to cut out overtime working; and the southern division of USDAW carried a resolution which stated that unemployment must be recognised as a deliberate Tory policy 'aimed at dividing the working class and weakening the struggle against the employers' onslaught on wages and living standards'. They called upon their executive to campaign for the TUC to organise the jobless:

'The TUC must:

Call on all affiliated unions to give the unemployed full trade union rights.

Demand that unemployment benefit is tied to a cost of living index prepared by the unions and the TUC.

Unite the employed and the unemployed in a common struggle to drive the Tory Government out of office and return a Labour government pledged to nationalise all basic industries under workers' control.'

This resolution recognises that 'the right to work' will be obtained only through the joint action of the employed and the unemployed, since it is the employed who have the greatest opportunity to exert pressure on both government and employers. *All* the working class must have the right to work. Our fight against unemployment must therefore be on a sound working-class basis; we must make clear the class nature of capitalism, and expose the role of its apologists in the trade union and labour movement.

Those who defend the employers on the grounds that 'the economic situation' demands that we must all tighten our belts, can rarely support their claim with facts. Plessey is faced with an occupation in Alexandria, because they are 'obliged' to close down the plant owing to a severe recession in their industry. Yet the company made a profit of £32·1 million in 1970, increased its dividend payment by 8 per cent, and paid two of its directors £61,388 and £50,000 respectively, in addition to their dividends for the year of nearly £100,000 each. Yet there are still 'trade unionists' who defend the plight of the poor employer, faced with the occupation of an 'unprofitable' plant.

REVOLUTIONARY OCCUPATION

Radek, at the Second Congress of the Communist International, in 1920, spoke in support of factory occupation as a means of fighting closures:

'One of the methods of fighting against the mass closing down of factories, wage cuts, and worsened conditions, is occupation of the factory by the workers, who will continue production against the wishes of the employer. With the prevailing hunger for goods, the continuation of production is particularly important, and therefore the workers should not permit the deliberate closing down of factories . . .

Capitalist arguments about foreign competition should in all circumstances be disregarded. The revolutionary unions must consider questions of wages and labour conditions not from the standpoint of competition between the robbers of different countries, but from the standpoint of maintaining and protecting labour power.

If there is an economic crisis in the country and the capitalists employ the tactics of pressure upon wages, it is the duty of the revolutionary unions to prevent piecemeal reductions in one industry after another, that is, they must not allow themselves to be split into several groups. The workers from the most essential industries – miners, railwaymen, electricians, etc. – must from the first be drawn into the struggle.'

It is these very industries, plus other nationalised concerns, such as the steel industry, which bear the brunt of the Tory Government's attack on wages, and which face the prospect of being sold off to private enterprise at give-away prices. (The Plessey fiasco is a warning of what can happen if this is permitted by the workers.) The unions representing workers in these industries have already united to press a joint wage claim. They should also be prepared to act together in the event of proposed hiving-off in any of their industries.

Let not this poem of Thomas Irving James, the son of an unemployed miner, be the epitaph of the unemployed in the future:

> 'Will they stand in groups again
> shabby, hungry, broken men,
> coughing, cursing, pacing . . . pacing,
> smoking, talking football, racing,
> hands thrust deep in trouser pockets,
> fingering their pitmen's dockets,
> wishing it had been a shilling,
> killing time, while time is killing –
> killing body, killing soul,
> dying slowly on the dole?'

REPEATING WRONG POLICIES

The slogan of the unemployed in the past, 'work or full maintenance', is not the answer. A redundancy payment and dole money are no substitute for a wage.

The comparatively new Claimants' Union, composed of those people claiming benefit from the State (including the sick and disabled, but largely the unemployed), scorn the 'right to work' demands of the trade unions. They say that the right to work is 'nothing but the *right to be used*, and does nothing to challenge the boss' *right to manage*'. The trade unions, it is claimed, are simply fighting for 'a few more jobs', even at the expense of the benefits which trade unionists have won over the years, and the answer offered by the Claimants' Union to this so-called 'sell-out' is to reject the trade unions, the TUC, and the Labour Party, and 'to get, by fair means or foul, every last penny that can be got from the state'. Furthermore, they claim that their objective is not simply to get a few more paltry jobs, but 'to struggle to build a society which is based on the real needs of all of us'.

Their argument has a number of serious flaws in it. First of all, 'getting every penny out of the state' means getting every penny they can get out of taxation, which comes largely, and bears most heavily, on the working class; so their aim of 'letting the government carry the can' for its policies hurts their own class more than anyone else. In other words, they reject the organised working class in the form of the trade unions, but wish to draw on their financial support while they fight their battles alone.

Secondly, the Claimants' Union aims to 'build a society which is based on the real needs of all of us', yet from the publicity which they hand out, it appears that only the unemployed are sufficiently virtuous to join in the fight. The houses, the schools, the hospitals we need will not be built by those who remain unemployed. The combined strength of employed and un-employed *within the trade unions* will be required to force the Government to release sufficient resources to increase job oppor-tunities in the public sector, and to make a start on the redevelopment which is urgently needed throughout the country. It is ironic that, with a million workers unemployed, workers are living in slums, or in the streets, sending their children to slum schools, and suffering in slum hospitals. *The Sunday Times* of 28 November 1971 made a similar point:

'There are grave needs for improvements on hospitals, schools, and other public services. And, of course, new long-term pro-jects as well. But we have Mrs Margaret Thatcher trying to dodge the comprehensive issue by not building secondary schools, we have local authorities frightened of the implications of expenditure for the rates . . . and worse still, we have some local authorities using restricted land-use planning as an excuse for avoiding needed expenditure.'

The unemployed alone will not force the Government to give the workers some of their money back, in order to provide more jobs and improve public services. The Claimants' Union attacks trade unions for not doing enough, for accepting too little and paying too high a price; but as I said before, the members must lead the leaders, and have no real excuse if the union moves in the wrong direction. This is one good reason why the un-employed should have full trade union rights, for they have even more reason to be militant than those in work.

Improvements in working conditions and wages have been won by the trade unions which the Claimants' Union so much despise. Yet one of the declared principles of the claimants is to refuse 'the stinking, low-paid jobs' offered to them, and hold out for better opportunities. This means, in effect, holding out for jobs in which wages and conditions have already been improved by trade union activity, and rejecting those where the workers' organisation has not been strong enough and militant enough to win improvements. If they really wished to 'build a new society', the poorly organised industries and services would be a good place to start.

BUILD CLASS UNITY

The whole of the working class must unite, employed and unemployed, black and white, Labour, Communist and Catholic, inside the trade unions and working-class parties which we have created over 150 years of struggle. They are our weapons to use in our struggle, and their power is there to be used by workers to take control of industry, land, banks, the social services, and all those things necessary to give the majority of the people – the working class – a secure and happy life, free of capitalist control and exploitations.

Bent on retaining their power and maximising profits for private industry, the Tory Government have persistently blamed unemployment on high wage settlements – workers pricing them-selves out of the market. Barbara Castle, speaking at the Labour Party Conference in 1971, accused the Tories of shedding

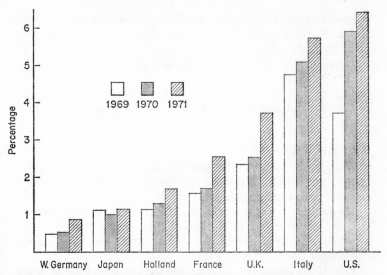

Unemployment: number of unemployed as a percentage of the working population. (Source: OECD)

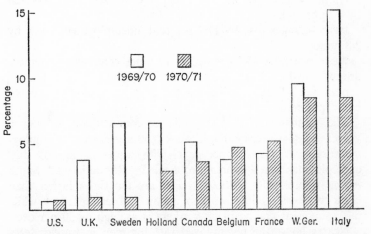

Purchasing power of wages (percentage increase). These are figures for the third quarter of one year compared with those for the third quarter of the previous year. (Source: OECD)

crocodile tears over the unemployment figures, and quoted Robert Carr as saying that 'the immediate cause of the present crisis in both prices and unemployment is the excess level of pay settlements'. We must not forget, of course, that in spite of Barbara Castle's scorn of this idea, the same theory was the keynote of the Labour Government's approval of *In Place of Strife*. The following figures refute this contention absolutely:

'DO HIGH WAGES CAUSE UNEMPLOYMENT?

What truth is there in the repeated assertions of CARR, DAVIES, BARBER and HEATH and other Tories that wages are too high and this causes unemployment?

Mr Barber, 21st April 1971, said "I am in no doubt whatever that the major cause of the increase in unemployment is the absurdly high level of pay settlements which we have experienced since the Autumn of 1969".

This is an absurd statement. One only has to look at wage increases and unemployment figures in other countries for 1969/70.

ITALY – Wages increase by 22·6 per cent, unemployment fell by 2·2 per cent.

JAPAN – Wages rose by 17·9 per cent, unemployment down by 2·8 per cent.

WEST GERMANY – Wages up by 12·1 per cent, unemployment dropped by 0·7 per cent.

DENMARK – Wages up by 9·8 per cent, unemployment down by 2·6 per cent.

The poor countries like India confound these assertions. Wages in India average 60p a week (£30 a year) and unemployment runs at over 25 per cent – with wages as low as this, unemployment is a worse problem. In Rhodesia and South Africa where white workers' wages are ten times higher than black workers' – white workers enjoy full employment while unemployment among black workers is as high as 30 per cent.

Nearer home the unemployed rate for men in Londonderry is 16 per cent, but wages are at least £5 a week less than the National Average.'

These statistics were circulated during the TUC-organised lobby of Parliament on 24 November 1971, when thousands of workers lobbied their MPs to demand the right to work. In Scotland, in June 1971, a demonstration of 100,000 Scottish workers highlighted the problems faced not only by workers on the Clyde but all over the country. A Youth Conference held in the Central Hall in London, and attended by 1,500 Young Socialists, focused attention on the situation of school-leavers, walking from the classroom into the labour exchange. The Institute for Workers' Control, planning a conference on the unemployment problem, decided to hold it on Tyneside, where 90,000 were currently unemployed.

These demonstrations of wrath over the Government's policy on unemployment were backed up by practical action from the AUEW, in the form of a national claim for improved wages and conditions. The claim included substantial wage increases for all categories of workers and increased annual holidays and a shorter working week of thirty-five hours. This would put more money in the workers' pockets, thereby increasing the demand for goods and opening up job opportunities. The Tories are naturally opposed to wage increases at any time, and are notoriously opposed to a redistribution of purchasing power in the form of a wealth tax.

A pamphlet produced by the Tory Bow Group, *Against Wealth Tax*, argues that 'Anyone who believes in freedom must be worried at the idea that the state may dictate how much property or wealth a man should own'.

Yet they have no hesitation about applying the same principals to control of wages, and they even dictate whether a worker should earn anything at all – by depriving him of a job. It is in the interests of the working class that wages should rise, not at the expense of prices but at the expense of the capitalists!

Demands for higher wages and shorter working hours can provide an immediate alleviation of unemployment problems, but they are not a long-term answer. We must direct our efforts towards changing the social order, establishing public ownership and the complete enactment of Clause Four of the Labour Party Constitution, thereby taking control of the economy out of the hands of the few who control the productive forces for their private profit and personal satisfaction.

Only by democratic public ownership and control of the means of production and distribution can we solve the problems of unemployment and poverty.

Chapter 9

Movements Towards Workers' Control in Basic Industries and Services

We want to see trade union representatives being able to invade the power of the bureaucrats in industry, limiting the dictatorial and unilateral authority of management and, above all, involving the workers through their unions in the decisions which affect their working lives.

Jack Jones (General Secretary, Transport and General Workers' Union)

'Democratic public ownership and control of the means of production and distribution.' Public ownership we have, but it is neither democratic, nor is it sufficiently extensive.

Furthermore, we have not taken full advantage of the opportunities so far created, for example in the field of municipalisation, and in the Co-operative movement. Labour councils have the power, and the duty, to establish municipally owned undertakings for the benefit of the community (see pages 65–68), but they are too often content to rely on private concerns to supply their needs. The Co-operative movement is *owned* by its members but, although this is a step in the right direction, it is not sufficient – members and workers in the movement should not be satisfied until they exercise complete control over their organisation. Likewise, 'the public' are the nominal owners of nationalised industries, and the employees in those industries number many thousands – yet control rests in the hands of a handful of individuals, and the nationalised industries are as far from being democratic as they were when privately owned.

Between non-democratic private companies on the one hand,

and non-democratic public industries on the other, there is a very tiny island of half a dozen firms which claim to be 'common-ownership enterprises'. These companies are members of an organisation founded in 1958, and now known as the Industrial Common Ownership Movement. The object of this organisation is 'to achieve democratic control of their own work by people at work', and the member-companies operate on the basis of all workers being equal co-owners of the company, and having an equal say in its direction, and in the distribution of profits.

Perhaps the best-known exponent of 'common ownership' is the Scott Bader Commonwealth, which, in the course of its twenty-one years' existence, has had an average growth-rate of 30 per cent a year. Its 350 co-owners produce an annual turnover of about four million pounds, and of the profits, 60 per cent is re-invested, 20 per cent distributed to the staff, and 20 per cent is donated to charities. The administration is supervised by an elected Community Council, although there is a Board of Directors which organises day-to-day business, subject to the control of the workers.

The Scott Bader Commonwealth recognises two difficulties which lie in the way of extending common ownership to other enterprises. 'The assumption of a responsibility by the workers far beyond their normal experience' – this is a 'problem' which workers should be only too willing to overcome. The second difficulty explains why, after thirteen years of the Industrial Common Ownership Movement, there are still only six participant companies, and that difficulty is 'the self-divestment of assets and powers by the original owners'.

WORKERS CAN GOVERN

We simply can't afford to wait to have common ownership handed to us on a plate. Workers' control must be taken, for it will never be given. But one thing the common-ownership experiments have succeeded in doing is in giving the lie to those who say that workers not only couldn't run an enterprise, but wouldn't, even if they had the opportunity. 'They need a boss to blame,' says William Davis, in an article entitled 'Why the workers can never run a business' (*Evening News*, 5 August 1971). The article explained why the UCS occupation was 'bound to be short-lived', and how neither the unions, nor the workers (nor, incidentally, private industry) really wanted workers' control. Mr Davis argued:

' "Power to the people" has always been an attractive battle cry. And ever since the Industrial Revolution people have argued that all would be well in British industry if only management would step aside and let the workers have a go.

The trouble is that, as a rule, it simply reflects a refusal to accept unpalatable financial facts. Never mind if a factory or shipyard cannot sell the stuff it makes; production must be maintained regardless. Earlier this year a trade union called for "the film industry to be nationalised without compensation and placed under workers' control". The same demand was made when Rolls-Royce went bust. It has been heard this week. And we shall hear it again as the Tories shoot down more of their "lame ducks". The Upper Clyde experiment is the latest in a number of "brave and desperate stands".

Alas, it's bound to be short-lived despite the current talk of possible orders from Communist countries for new ships. It's not that shop stewards don't know their way round a balance-sheet; nowadays most of them do. The snags are more serious. Who will meet the bills for wages and raw materials, and where's the money to come from once the current work in hand is finished? Which private shipowner would be ready to entrust large sums to an experimental worker-controlled concern? Two years ago a group of Merseyside trade unionists made a similar attempt when Sir Arnold Weinstock decided to close down three GEC-English Electric factories. An organisation calling itself the Institute for Workers' Control, with Jack Jones and Hugh Scanlon as Council members, applauded the move and produced a booklet.

"The occupation of the Weinstock plants," it declared, "will not lead into Utopia. It will be a hard and testing struggle. The workers will need massive support from the Labour movement. Unless their colleagues in other factories and industries collect large sums of money to aid them they will be starved out.

Unless a vast political and trade union solidarity movement arises they may be forced out."

They were. "The hard and testing struggle" never really got off the ground. Workers are, on the whole, less interested in idealism than in the financial backing for their weekly pay packets. It suits them to have bosses to complain to and to have shop stewards to complain on their behalf. They don't want to be their own bosses . . . It is even questionable whether the majority of workers are all that keen on nationalisation . . .

In Britain the TUC has never shown much enthusiasm for workers' control. A more fashionable term in recent years has been "participation" – giving workers more say in management. The TUC is no more keen on pouring good money after bad than the Tory Government. And it suits moderate trade unionists to keep the traditional division between "Them" and "Us". They know that the present system gives them far more effective "control". Union strength today is such that few managements dare to brush aside the shop steward's wishes. If a few lavatory attendants can bring a whole plant to a standstill (as they have done more than once) it is clearly absurd to pretend that workers have no power. If a long and costly strike at Ford can produce a package settlement of 33 per cent, as it did the other day, then it is farcical to pretend that workers are at the mercy of ruthless tycoons.

Still, I would dearly love to see the trade unions have a go. They have big investments in stocks and shares. I don't blame them for not wanting to put their money in something as risky as a shipyard, or indeed in any concern which is financially shaky. But I would warmly applaud a collective union decision to make a public take-over bid for a prosperous going concern (say a large electronics group) and let the workers show what they can do if they're given a fair start.'

The unions have, of course, already invested money in a 'shaky concern' – in the Fairfields shipyards, which continued to be run on capitalist lines, with subsequent financial failure, and loss of jobs. The workers' money has also bought the nationalised industries, paying handsome and crippling compensation to the former owners, which has prevented the economic running of those industries, while giving little or no real power to the workers. Hardly surprising if workers are not 'all that keen' on nationalisation, on those terms!

But it is a fallacy to suppose, as William Davis does, that workers don't want control, and are more interested in money than in 'idealism'. Under the present economic system, the emphasis must of necessity be on money; there is little incentive towards efficiency, when efficiency inevitably paves the way to redundancy and loss of pay. And the mere fact of being able to screw a wage rise out of an employer by means of a strike is no indication of workers' power; the fact that workers are obliged to go on strike to demonstrate their point of view shows how little real control they have over how their lives and jobs are organised.

Workers' power must not be limited to strike action; yet Mr Davis is right when he says that most workers do not want to go to the other extreme of being 'the boss'. The object of workers' control is not to develop a competitive spirit, but to make a collective effort to improve living standards for all; the aim is not to divide, but to unite. Workers' control is not 'idealism', but a practical economic system, providing security of employment, and greater co-operation and efficiency. In the words of Hugh Scanlon, President of the AUEW,

'Workers already have the knowledge necessary to effectively increase this country's material resources. We have probably the most industrially experienced work-force in the world. But why should workers bring forward constructive ideas for the efficiency of a plant if it means their employers' gain and with the possibility of their work-mates being made redundant as a result. Democratic self-management of industry by the workers themselves would release the long dammed up potential of the workers' hardwon experience.'

TUC AND WORKERS' CONTROL

There is increasing pressure from workers in many sectors of the community for this potential to be realised in the form of workers' control, and in spite of what William Davis has to say

about the TUC's lack of enthusiasm, the Agenda for the 1971
TUC Congress contained resolutions calling for more public
ownership, greater industrial democracy, and workers' control.
The National Union of Public Employees, for example, called
upon Congress to 'reaffirm its belief that an essential function
of the trade union Movement is to secure for workers and their
unions a continually increasing measure of control over their
work situations', and demanded that future TUC policies should
include 'measures designed to promote industrial democracy'.

The Greater London Council Staff Association introduced an
amendment to this resolution, reminding the TUC that industrial
democracy is as necessary in public services as in the private
sector, and urging 'the development of the principle of direct
participation by public service workers'.

The TUC's President, John Newton, has also put a strong case
for industrial democracy. In his inaugural address in 1969, he
declared that no one who has not experienced the effect of years
of confinement within the walls of mass production, without
apparent means of escape, can understand the debilitating effects
on the mind, the vocabulary or on the spiritual capacity of
human endurance. He went on:

'Where work gives little or no satisfaction to the workers, where
there is no freedom to exercise their skill, where men and women
do not determine how they do their work, where they have
become merely components in the production system, they have,
during their working lives, lost their identity as individuals.
Underlying many strikes is a protest against this unnatural
environment.'

Of course, the less self-determination the worker has, the
better the employer likes it. It's just a question of simple arith-
metic:

computer-programmed worker − appetite =
maximum profit + capitalist satisfaction.

Far from being prepared to sit back and become mindless
automatons, many workers in many industries are formulating
detailed plans for the operation of their industries by the
workers themselves. These plans are not coming from isolated

pressure-groups. More often, there are several plans in circulation for any given industry, ranging from mild reforms to outright workers' control, and the suggestions come from workers on the shopfloor, based on their appreciation of the current situation.

STEELWORKERS' CONTROL

Workers in the steel industry, for example, after fighting for the nationalisation – and re-nationalisation – of their industry, are now engaged in a two-fold struggle: to prevent the sale of profitable sections of the British Steel Corporation to private industry, and to extend their power over decision-making, which has so far been limited to an unsatisfactory system of appointed workers' directors.

Bearing in mind the situation facing steel workers in the 1970s, a situation of public-sector wages being held down, 'peripheral activities' under threat of being hived off to the private sector, and severe 'rationalisation' leading to redundancy, the co-operation which has only recently begun between the various steel industry unions seems long overdue.

It has only recently become standard practice, for example, for Works Councils to be based on trade union nominations (where formerly, the Works Council was a rival to the unions, and the unions were rivals to each other). Even with this welcome development, the Steel Seminar at the 1970 Conference of the Institute for Workers' Control reported that 'the actual identification of the demands that could effectively be made through Works Councils as opposed to individual Union negotiations was not seen by most of the group to be at all clear'.

Nationally, the TUC's Steel Committee has brought a little unity to the industry, but 'little is known by the rank and file of the work of the Committee and it is in danger of being very far removed from the problems and aspirations of the steel workers down below'. Between the TUC Steel Committee and the contentious Works Councils there is virtually no real organisation.

In a pamphlet on 'The Threat to the Steel Workers', the Scunthorpe Group put forward some proposals 'to bring a larger area of management policy under the control of the workers'. Their proposals include:

- Steel Committees covering all unions should be set up for each Works Group to 'frame common policies in consultation with the BSC'.
- Individual Works Committees should be set up to discuss domestic problems and elect delegates to the Works Group Steel Committees.
- Delegates from Works Group Committees should attend divisional and regional conferences to consult with trade union officials.
- The TUC Steel Committee should establish contact with Works Groups and Committees by
  (i) Publication of a regular bulletin.
  (ii) Calling of regular Works Group Committee conferences.
  (iii) Circulation of proposals for joint trade union demands for discussion and comment by Works Group Committees.
  (iv) Visits by the TUC Steel Committee to Works Groups.
- Works and Works Group Steel Committees should be given union funds in proportion to membership, to cover employment of a full-time secretary, correspondence, travel, conferences, sub-committees, etc.

The left-wing paper *Voice of the Steelworkers* goes further in its demands, and is more specific about the composition of committees. It proposes that:

- The unions should nominate half the members of the National Board for the steel industry, and that such members should retire after a five-year period of service.
- An operating board should work at Combine or Group level, and that half of its members should be elected by Workers' Councils.
- Workers' Councils, composed of 50 per cent trade-union-elected members and 50 per cent elected from shopfloor level committees, should have the right to information re costings and policy.
- Shop-, mill- and office-level committees elected by secret ballot should organise appointment of shop managers, deployment

of labour, hiring and firing etc., with right of appeal to a higher committee in the event of disagreement.

These proposals formed the basis of the unions' campaign against the inadequate system set up by the British Steel Corporation after its re-nationalisation – a system under which Lord Melchett reigned supreme, and was personally responsible for the appointment of 'worker directors' to the Steel Board.

The 'new' idea of having shopfloor representatives on the board of directors (it was generally hailed as a new idea, although socialists had been advocating this – and a lot more – for many years!) was watched with interest by trade unionists, and its failure has caused some critics to reject the whole concept of worker directors. This attitude amounts to throwing the baby out with the bath water, since it is not the idea which is wrong, but the method of putting it into practice.

If the choice of representatives rests with a Tory peer, instead of with the workers, it is hardly a surprise to find that the results are rather less than revolutionary. A report by Vincent Hanna in *The Sunday Times* (7 November 1971) quoted two of the worker directors extensively, and the following quotes are typical of their outlook:

'Of course, we're not really directors at all . . . We don't have anything to do with the policy.'

'I see myself as an ordinary manager too, not as a worker.'

'The big problem has been that workers won't trust us, we lose contact with them because we are appointed as individuals, not as their representatives.'

'A tub-thumping shop steward on the board would be disastrous. We have to be free to take management's side if we think it's right.'

'I'm a Socialist, but I'm not your Michael Foot type, I'm more of a Jenkins man; Roy, of course – not Clive.'

'I feel that unofficial strikes are never justified. They are usually caused by bad communications when management doesn't inform the workers of its decisions.'

Notice the word 'inform' – no asking or co-operating, only *telling*! And when the worker directors go back to the workers to *tell* them what has been decided on their behalf, 'they become tarred with the management brush and the accumulated suspicion of years'.

The answer is not less worker directors, but more – the more, the better – directly elected by the workers they represent, and required to report back to the electorate at regular intervals. Workers should have the right to withdraw their representative if he fails to protect their interests to the full extent of his powers as a director. With adequate safeguards, worker directors could prove to be a useful advance in the direction of workers' control.

William Meade, himself a steel worker, in his paper on 'Nationalised Steel' in the book *Can the Workers Run Industry?*, sums up the demands of the steel workers in two basic points: it is necessary 'to bring the unions together at every level and to connect the different levels democratically'; and it is essential for 'workers' representatives to be accountable to the workers they represent, both by being elected from, and by continuing to work among, their fellows'.

MOTOR-WORKERS' CONTROL

'The principle obstacle to be overcome is the fragmented character of the carworkers' militancy.' This remark from Tony Topham, a tutor at Hull University, characterises much of the progress towards workers' control in the motor industry, and provides the reason for the much-repeated call for 'one union for the motor industry'.

The one-union idea could probably best be achieved, however, not by a sudden migration of workers from the twenty-two unions which represent them at present – which would destroy at a stroke a hundred years or more of hard grind by trade unionists in a wide variety of industries, and gravely deplete the strength of the present unions – but by a 'Motor Industry Confederation of Unions', with a delegate national conference, and the power to conduct negotiations for the industry.

But this will not solve the immediate problems of workers at shopfloor level, and, with these problems in mind, the joint shop stewards' committees have united to form unofficial Combine

Committees, which have no official ties with either unions or management, and which act to improve earnings in the various plants of the same firm, and also attempt to narrow wage differences between firms. By spreading information on rates from plant to plant, these committees also promote a catching-up process among workers in lower-paid establishments. The committees exist to provide contact between workers in companies affiliated to the Engineering Employers' Federation.

The Ford Company, however, does not belong to the Federation, and instead conducts its negotiations on a company-wide basis with the twenty-two unions involved. Links between the Ford workers' unofficial Combine Committee and the similar committees in other car companies are much frowned upon by Ford management. At a Court of Inquiry into a Ford dispute in 1963, the company 'stated their determination to manage their establishments. They were very conscious how their control was being undermined by the skilful and ruthless exploitation by some shop stewards of the consultative machinery established by Agreement'. Their main objection was to the Joint Shop Stewards' Committee, 'this canker in the trade union movement' – which shows that such apparently minor activities can be effective enough to cause concern among those with financial interests to protect, because they are closer to the shopfloor and more directly representative of workers' opinions than the 'official' negotiators.

In spite of the objections of managements, the joint committees have done much to establish links between companies and between members of various unions, as well as between different plants in the same company. In addition, they put out feelers towards other industries. Many car manufacturers also have other major interests – for example, in aircraft production – and their workers in both industries belong to the same group of trade unions, and are often engaged in broadly similar work. The Combine Committees therefore maintain contact with workers in associated industries, and exchange information with the aim of narrowing differentials between workers on comparable jobs in a range of industries.

But what about the future? The Report of the Automobile Conference of the International Metalworkers' Federation in

1964 made the following proposals for the protection of trade unionists in the world motor industry:

I   Trade union demands should include:
- Business policy directed to healthy development of overall economy.
- Control of monopolies and market-political arrangements.
- Accurate forecasting and national planning of production.
- Maximum security of employment, if necessary by government intervention.
- Government intervention in siting and planning new plants.
- Safeguarding economic stability by agreement between unions, government and employers.
- Reduction of trade barriers between industrialised countries.
- Extensive state intervention in promotion of motor industries in developing countries.

II   Motor workers' demands should include:
- Protection of employment and social position of individual workers and continuous improvement in their standard of living.
- Full participation of workers in technical reorganisation, work planning and the whole running of their factory.
- A guaranteed monthly and annual wage.
- Improved public unemployment insurance.
- Companies to accept social responsibilities in decisions about production and investment.
- Reduction of working hours, longer paid holidays and earlier retirement pensions; protection of health and welfare.
- Improved training and re-training.
- Special protection of older employees.
- Improved job security and compensation for dismissal.
- Improved retirement pensions and other social benefits.

A Ford shop steward, in a *Voice of the Unions* broadsheet, called for 'full protection for convenors and shop stewards against arbitrary dismissals, the right to hold meetings on the premises in the workers' time, the right to have a say in and negotiate work loads and work times, 100 per cent trade unionism and a unified shop stewards' movement throughout plants'.

The IMF's demands and the Ford worker's suggestions would

be a prelude to the kind of control outlined by Bob Harrison (who was formerly a car-worker, and a teacher for the Workers' Educational Association) in a pamphlet, *Workers' Control and The Motor Industry.*

1. Nationalisation *with* workers' control.
2. The establishment of workers' Councils, representing all sections in the plant proportionally, meeting weekly, and controlling: organisation of production and systems of work, systems of payment and incentives, disbursement of the works surplus, some research and training, and relations with regional planning organisations.
3. The establishment of National Product Councils (for cars, buses, commercial vehicles, engines, instruments, tyres, etc.), elected from the Workers' Councils.
4. The establishment of a National Council, composed of elected members of the National Product Councils, to represent the whole industry in relation with the government and other sectors of the economy, with responsibility for the national investment programme, research and development, manpower and training, the export organisation, and the co-ordination of the Product Groups.

The National Committee of the AEU, not so detailed but equally blunt in its demands for the car industry, pinpointed the domination of the industry by foreign capital, when it passed the following resolution in 1968: 'National Committee, in the interests of our members and the nation, instruct the Executive Council to press for public ownership of the British car industry, starting with foreign-owned companies.'

The car industry must be nationalised by the next Labour Government, not in the same way that other industries have been nationalised in the past with bureaucratic control, but with real power for the workers through their democratically elected representatives.

How can this be achieved? It can only be achieved by increased activity on the part of the rank and file, which will only take place as the rank and file become more aware of the importance of control, and of the political implications of control in the hands of capitalist employers.

Rank-and-file activity and pressure for workers' control will increase as the workers come to realise that, to quote Bob Harrison again, 'any improvement in their lot will be achieved by themselves, or not at all'.

AIRCRAFT-WORKERS' CONTROL

The Plowden Report on the aircraft industry, and subsequent developments at Rolls Royce, have provided an overwhelming case for complete nationalisation. First of all, there is virtually no competition between private firms – and competition is held by the Tories to be the mainstay of private enterprise. There are two main categories of aircraft manufacture – BAC/Hawker Siddeley in airframes, and Rolls Royce in engines – and these are subsidised to the extent of 75 per cent or more on production and other costs by the taxpayer.

At the same time as absorbing huge government subsidies, battening on to the arms programme and defence spending (which gives private companies a dangerous vested interest in defence policy), and making unwarranted profit out of government contracts, these companies are also engaged in expanding their overseas interests at the expense of British plants.

The Confederation of Shipbuilding and Engineering Unions stated, in November 1971, that 'The British aerospace industry is continuing the decline of the past five years. The lack of any consistent policy of growth by British governments in the past has produced a situation unmatched in any other country'.

In support of this statement, the Confederation produced details of the numbers employed in aircraft manufacture in the USA, the EEC countries, Canada, Sweden, Japan and Israel. In each case, there was a substantial increase in the total numbers between 1960 and 1970 – in some cases the industry had doubled in size during that period – whereas the comparable figures for Britain were:

1960:	291,000
1967:	254,000
1970:	229,000

The Plowden Report advocated 'some degree of public ownership of the two main aircraft groups' in order 'to achieve a satisfactory framework for the industry's future'. They did not, however, recommend complete nationalisation, and advocated no interference in the aero-engines side of the industry, which was doing very nicely.

The Labour Government, while not going the whole way with the Plowden recommendations, for a time supported the idea of a State minority interest in the airframe department. But in 1967 even this was cancelled.

Not that aircraft workers would welcome a complete and 'straightforward' nationalisation such as that inflicted on the various groups of power workers, with no voice in the management of the industry. Present demands from a very broad base of aircraft workers go further than that, and the wide establishment of joint shop stewards' organisations and national Combine meetings of shop stewards have been followed up by demands for the takeover of the industry on a workers' control basis, without compensation. Under the present private system, workers have been framing demands for the opening of the books, not only at government level, but at shopfloor level too; for resistance to changes in work practice except under conditions of workers' control; and for examination of the books prior to productivity deals.

(But why submit to productivity deals in the first place, with or without opening the books? They amount to an admission by the workers that their share of the profit is already correct, and that they must earn higher wages by an increase in productivity. This is never true.)

Shop stewards have suggested the formation of workers' councils, to be composed of shop stewards and members of shopfloor gangs. The shopfloor gangs in the aircraft industry are already responsible for the allocation of work and the settlement of discipline questions. These workers' councils would form the basis of complete workers' control in a nationalised aircraft industry. As Alan Rooney, editor of *Aviation Voice*, says, however, 'all trade union representatives at national and plant level in any nationalised industry should be elected and sponsored by shop-floor workers, *to whom they should be responsible and accountable*', and this applies to workers' councils just as much as to worker directors.

Industrial Democracy in the Nationalised Airlines, a paper prepared by a nationalised airlines' Study Committee, has come up with some valuable suggestions for reforming their own present system of nationalised non-control – suggestions which might well be taken to heart by the manufacturing side of the industry, which is still struggling for public ownership.

As the paper points out, 'staff representation must exist at all policy-making levels within the firm, including the highest of all – the Board of Directors'. On the other hand, the simple trick of appointing worker directors, as has been done in the Steel Corporation, taking care to cut all ties with the shopfloor and giving shopfloor workers no say in their election, does not meet the conditions required by workers' control. Even the system of joint consultation in the nationalised airlines, while sounding a very high-flown concession to workers' demands, is not sufficient: 'it was never the intention that the system of joint consultation in airways should have any effect on the prerogative of management to take decisions.'

The following points were agreed by the Study Committee:

(*a*) Worker participation in management is the involvement of staff in all levels in the process of decision-making.

(*b*) The Panel system was not being used to its full and proper extent.

(*c*) That there should be direct representation of staff on the Board of Management of nationalised airlines.

(*d*) That such representation should be by not less than four members, or one quarter of the total Board membership.

(*e*) That the worker directors should be elected by the trade union membership of the airlines.

(*f*) No matter what election process be used, once elected a worker director would have responsibility to the whole of the airline staff membership.

The committee also put forward some plans for the election of worker directors, although recognising that these plans were in some ways defective, and gave room for improvement. They included division of the airline staff into a number of sections, each of which would be able to make nominations for worker directorships, each nomination backed by a certain number of endorsements ('to reduce the possibility of frivolous nominations'). All nominees would have to be members of an appropriate trade union. All members of staff would then be entitled to vote for the nominees in their section. The Study Group suggests the possibility of using salary packets as a means of distributing ballot papers, and of personal collection of completed papers, both of which ideas seem to be particularly open to abuse.

On election, the worker director should serve a similar period of service to other directors, at the same salary, with the same clerical and advisory facilities. Moreover, 'his job must remain open, and he must lose none of his rights as an employee', including pension rights.

With regard to the 'divided loyalties' of a worker director, the BEA Heathrow Branch of ASTMS points out that loyalty to the Corporation and loyalty to the workers should be essentially the same thing. The workers *are* the Corporation, and their interests must coincide. For this reason, the facilities for the reporting back of worker directors to their electors is vital to the functioning of such a scheme.

In conjunction with this, the machinery of joint consultation could also be improved in the following ways:

1. Lay members should be elected to the Trade Union side of the National Joint Council for Civil Air Transport in the proportion of one lay member and one full-time official.
2. The Staff Side of the National Sectional Panels should consist of lay members plus full-time officials.
3. The Local Panels should carry out their duties fully in accordance with their Constitution, discussing and deciding the answers to local problems without outside interference, either from management or unions.

All these proposals, however useful, will not function in a vacuum. *Aviation Voice* sees the problem of workers' control in relation to all other industries, whether they are labouring under the present difficulties of State control, or struggling against the private employer: 'It seems obvious that a "plan for aircraft" should be linked to a workers' plan for engineering as well as to a workers' plan for steel.'

The Confederation of Shipbuilding and Engineering Unions evolved, in the 1950s, an integrated plan for the public ownership of many sections of the engineering industry, and this plan is now being brought up to date. Such an exchange of ideas and interests will be a vital part of the struggle for complete control by the workers in all areas of the country's economy.

DOCK-WORKERS' CONTROL

The operation of the principle of recall seems to be sufficient safeguard in the election of worker directors, as proposed by the airline workers; provided that a worker director is directly accountable to his electors, democratic control is assured.

Not in the dockers' opinion, apparently! The proposals printed in *Humberside Voice* in 1965 not only reject direct representation of workers at national level, but suggest that no worker could remain uncorrupted, once elected to a place on the board. Their suggestions for dock democracy include:

1. Nationalisation of the industry under a National Port Authority.
2. Presentation of accounts and annual report to Parliament by the NPA in the orthodox manner of present nationalised industries.
3. The establishment of Portworkers' Councils with 'power of continuous supervision over the NPA at both national and local levels'. These Councils would have no direct representation on the NPA, but would have access to meetings, minutes, accounts, etc., and power to report to Parliament their criticisms of the NPA. They would also report back on proceedings to their members.
4. The NPA would become the sole contractor for dock labour, with responsibility for the determination of the total size of the labour force, and sending requisitions to the Portworkers' Councils of work to be done.
5. The National Dock Labour Board would be taken over by the Portworkers' Councils at both national and local level, and the Councils would then be responsible for hiring and firing (with an appeals procedure), promotion, safety, disposal of the

work-force on various jobs, health, welfare, recreation, and education facilities.

The demands do not include direct representation of workers on the National Port Authority, but it is claimed that the 'supervisory powers' of the Portworkers' Councils 'reinforce in a most important way the principle of accountability which, as nationalised industries are now operated, is quite inadequately applied'. The reason given for workers' non-representation is the possibility that representatives would be subject to a capitalist economy and its corrupting forces, since a nationalised dock industry would, under present conditions, be obliged to operate on the profit principles of private industry. 'The State is bound to reflect, and to impose on its public sector, today's priorities.'

There are several serious objections to these proposals as they stand. First of all, the 'supervisory powers' of the Portworkers' Councils over the National Port Authority are not 'powers' at all, in any accepted sense of the word. All they give is the ability to overlook the operations of the NPA and then, in the event of disagreement, to stand on the sidelines ineffectively whispering objections. This is not 'accountability'. There is no provision for appeal against the NPA's decisions, and – more important – no say for the dock-workers in the original formation of those decisions. How can the NPA be accountable to the dock-workers, if it is neither elected by the workers, nor committed to serving their interests?

The 'reason' given for non-representation is no real reason, if proper accountability were really enforced. The workers' representatives on the national authority would be (a) in continuous contact with their electors and responsible to them, and (b) subject to removal, should they fail to represent the decisions of Portworkers' Councils. Under such conditions, workers' representatives would become a steering force on the national authority, modifying its propensity to make decisions based on capitalist philosophy.

Workers should beware the tendency to avoid exposure to capitalist corruption to such an extent that they refuse all oppor-

tunities to take part in decision-making. Providing there is sufficient protection through accountability to electors, adequate
representation on national councils can be a valuable move
towards real control by workers. The purists, of course, prefer
absolute control immediately, or nothing. The result is most
likely to be nothing! As Mao Tse-tung said, one step is the first
step in a ten-thousand mile march.

Since the *Humberside Voice* demands were published in 1965,
much has happened in dockland. First of all came the Labour
Party's 1966 election promises, which held out hopes of much
more than *Humberside Voice* had modestly asked for. These
were followed by the Labour Government's White Paper in
1969, which actually offered much less, and provoked a 24-hour
token strike on 17 March 1970.

Labour's *1966* Plan for the Docks included:

1. Complete nationalisation.
2. Group Operating Committees at dock level, with 'the injection of a new radical element of industrial democracy'. Members
would include the Dock Manager and his principal officers, who
would be answerable to the rest of the committee for their
decisions. Remaining committee members would be directly
elected by the workers 'through the same trade union machinery
as is used or envisaged for the election of shop stewards'.
3. Group Operating Committee functions would include: efficient use of equipment and manpower, pay and productivity
questions, safety, the news-sheet, training for port-workers and
shop stewards, welfare, and the selection of supervisors (notice,
selection – not election!)
4. Representation of workers on management boards at all
levels of the industry.

Labour's *1969* Plan for the Docks had been watered down to:

1. Nationalisation limited to ports handling over 5 million tons,
with private ports continuing to operate in opposition, and
continuing to receive government grants.
2. Workers to have negotiation and consultation bodies, but
no real advances towards control.
3. Dock Labour Board to be replaced by Dock Labour Com-

mittees, with 50 per cent worker representation, but with powers only to rubber-stamp the activities of the national board.
4. Private employers to be subject to nationalisation proposals only after a delay, and with right of appeal.
5. Opening of the books discretionary.

The Dockworkers' Control Group issued immediate objections to these proposals, and called for

- The abolition of private employers on the docks NOW.
- Democratic management and control of the industry NOW.
- Portworkers' Councils to be elected by and from dockworkers NOW.
- The nationalisation of Felixstowe, and other private ports and wharves NOW.
- The preservation *and extension* of the joint control in the Dock Labour Board scheme NOW.

Their report finishes: 'Unless these things are done, NOW, then in five years' time, the dockers' militancy will be broken, the Labour scheme smashed, and dockers' security destroyed, with mass redundancies to follow.'

MINE-WORKERS' CONTROL

One industry which has suffered redundancy on a large scale over a number of years has been the mining industry. Yet in spite of the contraction in numbers, productivity has increased by 5 per cent or more every year for the past decade, and the level of wages has remained abysmally low. Part of the reason for the mine-workers' failure to improve their financial position has been the lack of rank-and-file control within their union, coupled with a total lack of control over their industry.

A *Voice of the Unions* broadsheet, compiled by mine-workers from various areas of the country and published in December 1969, sums up the miners' viewpoint:

'It is not possible to speak of Union initiatives but only of responses to the Board's initiatives throughout most of the past 20 years . . . The reason lies in the incompetence and lack of militancy of the National Executive . . .

What's gone wrong in the Union and in the industry is the failure of democratic control. The immediate battle for a 40-hour week only highlights a much bigger question. What control are the miners to have over their working lives?

Democratic control of our work requires democratic control of our Union. Indeed, the events of the last few years and the abject failures of our National Executive require this in any case. A combination of elected officials and a lay executive would create the conditions for militancy at the pit level to get through to policy making at national and area level . . .

Democracy isn't handed down from above, and doesn't depend only on getting the structure of organisation right. In the last resort it depends upon people at the base and their capacity to find ways of acting together to make the structure work . . .'

The broadsheet goes on to spell out a 'programme of action' for miners, which could provide a basis for the rank-and-file action committees recommended by the authors as a possible method of promoting discussion on workers' control at branch level:

'THE NATION AND COMMUNITY

1. A national cost-benefit study with evidence and findings openly published to determine a national fuel policy in the best long-term interest of the British people;

2. Simultaneous detailed examination of possible lines of diversification for the Coal Board into chemical production, etc., alone or in association with other nationalised industries;

3. Establishment of other publicly-owned enterprises in areas of run-down of the coal industry;

4. Guarantees of employment for all men made redundant, at negotiated union rates, on work of improving the amenities of mining areas, with or without retraining for necessary skills on this or other work;

5. Strong Union representation on special local development boards, set up to carry out local improvement, retraining, industrial development, etc.

THE COLLIERY AND INDUSTRY

6. Union control of pit management, including election of under-officials and veto on higher management appointments;

7. Union veto on Board appointments to major positions at area and national level, including membership of the Board itself;

8. National inquiry with major Union representation into causes of accidents and into safety and health in general;

9. Re-examination by the Union at every level of present earning differentials, including staff earnings, conducted jointly with other appropriate unions in the industry;

10. Union study of the costings of all pits and consideration of the implication of six-hour day underground, seven-and-a-half hour above and three weeks' holiday with pay, on the assumption of possible reductions in staff and manning.

DEMOCRACY IN THE UNION

11. Periodic election of all full-time officials at all levels;

12. A National Executive of lay members elected by areas from working miners;

13. Rationalisation of areas to come in line with Board areas, with assignment of greater funds to the centre where these can be more economically centralised.'

The mining industry is one of the few in which workers have suggested putting their own union house in order as a prelude to controlling the industry itself. Since these suggestions were made, a national miners' strike has taken place (January 1972) which points to increased militancy on the part of the workers, being the first national strike since 1926.

Before and during the strike, officials of the National Union of Miners called for the support of other unions in their strike – for example, members of the Transport and General Workers' Union were asked to help by refusing to move shipments of coal which were already in stock when the strike began. This created an interesting situation, in view of the new Industrial Relations Act, under which other unions can be penalised for aiding and abetting strike action, and a cooling-off period imposed on the original offender.

(The NUM's pleas for help were reminiscent of those of the Post Office workers, during their long strike in 1971, when other unions came to their assistance both financially and otherwise. Yet early in 1972 the Post Office Workers' Union turned their back on a million unemployed workers by recommending acceptance of proposals to cut back on the numbers employed in the service of the Post Office, by 'natural wastage' and stopping new recruitment. The UPW Paddington Branch Secretary asked 'How can the executive march for more jobs for the unemployed and at the same time advocate productivity deals which put more on the dole – and keep them there?')

CO-OPERATIVE CONTROL

The cases of workers' organisations taking action in their own interests, and at the same time against the broader interests of the working class as a whole, are unfortunately not isolated ones. This does not only happen in trade unions. The control of members and workers over the Co-operative movement, for example, is not sufficient to ensure that national policies always reflect the members' wishes. John Parkinson, a member of the Co-operative Party's national executive, writing in *Tribune* (10 September 1971), quoted the example of the North Eastern Society, where the members' council voted against Common Market entry, but was overridden by the decision of the Board to vote in favour of entry at the special Co-operative Congress on the Common Market. The national executive's recommendation of immediate entry was subsequently rejected by the Congress. John Parkinson remarked that the executive must be expected to give a lead, 'but not in such a way that they show indifference to the rank and file who put them there'; what is needed, he continued, is not a managerial revolution, but 'managers who act efficiently in implementing those policies which shall be determined democratically by elected members'. In other words, workers' control.

The amount of control exercised by Co-operative members can be measured by the fact that delegates voted unanimously in conference to oppose the Industrial Relations Act, yet the executive has supported the introduction of agency shops (against TUC policy) and generally recognises that 'the Act must be implemented'. This negation of democracy brought a comment from the *Workers' Press* (17 December 1971) that 'the spirit of Lanark and Rochdale has turned into its opposite, leaving the Co-op leaders standing shoulder to shoulder with the Tories and the bosses against the working class'.

EDUCATION CONTROL

While there are admittedly weak points in the framework of the workers' struggle, the increasing militancy of the working class – of which 'occupation' was a major feature during 1971 – is becoming evident. Workers are beginning to demand control over their work, their trade unions and their political organisations. But where does control begin?

Ideally, it should begin at school. Education is sometimes compared with industry – the school being the factory, the head-teacher in the role of manager, teachers as the workers, and the pupils being the products. Unfortunately, the analogy is usually taken too far. There is no reason why a head-teacher should maintain autocratic rule over staff and students, but this is all too often the case. Furthermore, education is the one industry in which the product can and must have control over its own production. Yet in the majority of schools, the only answer to 'Why?' is 'Because I say so'.

This is where the damage starts. As was pointed out in a *Tribune* article (31 December 1971), discipline problems often start with a head-teacher's insistence on petty rules, although the rules themselves have no intrinsic merit (what reason could you give for brandishing a tape-measure to ensure that the dresses of girls in a primary school were 'exactly two inches above the knee', according to rule?) *Tribune* explains: 'In any debate on these matters the question is not one of long hair, or short hair, nor of any particular style of dress, but one of conformity . . . It is the idea of uniform or, rather, of uniformity, which is the issue.'

The greater the docility and conformity of the products of the education factory, the more useful and the less troublesome will those products be when they are absorbed into the capitalist system to earn a living. Small wonder, then, that the Establishment roars its condemnation on the (rare) occasions when teachers show militancy, on the grounds that this is a bad example to the products in the factory.

What can pupils in primary and secondary schools do to improve their present situation? There are now many branches of the Schools Action Union, an organisation which disseminates information on pupils' struggles by producing its own newspaper from a central office in London. In this way, school children are kept in touch with the demands and successes of their fellows all over the country. The Union, a militant organisation, has supported strike action by its members, which has led on one occasion to expulsions, followed by a battle for reinstatement.

In a school in Wales, the headmaster has anticipated the demands of the students by holding elections for a student council. The first election had all the usual elements – hustings, ballot papers, polling booths – and one unusual element, an 85 per cent turnout, showing the amount of concern felt by schoolchildren over the democratic organisation of their work-place. One of the teachers described the council as 'the best way of getting grievances and constructive suggestions over to the staff'. It also has the advantage of raising the political awareness of the pupils, instead of forcing them into a position of powerless conformity.

After school comes, for the fortunate few, university or a college of education, both of which founts of learning have been until comparatively recently as rigidly disciplined as any primary school. After a long fight, students have won the right to elect representatives on the academic or governors' boards, and they have generally gained greater freedom within the universities, especially with regard to the organisation of the students' unions. Rather too much freedom for the students' unions, according to the Government, which issued in 1971 a 'consultative document', proposing changes in the system of financing the unions which would place them in a situation of dependence on the college authorities, and would price most students out of the market, as far as society subscriptions are concerned, by withdrawing subsidies and making them self-supporting. The document also suggested replacing the present automatic membership of the students' union by a voluntary subscription, although the student who chose not to be a union member would, under the terms of the document, still be entitled to all the benefits of membership. The students' unions which survived would be subject to a Registrar, in the same way as trade unions.

These few examples of the Government's proposals show remarkable parallels with the provisions of the Industrial Relations Act. Removal of subsidies from society subscriptions is aimed, not at the 'innocent' sports clubs, film societies, etc., but at the political societies (of which the left-wing ones are frequently the strongest); compare this with the system of 'opting in' to the trade union political levy, instead of the established system of 'opting out'. Also, the 'freedom' of the student to choose to be a member (or choose *not* to be a member) of a students' union, is paralleled by the freedom of a worker, under the Industrial Relations Act, to choose not to be a member of a trade union. In the first case, the student is entitled to all the benefits of membership, whether he joins or not; and the worker likewise benefits from, for example, wage rises won by the union, even is he is not a member of it. The result in both cases is to weaken union organisation.

The lesson to be learned from the 'consultative document' is that the students' struggles and the workers' struggles for control have the same roots, and that the Tory attack on students is part of the overall attack on the working class. A quarter of a million students demonstrated against the proposals of the consultative document on 8 December 1971, and the conference of the National Union of Students, held the previous month, passed a resolution recognising that the consultative document 'can only be understood as a part of a general attack on those sections of society which stand in opposition to the interests of the ruling class, in particular the trade union movement'.

The militancy and solidarity of the students, supported by the academic staff in many cases, led the Government to put their plans into abeyance in January 1971, on the grounds that they could not be implemented in time for the next academic year.

Perhaps the attack will be re-opened when a new quota of students straight from school have filled the colleges, and the present militant leadership has been absorbed into the community at large. Under 1972 conditions of unemployment, that militant leadership, and thousands of other students besides, will have little choice with regard to their life's work. Many of the products of universities and colleges of education will be obliged to drift into the teaching profession as a last resort.

On past records, militancy is an attribute which might be cultivated to great effect within the profession. Many teachers were conscience-stricken at the thought of going on strike, not appreciating that a teachers' strike was necessary *because* of the pupils, not in spite of them. Not only was it vitally important to improve teachers' salaries in order to encourage more and better people into the profession (and to prevent the disillusioned teachers from leaving it!), it was also a useful demonstration of militancy to the students, and was condemned as such by the Establishment, which is an adequate proof of its working-class value.

Teachers are now also making demands in fields other than that of pay, although as yet the demands are local or sectional rather than national. This is not surprising, since the unions representing teachers have so far been unable to agree on even so basic an item as salary scales. A conference of young teachers, held in 1971, agreed on a variety of suggestions for improving teachers' control, and these suggestions would be a sound basis for nationally co-ordinated demands. The young teachers' proposals included:

– State legislation to provide for the establishment of Staff Councils in every school.
– The Staff Council would have the right to participate in the determination of curriculum policy and school organisation.
– The Staff Council would be responsible for internal school finance, and for parent–teacher relations.
– The staff would be entitled to elect representatives on the governing board and on all educational decision-making bodies, and these representatives would have full rights as board-members.

One of the delegates to the young teachers' conference summed up the advantages of a Staff Council in this way: 'It would preclude the head-teacher from listening to us, then saying: "Thank you, now we'll do it my way." '

'REAL INDUSTRIAL DEMOCRACY'

Workers in many industries, nationalised and private, locally and nationally, have formulated plans for some degree of workers' control in their industry. However, none of these industries and services is working in a vacuum, and co-ordination and consultation between industries is of major importance in evolving a strategy for workers' control.

With such a strategy in view, the Tribune group of MPs issued a programme for the next Labour Government, which included:

- Public ownership of the insurance concerns, and the establishment of a Government insurance corporation and investment bank.
- Extension of public ownership in manufacturing industries, of which the aeronautical, shipbuilding and pharmaceutical industries are mentioned specifically.
- 'Unqualified acceptance by the Government and industrial management of the principle that those in representative positions at all levels in industry must be directly responsible to the workers on the shop floor.'

In order to achieve these objects, the Tribune group insists on the need for the active co-operation of the workers, calling for 'real industrial democracy'. The need for such co-operation is also recognised by the Belgian trade unions, which have produced detailed plans of action, and published these for discussion and amendment by the workers. *A Trade Union Strategy in the Common Market*, edited by Ken Coates, is a translation of these plans, which include the following 'Battle Lines for Future Action on Workers' Control'. The 'Battle Lines' were prepared by the Belgian General Federation of Labour (FGTB), an organisation representing three-quarters of a million workers, and affiliated to the ICFTU, but the application of such battle lines to the British trade union movement would be of great value in the progress towards workers' control:

'BATTLE LINES FOR FUTURE ACTION ON WORKERS' CONTROL

1. Democratic economic planning is an essential condition for

the extension of workers' control to various levels. Without such planning, workers' control risks coming to nothing in certain spheres. The institution of such planning is, therefore, a primary objective. Democratic planning is indispensable if we want the question of control of the holdings to be something more than a slogan.

It is by means of this planning that we must negotiate and if necessary impose a certain qualitative structure on investments.
2. Planning cannot be left in the hands of the technocrats, the bosses and the government. On the basis of claims from the workers, the trade union movement must define the objectives which should govern planning. This should be the subject of true negotiation as generally understood by our movement.
3. To make a synthesis of demands, which must be made within our trade union movement, we need an internal network of communications within our organisation which is sufficiently supple and efficient.
4. Such a network is indispensable if we want the presence of the FGTB in the various bodies to be something more than that of a hostage and if we wish to prevent the development of corporatism.
5. Particular attention must be given to problems of employment and qualitative and quantitative control of the labour market by the union organisation.
6. All trade union action in the area of consumption must be revised.
7. Workers' control must be exercised at all levels: regional, national, sectoral, and within the factory and financial groups. Apart from strengthening the union presence in the financial bodies. it does not seem that any new bodies should be set up at national level.
8. The powers of the union delegates in the existing organs should, nevertheless, be reviewed and extended. Decisions regarding hiring and firing should increasingly pass into the hands of the workers.
9. At sector level, formulae resembling those of the Control Committee should be set up following the resolution of the 1961 congress on the qualitative policy of investments:

– in sectors where a monopoly or a small number of large-size enterprises dominate the market
– where groups of enterprises exercise a determining influence on the development of whole regions
– in areas where there is immediate effect on private consumption: big distribution firms, housing, social goods, entertainment, public transport.
10. Systematization of workers' control and widening the powers of the workers demands a revision in methods of training and briefing to be put into operation by the FGTB.'

Of these points, the most important to the British trade union movement are numbers 7 and 8 – the extension of workers' control through all levels of decision-making, and the extension of workers' control over those organisations which have already been created by the workers – the trade unions and the Labour Party. Used to the full, and controlled directly by their members, these organisations would be dominating factors in the achievement of workers' control.

Workers' control over the industries and services will not be achieved until the workers control their own trade unions, political and other organisations.

Chapter 10

Workers' Control
Within Their Unions

Rise like lions after slumber,
In unvanquishable number,
Shake your chains to earth like dew
Which in sleep had fallen on you –
Ye are many – they are few.
Shelley: *The Mask of Anarchy*

'The emancipation of labour is neither a local, nor a national, but a social problem, embracing all countries in which modern society exists, and depending for its solution on the concurrence, practical and theoretical, of the most advanced countries;
. . . the present revival of the working classes in the most industrious countries of Europe, while it raises a new hope, gives solemn warning against a relapse into old errors, and calls for the immediate combination of the still discontented movements;

FOR THESE REASONS:
   The first International Working Men's Congress declares that the International Association and all societies and individuals adhering to it will acknowledge truth, justice, and morality, as the basis of their conduct towards each other, and towards all men, without regard to colour, creed or nationality.
   This Congress considers it the duty of a man to claim the rights of a man and a citizen, not only for himself, but for every man who does his duty. No rights without duties, no duties without rights;
   And in this spirit they have drawn up the following rules of the International Association:
1. This Association is established to afford a central medium of communication and co-operation between Working Men's

Societies existing in different countries and aiming at the same end; viz., the protection, advancement, and complete emancipation of the working classes . . .'

With these words, written by Karl Marx, began an attempt to forge international solidarity among workers. Today, more than a hundred years later, these principles of co-operation between countries have still not been put into practice; but within many individual countries, powerful weapons – the trade unions – have now been built by the working class to assist in their emancipation from capitalist exploitation.

After 150 years or more of struggle in Britain, we have forged a trade union movement which is over twelve million strong, and of these, 10,250,000 are united in the TUC.

Sufficient force now exists in the trade unions and working-class political parties to change society to correspond to the needs of the working class. But this cannot happen until the working class control their unions from the bottom to the top. It is useless to expect to achieve workers' control over industries and services unless trade union members have control over their own organisations, political and economic.

Trade unionists expect that trade union leaders should voice their demands and be under their control. Control can be exercised through agreed rules, and set out in union rule books. The AUEW (Engineering Section) rules are changed as members desire at least once every five years by a democratically elected rank-and-file rule-making body.

Democracy inside a union is vital in order to discover the will of the majority and to give effect to it. The criteria in all unions for union democracy should be:

1. The trade unions belong to their members.
2. The rule of the majority and the supremacy of the rule-book are of prime importance.
3. Protection of all members' rights and natural justice prevail.
4. Officials must be servants, not masters – control of them must be determined by members' policies, not by outside bodies such as employers or government.
5. Members' rights to internal and external democracy must be upheld.

6. The rights of members in internal opposition to express themselves freely must be maintained.

There must always be the right for members to fight for alternative policies and alternative leadership, and there must be freedom for all members to publish their views and criticise the administration.

ENGINEERS' UNION CONTROL

In the AUEW (Engineering Section), all members contesting for full-time offices have the right to write an election address to all members, and this is printed and distributed by the union without censorship. J. D. Edelstein, historian of trade union democracy, 'found that the AEU enjoys a stable democracy . . . with a structure which stimulates competition between relatively equal full-time officers or their backers . . . an electoral system which reduces inequalities and limitations on the power of the officials.'

So intent was Lord Carron, during his presidency of the AEU, on 'preserving' this democracy, that he launched an attack in the AEU Journal on the 'left-wing extremists' of the union who were responsible for launching the *Voice* papers, in particular *Engineering Voice*. Labelling us as 'agitators', and attaching the name 'communist' to as many names and organisations as possible, he 'exposed' our *Voice* meeting as 'a threat posed to the Union by those who take directions from sources made clear by their ideology'. *Engineering Voice*, he claimed, would be used as 'an extremist bid to take control of the Amalgamated Engineering Union', and its avowed intention of getting left-wing propaganda to branches, obtaining as much rank-and-file support as possible, and promoting left-wing policies and people as alternatives to the then current regime, was denounced in a long report and editorial in the union's journal as an attempt to 'negate our Union's democracy'.

What happened at that *Voice* meeting was simply a free discussion – in fact, an example of democracy in action – but such a discussion as was likely to undermine Carron's position, in time, by the very democratic process which he was anxious to protect. (Incidentally, the right wing have private *secret* gatherings.)

I myself was quoted as saying at the meeting that 'the grass roots of the union is in the branch' – presumably a dangerous thing to say in public! – and moreover Carron said I had attacked Jim Conway for his actions against AEU democracy; but Carron, protector of that democracy, did not bother to enquire into my allegations.

He concluded with 'an exhortation to the membership to be vigilant'. Which meant, I imagine, doing all possible to maintain the *status quo*!

(The 'democracy' of the union at that time was such that I was repeatedly prevented from speaking at meetings by the then Executive Council, although I was a nationally elected officer of the union and was invited to attend meetings by the members. Not for nothing was I referred to as 'The Prisoner of the Pope of Peckham'!)

A number of unions do not allow their members to come together in support of their candidates except at official meetings. Such a ban is restrictive and undemocratic, and it violates the civil right of free association. In this connection, and also on the right to produce and distribute papers, the International Commission of Jurists points out: 'Freedom of expression through the press and other media of communication is an essential element of free elections and is also necessary to ensure the development of an informed and responsible electorate.' Members should be allowed to communicate with each other through the official union organisation, and also to publish their viewpoints openly in their own newspapers.

In many trade unions, full-time officers are elected by a ballot of the membership, which gives democratic control, particularly if the officials have to come up for re-election at frequent intervals. In certain unions, full-time officials are appointed, but there is good democratic control by a lay or rank-and-file executive, which can remove officials if they are not satisfactory.

However, there are union leaderships which act in an arbitrary and dictatorial manner, apparently outside the control of the membership. This need not be so. Problems like the Pilkington dispute and the dockers' problems in the past arose because the

N

members allowed the Deakins, Carrons, Cannons, etc. to do as they pleased, instead of being active within the machinery of their union, fighting every inch of the way, and when necessary changing the structure of their union to bring it under members' control.

Democratic control is served by the separation of executive, legislative and judicial powers, such as exists in the AUEW (Engineering Section), and where the union policy is decided by a rank-and-file National Committee. In most British unions, ultimate authority rests with a delegate conference of the general membership, but the problem remains of compelling some executives to carry out the democratic decisions of Conference. The shorter the gap between delegate conferences, the greater the control over executive committees.

Trade unions also need to give attention to the method and basis of election of delegates. Representation, to be fair, should be on a proportional basis for each area as far as is practicable. Workers' control of unions can be extended by arranging official area or industrial sectional conferences to be held for the purpose of ensuring that the rank and file assist in policy-making.

However, the only real guarantee that we, as trade unionists, will control our own trade unions, is to be constantly active on the shopfloor, and – equally important – active in the branch. A 10 per cent turnout in a branch to vote in a union election shows how few branch activists there are!

The following account illustrates the kind of practice which is operated in a union, where the union controls the members and not vice versa:

'Nominees for regional council will be elected every two years, nominees will be grouped and voted on at branch meetings, the nominee getting the most votes will receive the votes of the whole of the branch membership, e.g. Total branch membership, 2,000, attendance at branch, 10, the nominee getting six or more votes will thus get 2,000 votes. In another branch, a nominee in the same group may get 50 votes, here however the branch membership is 200. So although no. 1 got less than one eighth of the votes that no. 2 got, he finishes up with ten times as many.'

The moral of this story is: don't let the machine control you – you control the machine instead. It is no use complaining outside, striking out blindly with 'What's the union ever done for me?', or becoming frustrated and apathetic. Organise and control. Use your branch, use your trades councils, and exert your power over the TUC. They have been built to serve our interests, and it is our individual responsibility to see that they do.

TUC CONTROL

Just as 'every nation has the government it deserves', so also trade unionists have the leaders they deserve, both in individual trade unions and ultimately in the TUC. In a chapter on 'The Dead Weight of Bureaucracy' in their book, *Incomes Policy, Legislation and Shop Stewards*, T. Cliff and C. Barker describe the 'creeping centralisation' of the TUC, and the gradual seduction of some of its leaders over a period of years by successive Governments, both Tory and Labour:

'With the centralisation of power in the TUC – a process already begun by the "wage-vetting" scheme – there will be an increased need, if the Incomes Policy is to work, to draw the trade unions closer and closer to the machinery of the State. This closer association between trade-union brass and State will be no new thing, however, but rather a continuation of a process that began a long time ago. In 1931–2 there was only one Government committee on which the General Council of the TUC was represented according to the TUC directory of committees; by 1934–5 the directory listed six such committees, and the number has been increasing steadily ever since.'

'Union officials,' say Cliff and Barker, 'are becoming less and less the *leaders* of the workers, and more their foremen.'

In the same way as foremen are encouraged to regard themselves as 'lower management', trade union leaders have been encouraged to collaborate with the Government on committees, and to climb the social ladder, away from the workers they represent, by accepting knighthoods and peerages.

The TUC's attitude towards the various Tory Governments

has not been one of unrelenting opposition. Indeed, the return of a Tory Government in 1951 prompted the TUC General Council to state (in the 1952 TUC Report) that:

'It is our longstanding practice to seek to work amicably with whatever Government is in power and through consultation with Ministers and with the other side of industry to find practical solutions to the social and economic problems facing this country. There need be no doubt, therefore, of the attitude of the TUC towards the new Government.'

As Cliff and Barker point out, the TUC 'saw to it that the cautious and moderate policy which they had pursued under the Labour Government was maintained under the Conservatives'. It is the practice of successive Governments to assure the continuity of foreign policies pursued by their predecessors. The TUC, by 'working amicably' with any and every Government, is encouraging the continuity of national economic policies, also, and in increasing its own representation on government committees, it is not increasing its influence over the decisions taken, but merely compromising its role as the workers' representative. In fact, the TUC has representation without power.

It is an easy step from working on government committees to accepting an 'honour' for services to the country, accepting a 'management' position in a nationalised industry or a post on the board of the Bank of England. Knighthoods have gone to

> Sir Frederick Heyday (G&MWU)
> Sir Sydney Greene (NUR)
> Sir Sydney Ford (NUM)
> Sir Tom O'Brien (NATKE)
> Sir Will Lawther (NUM)

while the House of Lords has been, and is, bristling with trade union leaders who have considered that a peerage from a Labour, or even a Tory, prime minister is not incompatible with the position to which they were elected by the members of their respective unions:

> Lord Carron (AEU)
> Lord Wright (NUAW)

Lord Collison (NUAW)
Lord Delacourt-Smith (UPW)
Lord Citrine (TUC)
Lord Cooper (G&MWU)
Lord Hill (Boilermakers)
Lord Williamson (G&MWU)

(It is worth noting that the distribution of appointments by Labour and Tory prime ministers has been equally impartial in its disregard of party boundaries, indicating that the degree of difference between the parties is not so great as might be expected; Aubrey Jones, for example, was the Tory MP chosen to head the Prices and Incomes Board by Harold Wilson; the Tory Lord Melchett was Wilson's choice for the leadership of the newly nationalised steel industry; Christopher Soames, an ex-Minister in a Tory Government, was the Labour Government's Ambassador in Paris; Lord Robens became leader of the Coal Board under a Tory Government . . . etc.)

Clearly, the large number of examples of full-time trade union officers who have been drawn into the machinery of 'the system' suggests that there is a widespread tendency for full-time officials to become more and more withdrawn from the members of their union. Cliff and Barker state that, according to the evidence of an extensive survey, 'most full-time officers rate themselves among the holders of middle-class posts,' so 'not surprisingly, very few trade union officials went back to the ranks after giving up their jobs, for whatever reason'. They quote the 'subsequent post of resigned officers' as follows:

Post in nationalised industry	48
Government post	25
Managerial post in private industry	14
Post in another union	11
Back to 'shop floor'	13
Own shop or business	7
Labour Party post	4
Elected Member of Parliament	4
Post with other organisations	9
Other	9
Unknown	122
Total	266

Cliff and Barker comment:

'Thus the trade union bureaucracy, rising above the rank-and-file membership of the unions, and feeling that it belongs to a group with a higher social status hardly ever thinks of going back to the rank and file. To this degree it is alienated from those it supposedly represents . . . The rank and file of the trade unions have to deal not only with the employers and the state, but also with the trade union bureaucracy. This, like the proverbial wheelbarrow, moves only so far as it is pushed and no further.'

RANK-AND-FILE CONTROL

The more frequently rank-and-file conferences are held, the more opportunity there is of ensuring that a full-time executive carries out the wishes of the membership. But to maintain even closer ties with the rank and file, elected lay committees could take the place of full-time executives. The lay members of these committees, both at national and district level, would be responsible to the members for decision-making, and their decisions would be carried out by administrative staff, who would be full-time employees of the union. The decisions would be made solely by the lay executive, the administrative officers having no vote in the process of decision-making. Members of lay committees would be subject to election and re-election, and would keep their normal jobs throughout their period of office.

The danger of such a system would be the same one which occurs between local councillors and administrative officers, for example, the town clerk, the borough surveyor, etc. All too often, the council is prepared to take the advice of these 'experts' instead of taking a decision independently and instructing the administrative staff to carry it out. The Merthyr Tydfil education authority, for example, defied the Tory Government (January 1972) by supplying free milk to school-children illegally, but they were forced to withdraw the supply because the treasurer and the director of education refused their consent to the scheme. The ultimate sanction of refusing financial support should not rest in the hands of one person.

The trade unions are not in such a vulnerable position as local councils with regard to finances and administration, since the elected officers of a union are better acquainted with the union rule-book than the union's administrative employees are, and are consequently better able to issue instructions and see that they are carried out, as well as maintaining control of their union's purse-strings. There must nevertheless be adequate checks on the lay executive from the shopfloor, and here again, the trade union has the advantage over the local council, since trade union members have – or can have – greater influence over the running of their organisation than the electorate has over the running of their local council.

One way in which the rank and file can exercise greater control over the activities of their executive, whether lay or full-time, is through their shop stewards. The shop stewards have power within their place of work, in a strictly confined sphere on the shopfloor; in the union machine, in the branches and committees, their power disintegrates. So, instead of using their own combined strength within the union machine when problems arise, shop stewards – often with the support of thousands of workers behind them – make their way as a delegation, cap in hand, to beg for the backing of the executive.

The growth of vast private combines in industry needs to be met with a similar growth in shop stewards' combines. This has been done to a small extent, but the general fragmentation of shop stewards' organisations means that combination on the part of the employers meets with insufficient resistance. The stewards act in isolation from their fellow stewards, and because of this, their great potential strength is lost. Recognising this potential, and fearing its repercussions on their own entrenched positions of authority, trade union officials in the past have declared shop stewards' combine committees unofficial, on the grounds that they are not in the best interests of the industry.

The TUC condemned the formation of combine committees in their 1960 Report, saying that their aim was to

'usurp the policy-making functions of unions or federations of unions. Unions are advised to inform their members that participation in such bodies is contrary to the obligations of membership . . . Unions should be more vigilant, and if, after a warning, a steward repeats actions which are contrary to the rules or agreements, his credentials should be withdrawn.'

The book, *Incomes Policy, Legislation and Shop Stewards*, quotes the following examples of the TUC's advice being put into practice:

'In 1959 the shop stewards' committees at Firth Brown (Sheffield) and Ford (Dagenham) jointly called a National Shop Stewards Conference. The Communist stewards play a leading role in both factories. The Executive of the AEU banned the Conference. Bro. Caborn, the convenor at Firth Browns, was suspended from holding office for one year.

The Power Workers' Combine was formed some time ago to fight for improved conditions in the power industry. As usual, the reaction of the full-time officials was rapid and hostile. The unions (ETU included) declared that following the last settlement the Power Workers' Combine was no longer necessary. On 14 November 1960 Frank Foulkes, President of the ETU and Chairman of the Electricity Supply Industry National Joint Council declared: "Unofficial bodies are not in the best interests of the industry."

Bro. Wake, secretary of the Combine, was then disciplined by the AEU.'

Cliff and Barker go on to make the point that the motto 'an injury to one is an injury to all' is not of purely ethical value, but makes financial sense too:

'The defeat of a strike or other form of action in a factory in the motor industry is a defeat for the workers in the entire engineering industry. And since other, worse-organised workers compare themselves with engineers, it is a defeat for the entire working class.'

The shop stewards, at the source of production, are closer to the demands of the workers than any national executive could be, and for this reason the shop stewards are in a better position than anyone else to ensure that the decisions of the executive correspond to the needs of the workers they represent. Organisations of shop stewards, therefore, must be encouraged and increased; combines must be strong enough not only to recognise the demands of the rank and file, but also to put pressure on officials at both district and national level, through the machinery of the union, to see that those demands are fought for and obtained.

The working class did not create the unions to be a disciplinary force, a rod for the backs of the workers, but in order to protect and free the workers from capitalism. The power of the rank and file must be maintained, so that the workers control the union and not vice versa. Part of the strategy behind industrial relations legislation is to force the unions to discipline their members, by imposing penalties upon them if they fail to do so. Even before the days of *In Place of Strife*, there was support in the Labour Government for the proposal that trade unions should be responsible for disciplining members who engaged in 'unofficial' strikes. The employers were, of course, in favour of this idea, and it was even suggested that 100 per cent union membership within an industry – a closed shop imposed by law – would be an effective sanction, in that a union could deprive a worker of his job by expelling him from the union, if he engaged in an unofficial strike.

Although many unions scorned the idea as being impractical, Ray Gunter, Minister of Labour, received the support of Sir William Carron and the AEU Executive, who stated in a memorandum to the Royal Commission on Trade Unions in 1965 that if a closed shop and the check-off system (payment of union dues by direct deduction from the wage-packet by the employer) were enforced by law, the unions 'would probably agree also to outlaw for ever unofficial strikes'. *The Times* of 9 November 1965 commented:

'A union agreement to outlaw unofficial strikes would represent only good intentions. Some unofficial strikes are directed as much against the unions as against the employers, and it would be hardly less difficult for the unions to expel a majority of workers in an undertaking than it would be for the Government to put them in gaol.'

Disciplinary action against unofficial strikers gained the support of the Labour Government, the employers, and some trade union officials. The illogicality of calling any strike 'unofficial' was never questioned; it was always assumed that the union's executive had the right to give its blessing to a strike or not, thereby either encouraging its success, or condemning it. Trade union officials are the employees of their members; they are not elected to sit in judgement over the electorate, but to support them in their actions when the need arises. It would indeed be virtually impossible to discipline large numbers of strikers. But the question would never arise if the members of unions exercised sufficient control over their elected representatives, and were sure of support in their struggles.

Organised workers can learn from their experiences; they can become aware of their organised strength; they can develop a working-class theory from their experience and practice. That experience is not limited to struggles with employers. The workers are often fighting not one battle, but two – against the employers, and against some officers who were elected to serve working-class interests. Once this is recognised, the strength of trade union membership is sufficient to change the course of the unions, and make them fulfil the purpose for which they were created – the emancipation of the working class.

To bring about changes in the relationship between trade union leadership and members, it is first necessary to make clear the political implications of trade union activity. Greater political understanding among trade unionists would have far-reaching effects. It would, for example, direct the workers' struggle against the system itself, and not only against an individual employer who is only a tiny part of the system. It would extend the struggle much more into demands for workers' control, instead of being limited largely to economic questions. And it would promote greater unity among members, and a greater awareness that 'an injury to one is an injury to all'. If workers felt that they shared responsibility for the well-being of fellow-workers, it would not be possible for strikes to go on for one or two years, as in the cases of Roberts Arundel and Fine Tubes. Concerted action by workers in associated companies or throughout the industry would quickly bring a satis-factory settlement. In the two cases mentioned, however, no joint action was proposed by the trade union leaderships, nor was it demanded by the members elsewhere sufficiently strongly.

CAN THE ECONOMIC WEAPON WIN CONTROL?

The working class must wake up to the fact that trade unions are not merely wage-negotiating machines. As Cliff and Barker put it:

'To limit oneself to economic demands, of course, is to deal with the *results* of the capitalist system as a system, and to miss the *causes*, the roots of the system. As Rosa Luxemburg, that great socialist revolutionary, put it, "Economic, trade-union struggle is a labour of Sisyphus". Sisyphus was a mythological king who was condemned to spend eternity rolling a huge stone to the top of a hill, from which it kept rolling back, so he had to start over and over again, incessantly heaving the boulder up the hill. As long as the capitalists own the means of production, workers – whether their wages are high or low – will still be oppressed, alienated, exploited. Capitalism cannot be abolished step by step. As Tawney put it: "You can peel an onion leaf by leaf, but you can't skin a tiger claw by claw." '

Of course we must attack causes and not only results, and this means more political activity and awareness within the unions at all levels. I cannot agree, however, with the con-clusion that 'capitalism cannot be abolished step by step'. Cer-tainly it cannot be abolished *by economic steps alone*, but workers can extend their control over their industry and em-ployers step by step, and in this sense the process is much more like the process of the onion than the tiger. On the principle of 'Much wants More', workers' advancement could progress to a stage where the capitalist tiger is seen to be merely a paper tiger in opposition to the combined strength of the working class. After which, the final onslaught of skinning the tiger can be accomplished.

A politically educated working class would also serve the purpose of safeguarding the interests of the entire working class, and not only of some sections of it. Will Paynter, in his book *British Trade Unions and the Problem of Change*, analyses the struggle between workers and capitalists in a way which tars trade unionists with the brush of selfishness, and he uses this as an argument for refraining from strike action in some circumstances:

'Some reservations must be stated against "free for all" tactics by workers and unions.

The first reservation, of course, is that no one wants to promote or engage in struggle for its own sake . . . There must always be a good reason for action, where the purpose involved justifies the means being used.

There are many meanings possible to the terms "action, struggle, fight", but usually they are meant to have a connotation with "strike". But whatever the term or the definition given to it, struggle or strike action is not an end in itself but a means to an end. The end must justify the means, and not all strikes satisfy this test.'

Will Paynter gives as examples of 'unjustified' strikes, the miners' strikes in which miners were promised a settlement if they went back to work – a promise which the miners perversely refused to accept! He also condemns lightning strikes which 'can be frivolous and over questions that are already being negotiated'.

What other means can be used for redressing grievances? If workers can solve their problems by speech alone, they do so; they do not take 'frivolous' strike action, because they know it hurts their pockets and their families. This being true, strikes, lightning and otherwise, should have the support of the union leadership and of other members in the union. Fully supported strikes are short strikes. Paynter argues that sectional strikes can be damaging, because they throw other sections out of work. The alternative is, to accept the injustice already being suffered, and turn the other cheek. He speaks of 'a few hundred men putting thousands temporarily out of work over a dispute they knew nothing about and the settlement of which would not provide any benefit to them'.

If workers recognised that their fellow-workers' struggles are also their own – that is, if they were more class-conscious and politically sensitive – they would willingly give their support to strike action, and would expect to get support in their disputes, in return. In that way, also, they would be glad to take action on behalf of pensioners, nurses, and others who, for various reasons, have limited bargaining power.

In the case of the miners refusing to return to work pending a settlement, Will Paynter argues that

'It was generally accepted in the mining industry that it was not in the interests of either the union or the employers to announce settlements while strikes were on, because the incidence of strikes were so frequent that such an inducement would have made things worse.'

The union leaders were clearly not able to forestall the need for strikes, by producing a settlement beforehand. Nor was the settlement made after the strike, since the announcement of a guaranteed settlement was used as a device for persuading the workers to go back to the pits. As is usually the case, agreement was reached not before or after, but during the strike – demonstrating that strike action is in many cases an effective and necessary supplement to verbal negotiations. The attitude taken by Paynter over the return to work, moreover, amounts to joining forces with the employers against the miners; the frequent occurrence of strikes would not be augmented merely by the timing of the announcement of a settlement, as he suggests. Indeed, strikes would not occur at all if there were no grievances among the workers.

On the subject of 'unconstitutional' organisations – for example, shop stewards' combines – Paynter seems surprised that such bodies should come into existence, often opposing themselves to the official union leadership, and in one particular case 'involving half the coalfield'. This 'problem' was dealt with by means of gentle persuasion, leading to an understanding on the part of the rebels that 'such divisions weakened the union in relation to the employer and if persisted in could lead to the union's collapse'.

Or perhaps, to the collapse of a leadership which was forcing its members to express their dissatisfaction in the form of unofficial organisations. If unions were really in the hands of the workers, there would be no need for such undercover activity, because the leadership would be fulfilling its role by responding to the needs of the membership.

CONTROL OF LEADERS – OR BY LEADERS?

In the last analysis, satisfactory agreements with employers are reached not as a result of clever negotiation by union officials, but by the workers' strength. Negotiations would have small hope of success, if the workers indicated in advance that they were not prepared to take strike action in the event of failure to agree. If the officials of the union show that they are less militant than the rank and file, on the other hand, then the rank and file has the right to remove those officers and elect others. In practice, this is done very infrequently (according to Cliff and Barker, only 3 per cent of elected officers were removed at the time of standing for re-election, over a period of thirty years). This is one of the rights which trade union members ought to use more readily. The attitude is often taken that defeat in an election would deprive an officer of his livelihood (do all officers, I wonder, have the same compassion in mind when negotiating redundancies for the members?) and he is dealt with leniently as a consequence. If elected officers felt that their security depended on their willingness to serve members' interests, trade union leadership would be a more faithful reflection of rank-and-file demands.

The same principle ought to apply also to the TUC but, in the case of the composition of the General Council, it certainly does not. Seats on the General Council are allocated to industrial groups, and the number of seats allotted to each group depends on the number of union members represented; Group 2 (Railwaymen) had three seats until 1970, when they were reduced to two, whereas Group 15 (Public Employees) showed an increased total of union members following the new affiliation to the TUC of the National Union of Teachers, and this group is therefore entitled to four places instead of its former three.

Some of the industrial groups, however, are composed of

small unions whose interests are widely different – for example, Group 13 comprises, Glass, Pottery, Chemicals, Food, Drink, Tobacco, Brushmaking and Distribution – and the one or two places allotted to such groups on the General Council cannot possibly represent adequately the members in all the unions. Group 13 covers fourteen unions, and has two representatives. This situation has led to a system of 'reserved seats' on the General Council. Some two-thirds of the places are distributed by general agreement *without election*, ostensibly to ensure that smaller unions get a fair chance of representation, although as Will Paynter says 'it is also generally recognised that the present system of voting involving Congress as a whole, guarantees continuity of election by the favoured few, under the rule of "the old pals act" '. Furthermore, an agreement between two or three big unions on voting for the General Council can determine the composition of the Council as a whole. Paynter calls this 'a rather phoney application of democracy'. Bryn Roberts, in *The Price of TUC Leadership*, goes further, suggesting that the 'old pals act' has been used to exclude the 'wrong type' of representative from the Council:

'If any member of the leadership (the General Council) retires or dies or is publicly disgraced, there will be no difficulty in filling the vacancy with the right type upon whom the leadership can safely rely.

Whatever the leadership does inside the Council always commands the necessary support outside the Council – thanks to the way the members of the Council, with the acquiescence of their respective Executives but without the knowledge of their rank and file members, use their block votes . . .

The miners, year after year, voted unanimously that Mr Arthur Horner, their General Secretary, should occupy a seat on the General Council, but the block votes of leaders of other unions who know little or nothing about the mining industry kept him off. But to disregard the wishes of nearly 700,000 miners in this way shows with what skill the TUC ballots are conducted. Nothing is left to chance. The exclusion of the Crusader or the critic or anyone likely to disturb the serenity of the General Council is of the utmost importance!'

Although the large unions exercise control to a large extent over the composition of the TUC General Council, Will Paynter argues that the General Council, once elected, has insufficient power to make its decisions felt in trade union circles. In order to fit itself for a new role – a role which sounds suspiciously like 'oracle to the trade union movement' – he suggests that some of the burden of decision-making should fall upon a new committee, composed of full-time TUC officials, who would form a sort of 'inner cabinet'. These officials would be elected from the ranks of national trade union leaders, and would sacrifice their job with their own union in order to work solely for the TUC. This, says Paynter, means that 'their appointment would need to be permanent and not subject to periodic election'. What's more, 'the salaries would obviously have to be attractive'.

What kind of control would the rank and file have in such a set-up? The answer is none. They would elect national officers to their own union, who would then be indirectly (that is, not by the rank and file) elected to the General Council, by a process far from democratic, subsequently to be exalted to the ranks of the elite, where they may do their worst without fear of having to face an election. There is no reason for absolving any trade union representative, whether shop steward or TUC official, from the necessity of standing for election; indeed, the higher up the ladder, and the greater the power attached to the job, the more vital is the need for accountability and elections.

Under the present system, the TUC wields very little power. Its 'power' depends on how far individual unions are prepared to fall into line with its policies. Speaking from experience as a national officer of the miners' union, Paynter confesses 'that the decisions of Congress had little significance for the union . . . Congress decisions were not really decisive in shaping the policies of individual unions.'

This has both advantages and disadvantages. The TUC has little or no real connection with the rank and file, who have far more control – if they choose to exercise it – over their individual unions. Far better, then, that unions should bear final responsibility for their own policies, which can be guided and affected by the members, than that policy should be inflicted from above by the TUC. On the other hand, a united front of unions, for example against the Industrial Relations legislation, in the form of the TUC could greatly strengthen the hand of the trade unions against the employers and the government.

At present, TUC policy can only be operated by the consent of member unions. At the Special Congress in Croydon (June 1969), which was held to discuss the White Paper *In Place of Strife*, the General Council gave itself greater powers to intervene in unofficial strikes and in disputes between unions, and to operate sanctions against offending unions. Will Paynter comments: 'The importance of the decision, however, is not whether the TUC can put sanctions into effect, but that affiliated unions were almost unanimously in favour of giving this power to it.'

When it came to the test, however, and the TUC recommended its member unions not to register under the Industrial Relations Act, the National Union of General and Municipal Workers, among other unions, chose to ignore the recommendation. The President of the NUGMW, Lord Cooper, is the Chairman of the TUC General Council.

Wider powers to ensure implementation of policies can only be given to the TUC when the structure of the TUC is changed, when it becomes more democratic, and is prepared to abandon its role as 'conciliator' in favour of adopting a steady position in support of the working class. The TUC must not have power to force upon member unions its policies of 'voluntary wage-vetting', or its antipathy to 'political' strike. The attitude taken by Bro. Paynter is the one which Barbara Castle tried to sell to the Labour movement throughout the period of the 1966–70 Labour Government, fortunately without much success:

'But the TUC must be given some power to prevent policies being pursued by one union that can embarrass or weaken the bargaining position of another in the same industry.

A wages policy, as stated previously, is not only a matter of securing a certain level of increase, but of making possible some orderly progress so that one section is not advancing at the expense of another and without regard to the interests of working people generally.'

o

This is a fallacy, for it presupposes that a wage increase refused by the car-workers or the toolmakers would automatically be given to the nurses or the dustmen. Certain groups of workers, either because they are poorly organised or because their bargaining power is weak (as in the case of nurses), fall into the category of 'lower-paid workers'. Their wages advance, not through union organisation and militancy, but mostly by comparison with the rising wages of other sectors. Therefore, holding the higher-paid sectors back has the opposite effect to that intended, and depresses the general level instead of raising it. Any wage rise for the working class is therefore a benefit to the working class as a whole, and it is divisive to suggest otherwise; any wage restraint likewise operates against the working class, in the same way as productivity deals are anti-working class, since it operates on the basis that workers are getting a full and fair return for their labour, which is not true.

Workers cannot afford to concede greater powers to the TUC while they continue to promote such policies as these. If the TUC exercised complete control over the policies of the trade union movement as a whole, the result would be to draw the trade unions into the web of capitalism, using the TUC as a force to discipline workers instead of protecting their interests.

The rank and file have no control over the composition of the General Council of the TUC, except to the extent that the General Council is composed of the elected officers of trade unions. If the rank and file elect militant officers in their own unions, the effect must ultimately be felt within the TUC. This change must be made quickly because, to quote Bryn Roberts, 'Under its present domination, Britain has no socialist future and . . . neither the trade union movement nor the Labour Party will ever be able to realise even its most moderate aims.'

Changes in the TUC will start in the branches of the trade unions. They will start with the rank and file, or not at all. When the rank and file control their own individual unions, they will also be able to control the TUC. The rank-and-file paper *Voice of the Unions* published a questionnaire for trade unionists, asking 'How Democratic is your Union?' Why not check it against your union's practice?

'HOW DEMOCRATIC IS YOUR UNION?

STRUCTURE:

Are top officials elected?

Are other officials elected?

Are Executive members elected frequently?

Is some authority devolved to:

Elected lay area committees?

Elected lay trade committees?

If so, do these include direct representation of shop stewards?

MEMBERS' RIGHTS (OF OPPOSITION)

Freedom to meet outside union structure.

Freedom to criticise leadership.

Independent appeal against disciplinary action.

ELECTIONS

Do individual members vote in branches or by post, or is Branch vote cast in block?

Can EC suspend members from election?

If yes above, is there effective independent appeal machinery?

Are ballots reasonably proof against fraud?

Must successful candidate secure majority of votes cast?

COMMUNICATION

Are full minutes and voting record of EC published?

Are verbatim reports of Conferences published?

Does union journal publish impartially letters and articles from members?

Is information about all members seeking election published?

Do members have right to visit branches other than their own?

Do members have right to circulate branches without EC permission?

Do members have right to write to Press about Union affairs?

If not, are penalties for infringement severe?

Do union leaders use national media to attack opposition?

POLICY-MAKING

Is policy determined by delegate conference?

Does basis of delegation give equal weight to all members?

Is conference managed by independently elected committee?
Does conference decide its own meeting-place?

RULE CHANGE
Are changes of rule decided by rules revision/delegate conference or general ballot of members.'

Chapter 11

Workers' Control Within Their Political Party

Revolution is the moving principle of the universe.

The economic demands of the workers' trade unions are not enough to change completely the nature of the society in which we live. The strategy and tactics of the trade unions, even when they succeed, will not create a revolutionary change. They will change the forms in society, but not its capitalist content.

Perry Anderson, writing on 'The Limits and Possibilities of Trade Union Action' in *The Incompatibles*, sees in the very existence of the trade unions a tacit recognition that there are 'two sides in industry', and an acceptance of perpetual opposition between those two sides. This continues, Anderson says, in spite of the fact that

'All mature socialist theory since Lenin has started by stressing the insurmountable *limitations* of trade union action in a capitalist society. This emphasis emerged in the struggle against the various forms of syndicalism and spontaneism endemic in the European working-class movement in the early years of the century. The belief that the trade unions were the chosen instruments for achieving socialism was the main tenet of syndicalism, the revolutionary version of exclusive reliance on trade unions. For this tradition – De Leon, Sorel, Mann – the general strike was the weapon which would abolish capitalist society. The reformist version was simply the belief that trade union wage demands could ultimately lead to a transformation of the conditions of the working class, without any change in the social structure of power. Both of these currents were rejected by the central tradition of European socialism. Marx,

Lenin and Gramsci were all emphatic that trade unions could not in themselves be vehicles of advance towards socialism. Trade unionism, in whatever form, was an incomplete and deformed variant of class-consciousness, which must at any cost be transcended by a growth of *political* consciousness, created and sustained in a *party* . . . As Gramsci once wrote, trade unions are "a type of proletarian organisation specific to the period when capital dominates history . . . an integral part of capitalist society, whose function is inherent in the regime of private property".

In this sense, trade unions are dialectically both an opposition to capitalism and a component of it.'

Trade unions certainly grew out of the conflict between labour and capital, but, having developed out of this conflict, they can and will be used as a power-lever to change society in the interests of the proletariat, even after private capital has been defeated. As I said in Chapter 2, there will be an uphill struggle both before and after the balance of power changes, no matter what means the workers use to gain control.

Anderson's contention that 'trade unions have no built-in socialist horizons', depending on capitalism for their existence, is neither true, nor helpful to the working-class movement. He writes:

'Marx saw socialism as the suppression of class society by the proletariat, and therewith the suppression of itself. This dimension of "auto-suppression" is lacking in a trade union. As institutions, trade unions do not *challenge* the existence of society based on a division of classes, they merely *express* it. Thus trade unions can never be viable vehicles of advance towards socialism in themselves; by their nature they are tied to capitalism. They can bargain with the society, but not transform it.'

According to this definition, trade unions are a millstone round the neck of the working class. Yet many trade unions in this country have socialist or common-ownership principles embodied in their rules and constitutions, and it was the trade unions which, in the early part of this century, came together to form their own political party, the Labour Party. But, as with most arguments, there is a grain of truth in Perry Anderson's argument. The element of auto-suppression which he mentions is not to be found in the trade union movement *at the moment*; and the trade unions cannot be vehicles of advance towards socialism *in themselves*. The initial impetus of establishing the trade unions and a working-class political party has slowed down to a steady stream, in which the employers' gains are partly matched by gains for the workers without any major change in the balance of power. And the Labour Party, purpose-built by the trade unions for the achievement of socialism, has so far failed to live up to expectations. The trade unions cannot transform society by themselves. Neither can the Labour Party do the job without the support of the workers, of whom a large proportion are organised into trade unions. It is time, then, that the trade unionists took to heart, and put into practice, the advice of Lenin, in *What is to be done?* Lenin makes it quite clear that economic demands are merely a subordinate part of a revolutionary struggle, whereas the Labour Government of 1964–70 (and of course the post-1970 Tory Government) made the economy in general, and the wage demands of the trade unions in particular, the pivot of their activities. 'When the economy is right', we are told, the road will be clear for more nationalisation and socialist advances. Lenin, on the other hand, puts economic issues firmly in their place:

'Revolutionary Social-Democracy always included, and now includes, the fight for reform in its activities. But it utilises "economic" agitation for the purpose of presenting to the government, not only demands for all sorts of measures, but also (and primarily) the demand that it cease to be an autocratic government. Moreover it considers it to be its duty to present this demand to the government, not on the basis of the economic struggle *alone*, but on the basis of all manifestations of public and political life. In a word, it subordinates the struggle for reforms to the revolutionary struggle for liberty and for Socialism, in the same way as the part is subordinate to the whole . . . Social-Democrats *must under no circumstances* create grounds for the belief (or the misunderstanding) that we attach greater value to economic reforms than to political reforms, or that we regard them as being particularly important . . .'

Under such a programme, the trade unions would be a political spur to the Labour Party, and would be in a position to control the policies of the Party, and of a Labour Government, to a much greater extent than they do now. The question remains, how is this to be done? How are the workers to be persuaded that their trade unions must not be limited to an economic sphere? The politically conscious workers must undertake the political education of their fellow workers, as Lenin says:

'What does political education mean? Is it sufficient to confine oneself to the propaganda of working-class hostility to autocracy? Of course not. It is not enough to *explain* to the workers that they are politically oppressed (any more than it was to *explain* to them that their interests were antagonistic to the interests of the employers). Advantage must be taken of every concrete example of this oppression for the purpose of agitation (in the same way as we began to use concrete examples of economic oppression for the purpose of agitation). And inasmuch as *political* oppression affects all sorts of classes in society, inasmuch as it manifests itself in various spheres of life and activity, in industrial life, civic life, in personal and family life, in religious life, scientific life, etc., etc., is it not evident that *we shall not be fulfilling our task* of developing the political consciousness of the workers if *we do not undertake* the organisation of the *political exposure of autocracy in all its aspects*? In order to agitate over concrete examples of oppression, these examples must be exposed (in the same way as it was necessary to expose factory evils in order to carry on economic agitation).'

Trade union activity has a severe limitation, in that it tends to restrict agitation to the sphere of industry. Lenin points out the necessity for widening the scope of political education to cover all aspects of life. This necessarily means the education and involvement of some groups of people *outside* the working class to take part in the workers' struggle.

TRADE UNIONS—REFORMIST OR REVOLUTIONARY?

The working class cannot transform society alone. They need a political party which has a real revolutionary theory of Marxism, and it must have unity with Marxist intellectuals and with some middle-class elements who must be won over to socialist beliefs. As Perry Anderson says, these people 'are bound by no inevitable ties to the socialist movement', but 'their allegiance is created, *against the grain of the social structure*, by the work of the revolutionary party itself.' It is true that the trade unions in this respect need a political party to draw together all the elements of the socialist struggle. But it is equally true that the intellectual and middle-class elements, whose natural inclinations tend towards exerting authority, must not be drawn into the party on the promise of future power, but on the basis of serving working-class interests. This means that the workers will control the political party, and power will not fall into the hands of those who wish to use the party as a stepping-stone to personal authority. This means that the trade unions will be the most important component in a revolutionary political party, though not in their current role as defenders of the workers' *economic* rights alone.

Among the 'limitations' of the trade union movement, Perry Anderson lists the strike weapon:

'As a political weapon, strikes are nearly always profoundly ineffectual. No general strike has ever been successful. The reason is that socialism requires a conquest of power, which is an *input* of action, an aggressive *over-participation* in the system, which abolishes it and creates a new social order. The general strike is an abstention, not an assault on capitalism. In some cases, it has actually *demobilised* a working class in a political crisis . . . The strike is fundamentally an economic weapon, which easily boomerangs if used on terrain for which it is not designed. Since the nature of the economy as a system is ultimately a political question, it follows that strikes have only a relative and not an absolute efficacy in the economic struggle itself. This is another reminder that trade unions cannot put in question the existence of capitalism as a social system.'

The lack of success of general strikes so far has not been the fault of the weapon itself, as Anderson suggests, but largely the fault of the user. The reason for the failure of strike action, whether the strike has been for 'economic' or 'political' ends, has been the low level of political education among the working class, and their unwillingness to co-operate to the full without seeing the absolute necessity for strike action.

A great many people, both within the working class and outside it, are of the opinion that most workers will strike unquestioningly at a word from their shop steward or a trade union officer. This idea has been carefully propagated by the mass media, and is trotted out from time to time in support of various campaigns, such as 'trade unions wrecking the economy', 'Communist influence/Reds under the Bed' and so on.

The workers are not sheep. They do not follow without question whatever course of action is proposed by their leaders. They first require strong arguments and examples to demonstrate that action is necessary, and that action could be successful. Once convinced of this, the unity and strength of the working class are powerful weapons.

But the theory of the spontaneous strike dies hard. It has its supporters among left-wing militants, as well as among those who have a capitalist axe to grind. Some 'militants', for example, claim that a more militant trade union leadership would merely have to 'call a general strike' and the whole of the trade union movement would be out on the streets, no questions asked. There is no doubt that a more militant leadership *elected by the workers* would have a better chance of satisfying trade unionists that a general strike was not only essential, but could also be a success; but the job of rousing the workers to political consciousness would still have to be done first.

The political education of the working class has never been of such a high standard as to enable a general strike to be successful. The apparent strength of 'them' – the employers, the Government – has always seemed too great for a working class not yet conscious of its own strength. But this is not to say that the working class will never use a general strike success-fully – even a babe in arms, unable to lift a finger in its own defence, grows into a strong adult.

Working-class leaders have always approached the idea of a 'strike for political ends' with some delicacy. On the question of the Industrial Relations legislation, the AUEW called for a series of one-day strikes which were little more than a token stoppage, and the TUC refused to give its support to any strike action at all, although the more militant among the rank and file were calling for a general strike. A strike against legislation of this kind, against a Government responsible for mass un-employment, or against a Government responsible for depressing the living standards of millions of workers in publicly owned industries, could be 'successful' in the sense of bringing down the Government and forcing an election, provided that the rank and file gives its full backing to the strike under a strong and militant leadership. The trade unions could have forced the Tory Government into submission on the Industrial Relations Act, if the struggle had been better led.

INTELLECTUALS, YES – ELITISTS, NO!

So the effectiveness of strikes depends upon the class-conscious-ness and solidarity of the working class, and upon the militancy and strength of the leaders they elect. The need for a revolu-tionary political party, therefore, is not because the workers are not capable of winning the struggle alone, but because a political party is a common point of reference for all workers in all unions, and because it draws into the struggle those members of other classes who recognise that their interests lie with the workers. While agreeing with Lenin's proposition, that members of other classes – the intellectuals and the bourgeoisie – must be a part of the workers' struggle, I cannot, however, subscribe to his reasons for including them. Lenin says, in *What is to be done?* :

'The history of all countries shows that the working class, exclusively by its own effort, is able to develop only trade union consciousness, i.e. the conviction that it is necessary to combine in unions, fight the employers and strive to compel the government to pass necessary labour legislation, etc. The theory of socialism, however, grew out of the philosophic, historical and economic theories elaborated by educated representatives of the propertied classes, by intellectuals. By their social status the founders of modern scientific socialism, Marx and Engels, themselves belonged to the bourgeois intelligentsia.'

Perry Anderson goes even further, stating categorically that without the privileged classes, there would be no theory of socialism. He goes on: '. . . only if some members of these strata go over to the cause of the working class can a revolutionary movement be born. For without a revolutionary theory, there can be no revolutionary movement.'

The extent to which the working class depends upon the 'educated representatives of the propertied classes' for its socialist theory is in turn dependent on the political level of the working class itself. The British workers, including the unskilled, skilled, technical and professional members of the working class, can learn, and in the past have learned, from the revolutionary experiences of others, as well as from their own experiences, and are fully capable of developing their own strategy and tactics.

The theory of 'the elite of expertise' is a dangerous one for the working class. The workers must not believe that they need an elite to think on their behalf, otherwise they get saddled with petty-bourgeois intellectual 'experts', who are a dead-weight for the working class to carry. Marxism has been expounded by Marx himself, by Engels, Lenin, Mao and others; the proliferation of an elite breed of intellectuals to interpret their theories is reminiscent of the establishment of clergymen to interpret the bible – the greater the number of interpreters, the more plentiful the points of disagreement, and so the more schisms and sects and irreconcilable factions. In order to think like a revolutionary, you have first to act like one – and that does not mean dividing the working class against itself, but working for its unity.

Lenin implies, in *What is to be done?*, that the bourgeois intelligentsia are a unifying factor in a revolutionary party, since they provide the necessary breadth of outlook, and the ability to recognise and respond to 'all cases of tyranny – no matter what class is affected'. The trade union movement is so self-absorbed that it is not equipped to teach the workers to observe 'every other social class in all the manifestations of its intellectual, ethical and political life', whereas the bourgeoisie within the political party, with their educational and cultural advantages, are well able to do so. Perry Anderson supports this idea, claiming that trade unions have 'only a sectoral power-potential' – the power of labour withdrawal or factory occupation – whereas a political party including the bourgeois elements is a 'polyvalent potential of revolutionary action'. That is, the middle class provide capital, which can be converted into resources for elections, mass media control, political education, etc., whereas the workers 'only' provide labour, which is a commodity of limited convertibility. This means, says Anderson, that 'A political party is by its nature flexible and versatile where a trade union is fettered and immobile'. Capitalist ideology says that capital produces goods, and without money in one form or another, nothing could be produced. In other words, the money does the work.

Perry Anderson's idea is based on the same belief, that no work will be done unless the money is there to support it. It would be more true to say that money will buy nothing unless the workers choose to make it. The 'limited' potential of the trade unions is therefore greater than the 'polyvalent' potential of the party, in that labour can be withheld or applied independently of money. It depends more on the political education of the workers, than on cash. If the workers chose to print socialist material rather than Tory material, or to broadcast socialist programmes in preference to any other, nothing short of armed force would prevent them.

There is no reason why this level of political understanding cannot be achieved. The organisation of the workers has grown in strength over the years; the gains made, though they appear slight individually, are considerable when viewed as a whole. Anderson accepts that ' "encroaching control" is not a myth', but declares that 'the results have been disappointing so far'.

Nevertheless, a worker acquainted with conditions at the end of the last century, if transported into the 1970s, could be for-given for thinking that socialism had arrived in Britain – at first sight, anyway! Shorter working hours, improved living stan-dards, national health service, unemployment pay, sick benefit, free education, and so on! And in other ways the working class has advanced, too. In organised strength, in its willingness to use that strength in strike action, and lately in occupations.

OCCUPATION – A POLITICAL LESSON

Until recently, occupation of a factory was virtually unheard of. 1971, with the provocation of massive unemployment, saw the beginning of half a dozen occupations, most of which were concluded with some success, i.e. the saving, if only temporarily, of some jobs. Time was when strikes could not take place because of the workers' lack of organisation; time could bring about a dramatic increase both in the number of occupations, and in the degree of their success. Although it is not at present possible to take over a factory and continue to produce goods, there is no reason why this should not be done in the future. Perry Anderson describes occupation as 'no more than a dramatic form of picketing', since the operation of a plant 'is naturally impossible in modern industry, where circulating capital is necessary to keep any industrial installation going at all'.

Certainly it is not possible for a single plant to continue to produce, as its sources of supply from capitalist-controlled plants elsewhere would quickly dry up. But it is a mistake to suppose that it is the circulation of capital which prevents occu-pation for production purposes. 'Encroaching control', the result of the workers' struggles, has evolved a new weapon, occupation, which has at present only a limited application. A situation can be foreseen, however, in which occupation will be as common a form of action as strikes are today, and under these circumstances, the possibilities of mutual aid in keeping up supplies between occupied factories would be greatly increased. But just as the success of strikes increased with the growth of the workers' belief in their own power, so also will the development of occupations into takeovers be directly related to the growth in political awareness of the working class, and their willingness to exercise the power of labour over capital.

Factory occupation is not merely a symbolic protest. Political lessons can be learned from occupation, among which is the need for a revolutionary government which will take the means of production out of the hands of capital, under the direction and control of the working class. So, although one or two attempts at occupation may appear symbolic, the growth of occupation as a form of protest contains the seeds of workers' control and socialism, in that it is a challenge to the private ownership of property.

That challenge must come from the workers. It must start with the rank and file, and express itself in the choice of a militant trade union leadership, and ultimately – through the activities of the trade unions – in a revolutionary leadership in the Labour Party. In a democratic society, the degree of militancy is dictated by the workers, and reflected in their election of leaders for their political and economic organisations. Unless force is to be used to oust unsatisfactory leaders, a course of action which would not attract the support of the vast majority of the working class, the election process will decide the type of leadership which has the support of the workers.

TRADE UNIONS AND THEIR POLITICAL PARTY

Breakaway-groups of militants, forming themselves into 'revolutionary parties', have gained only minimal support. The bulk of the workers look to the Labour Party for leadership, if only by turning out to vote at general or local elections. It is a mistake to talk about an 'alternative leadership' as if it were merely a case of installing revolutionary leaders in positions of power. Between twelve and fourteen million people choose to 'vote Labour', however misguided their selection of candidates may be, and these votes cannot be overridden by a revolutionary minority, however noble their motives.

Lenin was therefore mistaken when he took McLaine to task for claiming that the Labour Party was 'the political expression of the trade union movement'. Lenin said, speaking of *The Communist Party and the Labour Party*:

'Of course, for the most part the Labour Party consists of workers, but it does not logically follow from this that every workers' party which consists of workers is at the same time a "political workers' party"; that depends upon who leads it, upon the content of its activities and of its political tactics. Only the latter determine whether it is a political proletarian party. From this point of view, which is the only correct point of view, the Labour Party is not a political workers' party but a thoroughly bourgeois party, because, although it consists of workers, it is led by reactionaries, and the worst reactionaries at that, who lead it in the spirit of the bourgeoisie and . . . systematically deceive the workers.'

Certainly, it does not logically follow that every party which consists of workers is necessarily a political workers' party. But neither does it follow that every political party with revolutionary leadership, activities and tactics is necessarily a *workers'* party.

At the present time, the Labour Party has the active support of some workers, and the passive support of many workers. The trade union movement, representing the working class, *is* the Labour Party – in the sense that trade unions breathe financial life into the party, and exercise great control (though not sufficient control) over it in the form of block votes. No other party commands so much working-class support as the Labour Party. This, then, is the workers' party, 'the political expression of the trade union movement'.

The workers exercise their choice of leadership directly, in the selection and election of parliamentary candidates, and indirectly, through the strength of their trade unions at the Party Conference. The weaknesses, the reactionary tendencies, the bourgeois leadership of the Labour Party, as well as its successes, are the responsibility of the working class. But they are to an even greater extent the responsibility of those who consider themselves to be revolutionaries, who consider the Labour Party to be beyond redemption, and who choose to direct their energies into building tiny 'revolutionary parties' – which have all the ingredients of revolution, except the backing of the working class.

Lenin was right to say that the Labour Party was in effect only an imperfect tool for the workers' use. Nevertheless, it has greater potential for the British working class than any other party. Revolutionary tactics within the Labour Party therefore have a much greater chance of getting proletarian backing, than the same tactics operated outside the mainstream of working-class politics. As Lenin went on to say, fighting against bourgeois leadership *within* the party can have a great effect on the masses:

'Under such circumstances, it would be a great mistake if the best revolutionary elements did not do all that was possible to remain in such a party. Let Messrs. Thomas and the other social-traitors, whom you call social-traitors, expel you. This will have an excellent effect upon the mass of the British workers.'

In other words, forcing the leaders to show their political colours has a salutory effect on the Party as a whole. While saying that 'What we want are new parties, different parties. We want parties that will be in constant and real contact with the masses and that will be able to lead those masses', Lenin was 'convinced' that 'the decision to remain in the ranks of the Labour Party is really a correct decision', although he admitted that 'a large section of the best revolutionaries' were against affiliation to the Labour Party 'because they are opposed to parliamentarism as a means of struggle'.

CONTROL WITHOUT POWER

The next Labour Government must be forced to socialise, or it must be exposed. We must destroy blind faith in Labour Party leaders, by convincing the working class that democracy is not confined to a vote every five years, followed by impotent discontent until the next election. Parliamentarism is not democracy under these terms. The trade unions and individual party members gained a small victory when they forced the Labour Government to withdraw its anti-working-class trade union legislation, thus demonstrating that a Government must bend, if not break, under the weight of opinion of the workers. The task of militants is not to desert the workers, but to help in the political education of both active and passive Labour Party suporters; this must be done *before* an election, to make sure that revolutionary candidates are chosen and elected, and *after* an election, to ensure that the elected Government carries out the wishes of its electors.

The degree of militancy shown by the electors reflects upon the Government to such an extent that the real advances made by a Government are always the result of rank-and-file pressure. This pressure need not always be used negatively – for example, in *stopping* the Labour Government from going ahead with *In Place of Strife* – but can be applied positively, for example, by demanding more nationalisation, and forcing the government to nationalise *with workers' control*. The workers, exercising their right to control their country, could dictate the terms of nationalisation – expropriation, with no further control for the previous owners, etc. – and the extent and speed of nationalisation would be in their hands alone. While it remains in the hands of a reactionary leadership, power will be abused; so it is necessary for the workers to learn the relationship between control and power, if they are to stop their exploitation not only by the capitalist class, but also by a small number of 'Labour' leaders.

British 'democracy' today consists in 'control without power', and Lenin exposed our democratic system as an illusion when he wrote about controlling England:

'Control without power is an empty phrase. How can I control England? In order to control her I must capture her navy. I know that uneducated masses of workers and soldiers may naively and unintelligently believe in control, but it is sufficient to ponder over the fundamental element of control in order to realise that this belief is a retreat from the fundamental principles of the class struggle. What is control? If I write an order or a resolution, they will write one countermanding it. In order to be able to exercise control one must have power. If this is not intelligible to the broad mass of the petty-bourgeois bloc, one must have the patience to explain this to them, but under no circumstances must we tell them lies. And if I obscure this fundamental condition of control then I tell a lie and play into the hands of the capitalists and imperialists. "Please control me, but I will have the guns. You be satisfied with control," they say.'

'Control without power' is only nominal control, and this is the kind of control the working class has been content with up to now. Furthermore, this is the kind of control which Labour Governments have been content with, since real power has remained in the hands of the capitalists, no matter what the colour of the Government.

PENALTIES OF NOT CONTROLLING

The trade unions in the early 1900s, having been lied to and cheated by previous Tory and Liberal Governments, decided to establish their own working-class political party, which they would control, and which would represent their interests in the House of Commons. So the Labour Party came into existence in 1906.

The experiences arising from the treachery of Ramsay McDonald, Snowden, Clynes, Jimmy Thomas, etc., taught the working class some things, but not enough to make them exercise the control they could have done through their trade unions, which could have controlled the party by sheer numerical strength as well as financial power.

The 1945–50 Labour Government was the first Labour Government to have an absolute parliamentary majority. It could have taken control of all the commanding heights of the economy. It could have made real inroads into the power of the capitalists. It could have strengthened the power of the working class through workers' control in many aspects of the nation's economic and political structure. It could have weakened the capitalist state apparatus and made the way easier for the transition to socialism in Britain.

It did not do this in its five years of power. Whilst they nationalised a few industries and services, they left control in the hands of the previous owners or appointed other anti-socialists to positions of power. The workers in the under-takings were not given, and did not take, any real control. The welfare services which they had previously expanded, the Government proceeded to cut back in 1951, which caused a section of the then left wing, Nye Bevan, Harold Wilson, Free-man, to resign from government positions. Labour Govern-ments which have since been elected have not satisfied the needs of the working class any better than these early efforts did, and have not brought us any nearer socialism.

In 1962, about fifty left-wing trade union leaders and Labour MPs founded a new paper, *Union Voice*, which would spell out for the rank and file the most urgent tasks facing the Labour Party. Our aims in sponsoring such a paper were declared as follows:

'1. The election of a Labour Government as soon as possible.
2. The implementation of Clause IV, i.e. "To secure for the workers by hand or by brain the full fruits of their industry and the most equitable distribution thereof that may be possible, upon the basis of the common ownership of the means of pro-duction, distribution and exchange, and the best obtainable system of popular administration and control of each industry and service."
3. For World Peace and Socialism.

The role of this paper will be to create unity and clarity amongst all socialist trade unionists on the great problems facing our movement. We shall fight against unemployment and the pay pause, in support of workers' demands for wage-increases and shorter working week, and increasing Trade Union member-ship . . .

We shall struggle to bring to an end this disastrous Tory Government as quickly as possible.

We stand for the democratic right of the Annual Conference of the Labour Party to decide the Party's policies . . .'

Union Voice was launched successfully, and has fought for the adoption of socialist policies on every front. But the 1964–6 Labour Government antagonised the organised trade union movement with its attacks on wages through the prices and incomes policy, and this conflict deepened during the period of the 1966–70 Labour Government, as a result of the anti-trade union industrial relations policy, *In Place of Strife*. During this period, nearly all the local councils where Labour had had a majority were swept from power by the working class, who were demonstrating their resentment against the national policies of the Government.

All this resulted in the working class turning against the Labour Government in the 1970 general election, either by abstaining from voting, or voting against them, and a Tory Government was returned to power.

Considerable antagonism developed amongst the activists of the Labour Party in the constituencies. They complained that the Labour Party had not, when in office, carried out National Labour Party Conference decisions on a number of issues, particularly on prices and incomes. It seemed that the Parliamentary Labour Party was a power apart from the Labour Party organisation, and acted as a supreme authority. But the following quotation from the *Militant International Review* (Summer 1971) should have been applied to the Labour Party as much as to trade unions:

'Any one who considers himself a socialist and is not prepared to work inside the unions with reactionary leaders can in no way be classed as a revolutionary. Lenin once said "that if necessary we will work within these unions in order to win those backward elements to socialism".'

Instead of taking this advice to heart, many members either left the Party, or simply became too discouraged to put up a struggle against the policies of the parliamentary party.

INTERNAL DEMOCRACY

But where does power rest in deciding these policies? In the election of the National Executive of the Labour Party? In the selection of parliamentary candidates? In the selection of the party leader?

The Labour Party membership is made up of 700,000 individual members, 22,000 Co-operative and Socialist Society members, and 5,500,000 affiliated trade union members. It is clear from these figures that the block votes of the trade unions *can* determine the policies of the Party's Annual Conference, and it is therefore a false contention that the trade unions are merely economic institutions with no political interests or means of exercising political influence. Trade unions *can* determine Party policy; in fact, this power is not exercised by the membership of the unions very often, because the right-wing leaders who in some cases control the block vote of their union delegation use the votes to support the National Executive or right-wing members of a Labour Government.

This need not be so. Trade union members should exercise their control to make certain that those delegates and leaders who attend the Annual Conference represent the point of view of the membership and put forward their demands. Each trade union delegation meets prior to the opening of the Conference to decide how their union's votes should be used, both on the resolutions and in the election of the National Executive, which contains a majority of trade union representatives.

It is no use any of us simply sitting down and complaining. We have both the right and the opportunity to control, and we must exercise our power.

However, having taken a part in the decision-making of the Party Conference, it is also our responsibility to see that conference decisions are carried out by the Parliamentary Labour Party. The following quotation, taken from an article on the Labour movement in the *Morning Star*, analyses the position with particular reference to the debate on the Common Market:

'Already Wilson has made it clear that he and the Parliamentary Labour Party will not be bound on the Common Market issue by Labour Party Conference decision, either on July 17th [1971], or in the autumn.

He says this is a restatement of the constitutional relationship between the mass party and the Parliamentary Labour Party.

This so-called constitutional relationship is a cynical Tory Party invention. With the extension of the vote in the 1870s, the Tory and Liberal leaders of the time had to create mass parties to provide the necessary organisation to turn out the new voters.

The MPs were christened the "Parliamentary Party" and made independent of the annual conference or executive bodies of the mass parties.

It was Ramsay MacDonald who brought this Tory practice into the Labour Party.

By 1929 he was assuring King George V that his Labour Cabinet paid no attention to the Labour Party EC or the Labour Party Conference. When challenged by Churchill in 1945, Attlee laid down the same doctrine. It's been Right Wing credo ever since.

The sooner the Labour Party Conference decisions are made binding on the Labour leaders the better.'

And the sooner trade unions act to make it so, the better!

Anthony Wedgwood Benn, quoted in *Labour Weekly* (5 November 1971), complained of the outmoded belief of some political leaders in the 'divine right of Parliament', but he did not suggest that Conference decisions be made binding on the Parliamentary Party – only that they 'must be treated with greater respect'. In other words, the Party Conference would control the decisions, and the Parliamentary Party would have the power to reject them if they wished, while treating them with all due respect, of course. The same illusion of 'control without power' is apparent in Wedgwood Benn's attitude to workers' control in industry. Robert Vitak, writing on the Czechoslovak experience of workers' control, in *The Socialist Register 1971*, comments: 'When Anthony Wedgwood Benn, for example, came forward last year with his contribution he was quite explicit in his view that "real workers' control" would fit comfortably within the existing relations of power.'

Vitak went on to quote a Fabian Tract, *New Politics: A Socialist Renaissance*, in which Benn said:

'Certainly there is no reason why industrial power at plant or office level should be exclusively linked to ownership of shares, than that political power should have been exclusively linked to the ownership of land and other property as it was in Britain until the "voters control" movement won its battle.'

On the contrary, there is every reason to believe that workers' control cannot be complete while society permits the private ownership of the means of production. Encroaching control can improve the situation and teach the workers to demand more, but while power remains in the hands of capitalists, ultimate control rests with them, too. When workers' demands for control begin to endanger their system, they will demonstrate where control really lies by the use of force, and that will be the crucial point for determining who is to have control in the future.

Similarly, although we all have the right to 'control' the government by means of a periodic vote, this does not mean that we have 'won the battle' for democracy. Voters have this minimal 'control'; the *power* is with the capitalists, whatever the government.

Within the Labour Party, therefore, it is not enough to give nominal control to the rank and file, while reserving the real power to the Parliamentary Party – or, in the case of a Labour Government, to an even smaller group, the Cabinet. Norman Atkinson (*Labour Weekly*, 7 January 1972) has been more explicit in demanding that the decisions of Conference be carried out. As he said:

'It would be a tragedy if Labour's policy-making plan "Participation 72" suffered a lack of response due to the Party's deep suspicion that Conference decisions count for nothing . . .

The NEC – as custodians of Conference decisions – must make it absolutely clear that every policy decision which conference supports by a two-thirds majority will be included in the election manifesto and will become binding upon the next Labour Government.

Annual Conference is Labour's highest policy-making authority, and failure on the part of Labour MPs to accept the principles Conference decides must inevitably lead to the disintegration of the Party.'

We must not be led into the error of believing that, providing we elect 'good' people, we can safely leave them to do a 'good' job. The rank and file must control policy *at all times*, and since it clearly does not do so at the moment, the time is ripe for the rank and file, through the constituency parties and the trade unions, to campaign for their right to control national policies.

CONTROL OF PARLIAMENTARY CANDIDATES

But the area where the central struggle for power and workers' control must take place is in the selection of parliamentary candidates, who become after election to Parliament, the Parliamentary Labour Party, who can exercise real political power. (Whether they do so or not depends upon the pressure and militancy of the rank and file.)

The National Executive of the Labour Party reported to the 1969 Annual Conference:

'By July 1969, the National Executive Committee had endorsed 236 candidates, of which 213 have been selected on the responsibility of constituency parties, 16 are sponsored by trade unions, and 7 by the Co-operative Party. Only a small number of constituencies had not then set in motion the procedure for selection.

On a number of occasions in recent years the National Executive Committee has given consideration to the compilation of "List B" of available parliamentary candidates, but in doing so has been limited by the decision of the 1948 Annual Party Conference that the list of available candidates be compiled from nominations received from constituency labour parties and affiliated organisations. To enable the whole question to be looked at afresh the National Executive Committee recommends Conference to rescind the decision of the 1948 Annual Party Conference, so that when the Committee reviews the procedures after the next General Election it would not necessarily be bound by that decision.'

The Conference agreed to the National Executive's request. The lists 'A' (of sponsored candidates) and 'B' (of unsponsored candidates) are purely advisory lists. It was the practice until 1971 that any person who was a member of the Labour Party for no matter how short a time could be nominated as a candidate for selection by any constituency party; this has been sensibly amended, to make two years' membership a condition of nomination.

In the 1970 General Election, of 618 candidates chosen by constituency Labour Parties, 137 were trade union-sponsored candidates, 28 were Co-op candidates, and 453 were unsponsored. The Parliamentary Labour Party after the election was composed of 15 Co-op MPS, 114 trade union MPS, and 287 constituency-supported MPS. Taking into consideration the overwhelming membership of trade unionists in the Labour Party, and the fact that the bulk of the finance of the Party comes from the trade unions, this balance of representation is very unsatisfactory.

None the less, this is the fault of the trade unionists themselves. If all trade union branches in each constituency not only paid affiliation fees but also elected their full complement of delegates to the local constituency Labour Party, they would have a majority vote at the selection conferences, as well as being able to determine party policies. But this is not done. I know this only too well, as a result of being the national political officer of a union which has over 850,000 members affiliated to the Labour Party. Only a very small percentage of our 2,750 branches affiliated to the local constituency party have any delegates elected to their CLP.

This means that when one of our union's parliamentary candidates is nominated for a parliamentary seat, he is generally not chosen, because our branches are not represented at the selection conference. For example, in one constituency we have 34 branches, who could have had about 170 delegates at the selection conference. Only *three* of our possible quota attended. Our candidate did not stand a chance. Several other examples demonstrate that where we could have had between fifty and a hundred delegates, only 10 per cent on average were present at the selection conference, and our candidates lost by between two and ten votes to other candidates who were middle-class professionals or upper-class 'gentlefolk'.

In engineering centres like Coventry, Sheffield, Birmingham and Manchester, one would think that it would be easy to get a trade union engineering candidate selected, but this has not proved to be the case. Coventry, for instance, now has three parliamentary seats, and will have another one, arising from redistribution, in future elections. In this city, the AUEW branches could have about 400 delegates to the CLPs and could in fact determine who the parliamentary candidates were, but they have been slow to take advantage of this power.

Due to Richard Crossman, one of the Coventry MPs, stating that he would not be contesting the next general election, and the provision of a new seat through redistribution, the opportunity arose for Coventry engineers to select two of their trade union candidates to represent them in the House of Commons. In the case of finding a successor to Richard Crossman, the trade unions exercised their right to elect delegates to the selection conference, and as a result Mr G. Parks, a shop stewards' convenor, was chosen by the constituency to fight the seat.

If *all* the trade union branches which are affiliated to their constituency parties were to unite in their efforts to get working-class candidates into parliament, by electing the maximum number of delegates to selection conferences and agreeing to support each other in the exhaustive ballot method (that is, if one trade union nominee is defeated, the votes of all the trade unions are used in support of the remaining trade union candidate), the proportion of trade union members of parliament would be very much increased. This would be more representative of the membership of the Labour Party as a whole, and it is the only way to change the middle-class character of the Parliamentary Labour Party.

In a by-election in 1971, a good engineering union candidate was defeated at the selection conference, in an engineering and solidly working-class constituency, by a gentleman lawyer who drove up to the conference in his Rolls Royce. In spite of the fact that all the trade union delegates agreed to support the engineer, he lost by a small margin of votes because the ladies of the party – who do the dry-as-dust work in the Party machine and who take the trouble to attend regular meetings and selection conferences – decided the lawyer was such a nice man: good speech, good dress, nice manners, and a university degree too. Sure to make a good impression. These trade union candidates, well, some of them are a bit rough and ready . . . they tend to call a spade a – –.

Another typical case was that of a young lady candidate, not long out of college, excellent elocution, good middle-class background. She knew all about the workers' problems – she had read about them, no doubt, and written about them, too, and was all ready to lead the workers to socialism. She was chosen as a Labour candidate, and will no doubt soon be a member of the Parliamentary Labour Party. *The Observer* gave this little thumbnail sketch of her:

'Diana Jeuda is 30 and head of the Research Department of USDAW. She has worked in the Labour movement ever since leaving London University with a first in history and an MA in manpower studies. She was married last year to the chairman of the local Labour Party, a management consultant.

She is reluctant to talk about herself or her background, perhaps because her father, Martin Jukes QC, is Director-General of the Engineering Employers' Federation.'

I am sure that Diana Jeuda and others like her who aspire to be Labour Members of Parliament act in good faith and from the best motives. But the working class is capable of producing its own leaders, men and women who understand working-class politics as a result of their own experience and who are well equipped to represent the workers in Parliament. There is no shortage of such candidates at selection conferences, yet *Labour Weekly* announced (4 February 1972) that nearly half of the Parliamentary Labour Party was composed of teachers, lecturers, lawyers and journalists, and of the sixty-four candidates so far chosen to fight the next election, exactly half were from those professions; there were 'only three trade union officials, two post office workers, six engineers, but nine managers, executives or administrators'.

The reason suggested for this trend was that lecturers, lawyers and journalists are 'best trained and equipped to make a good impression in a 15-minute speech', and the selection committees 'often seem to go for the smooth talker, the man who can give a good instant impression'. The answer? *Labour Weekly* says:

'Perhaps selection committees should ask more searching questions about their candidates, their background, their work for the local party, whether they send their children to state schools, whether they belong to private health schemes, why they want to be MPs.'

Of course. But a more important factor by far is ensuring that selection committees are not biased in favour of the middle-class candidate, and this must be done by mobilising trade union delegates to attend conferences.

CONTROL OF MPS

Following the disastrous policies of the Labour Government up to 1970, members began to question the necessity of having a rank-and-file membership at all, when its declared policies and decisions were virtually ignored by its 'representatives' in Parliament. Mike Casselden, a correspondent to *Labour Weekly*, probed the reasons for the breakdown between electors and elected:

'Is the answer that Labour can no longer be effectively represented by middle-class professionals such as solicitors, barristers, etc., who have middle-class aspirations and ideals? Can they only react in a philanthropic manner towards the working classes as "liberals" with a desire to treat the malaise of capitalism rather than eliminate it?'

(31 December 1971)

John G. Owen, a correspondent to *The Observer*, claimed that a party so curiously represented in Parliament as the Labour Party calls into question the whole concept of democracy. Replying to an article by Polly Toynbee on factory life, Mr Owen wrote:

'I assume Miss Toynbee is typical of the lucky few of her generation, those who are well-educated and have no worries about money. I have seen many of the type who eventually would like to become Labour MPs. This raises a major problem in present-day politics: how can a person who has received full-time education up to the age of 21 and has never mixed with the mass of the people hope to represent them? I feel that it makes a mockery of any fiction that Britain is a representative democracy. It is one of the sad failures of the present day that the leaders of the Labour Party are mere theorists who play with nice political ideas while the people of the country cry out to be heard.'

The movement of the Labour Party towards intellectuals, coupled with the backsliding on policies which has led to industrial relations struggles with the trade unions, wage freezes, introduction of health-service charges and so on, must be seen as an incipient danger to the Tories. Unless the rank and file rouse themselves, there will be little to choose between the Tweedledum Party and the Tweedledee Party. Gerald Nabarro noted the trend in his book, NAB 1:

'Of course, party images and the composition of parties change over the years and not always for the better. The Labour Party, fearful of too much Keir Hardie, Clause 4, clothcap Socialism, heavy watchchains and Trade Unionism, have overplayed the bias towards academics and the parliamentary party now contains all manner of pedagogues and prosaic theorists who look down their noses at the horny-handed sons of toil who made their party in the first place. The pendulum has swung too far towards the intellectuals and away from the working men.'

Naturally enough, having selected, slaved for and elected candidates whose background and interests are not wholly in sympathy with their own, members of constituency Labour parties are unpleasantly surprised when the parliamentary activities of their chosen representatives don't match up to expectations.

It was reported in the press that Mr Christopher Mayhew had spoken to the GMC of the Woolwich Labour Party, and declared his support for the Tory White Paper on Industrial Relations. When the first part of the Industrial Relations Bill was voted on, he abstained, and

'this action so disgusted ordinary members of the Woolwich Labour Party, and particularly the affiliated trade unions, that the executive committee proposed a resolution "regretting Mayhew's actions and reaffirming their own total opposition to the proposed legislation".'

In his own defence, Mayhew is reported to have said: 'I am not a delegate of the local Labour Party – no MP is', and followed this up with remarks about 'the national interest' and his right to 'say what he thought fit'.

When the GMC voted on their resolution, however, Mayhew received only three of their eighty votes.

After voting with the Tory Government on the question of entry into the Common Market, a number of Labour MPs came under attack from their constituency parties. The divisional management committee in the Barnsley constituency 'severely reprimanded' Roy Mason, but one of the committee members, George Wilkinson, said afterwards:

'I seconded the resolution severely reprimanding Roy Mason, but it didn't really go deep enough for me.

I wanted his resignation. A man who votes with the Tories is voting for Tory policies all the way round.

One million unemployed and the Common Market are part and parcel of the same thing. We are fighting like hell for wages and Labour MPs vote with the Tories.'

Mason, an NUM-sponsored MP, said that he 'had to vote with his conscience' – in spite of the fact that his union, the TUC, and the Labour Party Conference all voted by large majorities against entry. Nor was he the only well-known name to come out on the side of the Tories: Roy Jenkins, Shirley Williams, Michael Stewart also 'followed their consciences'.

These, and the other more obscure but equally conscience-stricken voters and abstainers on the Common Market issue, received the support of a *Labour Weekly* correspondent, R. G. Thurston (10 December 1971), whose letter provoked a response the following week from Fred Silberman: 'Mr Thurston asks whether one can seriously consider that the Labour Party could afford to lose Roy Jenkins and Co. A more pertinent question is can the Labour Party afford to keep them and maintain any credibility with the working class?'

The question often arises of what action can be taken by a constituency when their MP rejects their expressed wishes. On this issue, it is worth quoting at some length the article by Francis Flavius in the *Tribune* of 15 October 1971, in which he discusses not only the morality of voting against one's constituency, but also the remedy under the Party's constitution:

'A number of political commentators have been suggesting that there is something improper about Labour constituency parties telling their Members of Parliament what they will feel about them should they go into the lobbies to vote with the Tory Government on the Common Market.

There is nothing improper about such pressure. Indeed, anyone who takes the trouble to read the constitution of the Labour Party will discover that both the rights of the Member of Parliament *and* the constituency party are carefully considered. The idea that a Member of Parliament who has lost the sympathy of his local party should be allowed to ride roughshod over their views is the very negation of democracy.

Some papers are suggesting that there is something anti-democratic about local parties telling their MPs that they will not support them for re-adoption at the next general election. In fact, quite the opposite is the case: those Members of Parliament who believe that they can continue to defy the will of democratically-organised party conferences and their own local parties do the gravest damage to democracy in Britain.

Now let us look at the facts of the situation. Take the example of the Clapham (Wandsworth) Constituency Labour Party which decided in January 1970 that it no longer wished to continue with Mrs Margaret McKay as its Member of Parliament.

It passed a resolution by 21 votes to 14 asking the National Executive Committee of the Labour Party whether it could decide to set up a selection process to choose a new candidate. In fact, the Clapham party did not even need to ask the NEC's permission. Under Section 7, Clause 6 of the rules pertaining to parliamentary candidates, the constitution says: "If at any time the party is represented in Parliament by a member of the Parliamentary Labour Party, procedure for the selection of a prospective candidate shall not be set in motion until an election is imminent . . . unless (a) such representative intimates his or her intention to retire, or (b) the general committee, on securing a mandate from the affiliated and party organisations intimates by resolution that he or she must retire." . . .

Already some local Labour Parties are considering action of this sort where Labour pro-Marketeers have indicated that they will defy conference decision and vote with the Conservatives.

Under the democratic constitution of the Labour Party every party has the right to tell its MP that he or she will not be re-selected as the Labour candidate for a future general election. There is nothing improper about that – unless, of course, you believe that MPs have some divine right to rule, and I don't know many who would claim that!'

Some parliamentary candidates, speaking to CLP members at selection conferences, promise to carry out party policy, the wishes of the constituency, and carry out the mandate of the members (in spite of the fact that any or all of these might be at variance with each other at one time). In their anxiety to get a seat, they say in effect: 'This is my policy, and these are my principles, and if you don't like them, I'll change them.'

How different it is, once they have been selected and elected to Parliament! When CLP members meet to challenge an MP on his actions in the House of Commons or at Parliamentary Labour Party meetings, he declares that he is not the representative of the local Labour Party in Parliament, but the representative of the electors in the constituency, and that his actions must be dictated by his conscience. He ignores the fact that he has been elected on the basis of Labour Party policy and the members' money, and their activity in the constituency over a number of years. It is worth bearing in mind the words of Harold Wilson, at the Labour Party Conference 1971, when he said:

'There is not one Labour Member of Parliament who could have been elected by his own efforts. He is where he is, because of the efforts and dedication of thousands upon thousands of those represented by delegates here today. And he is elected to be in his place, and to do the job he was sent to do.'

If only Wilson, and the rest of the Parliamentary Party, remembered this in office, as well as in opposition! Anthony Wedgwood Benn, in a statement made on 31 October 1971 as a contender for the post of Deputy Leader of the Labour Party – the current holder being pro-Marketeer Roy Jenkins – claimed that:

'If every Labour MP had voted together, the Conservative Government would have been defeated; Mr Heath would not have remained as Prime Minister; the Cabinet would have collapsed; and a general election would have been inevitable.

It is no wonder that the Labour and trade union movement made up of millions of ordinary people who sent us to Parliament to represent them are so dismayed at our tragic failure to defend their interests.'

So the constituency parties have every right to complain – but not, it seems, too strongly. Mr Wedgwood Benn, in his other role as Chairman of the National Executive Committee, was reported, three days earlier, to have

'ruled out of order a motion moved by Mr Alex Kitson and seconded by Mr Len Fordern which said that "where MPs act contrary to the collective decisions of the Annual Conference and Parliamentary Labour Party", this should be drawn to the attention of their respective constituency Labour Parties.'

(*Morning Star*, 28 October 1971)

The 1971 Labour Party Chairman, Ian Mikardo, speaking at a Tribune meeting, defended the right of CLPs to get rid of their MP, although he said that, in the long run, constituency parties get the MPs they deserve, 'because it is they who choose them and can change them'. If they choose 'the slickest talker and the best salesman' instead of 'the hardest workers or the best socialist', they get their just deserts if their Member does not act on their decisions, nor even on national policy decisions.

Some CLP delegates have been so incensed by this attitude on the part of their MP and hold such fundamental opposition to his or her political position on so many issues, that they have attempted to select a new candidate at the earliest opportunity. But this course of action has been found to be extremely difficult, and in fact it has rarely been possible, as the national party machine protects its own candidates.

Here is a most important area where workers' control must operate: power to remove the MP as their candidate must always be in the hands of the CLP.

The 1970 Annual Conference of the Labour Party had before

it a report from the National Executive, which it accepted, dealing with the procedure for removing a candidate:

'MEMBERS OF PARLIAMENT

The National Executive Committee gave consideration to the procedure by which a Constituency Labour Party could decide that its Member of Parliament should retire at the next General Election. Under the present rule there is no provision for a Member of Parliament against whom such action is taken to have a right of appeal. The National Executive Committee considers that there should be such a right of appeal and has submitted an amendment to clause XII, Section 7(*b*) of the model rules for the Constituency Labour Parties which would provide for this . . .

The National Executive Committee considered also that the procedures for invoking this rule should be clearly laid down and should include the right of a Member of Parliament to reply in person to criticisms by a constituency Labour Party before a decision is taken under the provisions of this clause.

Therefore Conference is asked to approve the following procedure in carrying out the provision of Clause XII, Section 7, sub-paragraph (*b*):

(*a*) A special meeting of the Executive Committee of the constituency Labour Party shall be held to decide whether or not to recommend the General Committee to consider that the Member of Parliament must retire at the next General Election.

(*b*) The Executive Committee recommendation shall then be considered at a meeting of the General Committee.

(*c*) In the event of the General Committee approving the recommendation, a special meeting of the General Committee shall be convened at not less than four weeks' notice to consider a resolution that the Member of Parliament must retire at the next General Election.

(*d*) The Member of Parliament shall have the right to attend and be heard at meetings of the Executive Committee and the General Committee where this procedure is invoked.'

If the members of a CLP are not satisfied with their Member of Parliament, therefore, the remedy is in their hands.

NO BANS OR PROSCRIPTIONS

Furthermore, action must be taken by individual members of the Labour Party, and by trade unionists, to stop the heresy-hunting that takes place against those members on the left of the Party, by the right wing of the Party, as in the cases of Iltyd Harrington, Tom Braddock, Bill Dow, Ken Coates, Richard Fletcher and myself and others, many of whom have between fifteen and forty years' membership of the Labour Party. Unlike the ex-Liberals and ex-Tories who have in the past joined the Labour Party, and within a year become Labour candidates, like Megan Lloyd George (N.B. this practice is no longer possible), we find that even after being elected on to our union's parliamentary panel, and then being selected by our CLP delegate conference, the National Executive refuses to endorse us without giving its reasons. In one case, more than two hundred CLPs protested against the decision, as well as the union leadership. Thus we have found ourselves investigated by a few members of the NEC (as I was by George Brown, Ray Gunter, Joe Gormley and Len Williams, then General Secretary of the Labour Party), to decide whether we were fit and proper candidates.

In such cases, an arbitrary decision is taken, and it is useless to try to appeal to the Annual Conference against the decision. There is never enough time for Conference to consider all the serious issues in the resolutions on their agenda. Consequently any appeal is dealt with brusquely, with the platform heavily weighted against it. It is clear that the only way to deal with appeals of members against NEC decisions is by an Appeal Court elected by the Annual Conference of the Party, and consisting of constituency and trade union representatives. This method is the one used in the AUEW, where decisions of the Executive Council can be challenged before a Final Appeals Court of rank-and-file members, which meets each year, and whose decisions are final and binding on all concerned.

This internal Party democracy is a matter for workers' control. The left wing of the Labour Party stated the wider effects of such control in their statement, *A Role for the Left?* :

'The extension of democratic control is the key issue in the struggle for socialism. It is the one demand which can unite MPs, trade unionists and Party members, and which is applicable to all the situations with which we are faced. It means the control of housing by tenants, and not officials; of regional planning by elected councils and not by men from Whitehall; of industry by employees and not by owners or the state; of the health service by patients and doctors; of education by parents, teachers and pupils, and so on, throughout the range of human activity.'

The NEC statement to the 1971 Annual Conference of the Labour Party ('Building a Socialist Britain') took up the same theme:

'If we are to get rid of this sense of remoteness and frustration, we must extend the democratic process into the workplace, and into the public services . . . In opposition, we shall continue to work out plans for improving the quality of our democracy – with the major aim of giving more power to the people.'

Starting, I suggest, by giving more power to individual members of the Party at the Annual Conference, and respecting decisions taken there.

On 'tackling the weaknesses in our Party structure', the NEC Report goes on:

'[we must put] more effort into developing the political strength of our movement – through education, and attention to the needs of our internal democracy, including the relationship between the NEC, Annual Conference and the Parliamentary Labour Party, whether in Government or in opposition . . . In future Conferences we shall build policies to guide the Party back to power, and build a socialist Britain.'

But if we allow the Party to continue on the lines of the last Labour Government, we shall find the Parliamentary Labour Party once again trying to 'build a socialist Britain' on the foundations of capitalism, leasehold.

Now is the time for the working class, through their union branches, to increase their political understanding, move into the CLPs, and with the individual members of the Labour Party,

– *take control* of the Party organisation.
– *elect* the leader, deputy leader and general secretary of the Labour Party annually at the Party Conference.
– *make* the policy of the Party correspond to working-class needs.
– *select* local council and parliamentary candidates who are real socialists, and not professional politicians.

If this is done, the trade unions can play a leading role in the creation of a socialist party in which the Annual Conference delegates, the National Executive Committee, the Parliamentary Labour Party and the Party Leader will be united in their efforts to destroy the present capitalist society and replace it with a worker-controlled socialist society.

This change will involve the setting up of a new kind of Parliament, to which the workers will elect their representatives from the places in which they work, and a new kind of State, based on workers' power.

Chapter 12

Elitism

When Adam delved and Eve span,
Who was then the gentleman?
John Ball

'The increase in the number of large private balls is staggering. more than 250 of these took place this summer, each with 400 to 800 guests. A few had more than 1,000 and most were in the country . . .' The 'economic elite' clearly have problems. One of those problems, as evidenced by the above quotation (*Sunday Times Magazine*, 17 October 1971), is how to spend their surplus time and money.

This book began with evidence of economic elitism, demonstrating the vast power which rests in the hands of a tiny minority of people in Britain: 90 per cent of the personal wealth in the possession of 10 per cent of the people; 75 per cent of ordinary shares on the stock exchange controlled by 2 per cent of the population; massive salaries creamed off the wealth produced by the workers, and given to company directors, stockbrokers and the like.

Far from wishing to flaunt their ill-gotten gains, the moneyed elite seem anxious to prove that surtax and death-duties make it hard to turn an honest penny. The *Sunday Times Magaine* goes on:

'The full list of private balls used to appear in the *Times*. Not any more . . .

Fathers are often anxious to have a big "do" for their daughters, but, with 900,000 unemployed, if they are directors of public companies they don't want people beyond their relatives and friends to know anything about it.'

One of the non-taxable benefits of economic security is increased leisure time. In the words of Marx: 'True wealth is the developed productivity of all individuals . . . Then no longer labour time, but free time is the measure of wealth. Using labour time as the measure of wealth places wealth itself on the foundation of poverty . . .'

Tom Mann, in his pamphlet *The Eight-Hour Day by Trade and Local Option*, published in 1892, argued that it is an error to believe that it is our 'duty' to produce as much and consume as little as possible. Orthodox capitalism invariably tells the working class to increase productivity and at the same time to tighten their belts and forego wage increases; which means in effect, producing more and being unable to consume what they produce, because they have neither the time nor the money to do so. Yet it is plain that, under capitalism, those who produce least of all are responsible for consuming the most. These are the economic elite – the people who have the leisure to consume what the workers produce and cannot afford to buy.

It is true that a million or so unemployed workers also have plenty of time to consume the products of those who are working. But their free time is enforced idleness, not leisure, because it is not supported by economic independence. At the present time, leisure is restricted to the elite who have money to buy it; it is also restricted *by* the elite, who have a monopoly over Freedom of Time. Tom Mann said:

'The demand we, as workmen, now make is for
LEISURE, NOT IDLENESS.
Leisure to think, to learn, to acquire knowledge, to enjoy, to develop; in short, Leisure to Live.'

The eight-hour day is no longer the workers' goal. The forty-hour week has been established, and trade unionists are engaged in the struggle for a further reduction to thirty-five hours. But for large numbers of workers, there is no more leisure than there was in Mann's time, since they work long hours of overtime in order to supplement low basic rates of pay. Overtime is detrimental both to the worker who does it, and to the unemployed. To the unemployed, of course, since overtime removes the necessity for employers taking on more full-time workers; and to the worker himself, overtime is detrimental not only because it deprives him of leisure, but also because his average earnings appear artificially high, a fact which depresses the workers' chances of negotiating an adequate basic rate. It is time that the working class rejected overtime working and demanded a living wage for a normal working week.

This alone, however, will not eliminate economic elitism – only a complete change of the system in which we live will do that, by bringing the economy under the control of the working class. In the meantime, workers who are struggling, through their trade unions, for better wages and working conditions and more control over their work, often find that they are struggling against trade union elitists as well as against the employers.

An American Marxist paper, *The Spartacist*, writing on 'Syndicalism and Leninism' (November 1970), expresses the belief that such elitism within trade unions is a result of the trade unions' necessary contact with capitalism; but the paper also suggests how this pitfall can be avoided:

'The existence of strong working-class institutions under capitalism – unions or parties – necessarily creates the objective basis for privileged bureaucracy. A sure-fire cure for union bureaucratism is not to have unions at all! The corollary, of course, is that the workers are then completely at the mercy of the bosses. There is no mechanical solution to the problem of democracy. The only answer is an aroused and conscious working class which controls its own organisations, whether these be hundred-man factory committees, unions of hundreds of thousands or mass parties numbering in the millions.'

TRADE UNION ELITISM

The working class in control of its own organisations! At the present time this is patently not the case. After striking for six weeks, the miners received an offer of increases from the Coal Board amounting to about three-quarters of their claim (February 1972). There had been 100 per cent solidarity in the strike, and successful picketing of power stations, preventing fuel from entering. Yet the miners' union leaders provisionally accepted the offer, pending the result of a ballot of their members, and immediately 'ordered' the pickets to withdraw, allowing fuel to reach the power stations nearly a week before rank-and-file miners had the opportunity of expressing their acceptance or rejection of the terms in a ballot.

This action reflects the same attitude as that expressed by Jim Conway, who, as General Secretary of the AEU, was quoted in *The Financial Times* (25 March 1970) as saying: 'If we [managers and trade union leaders] want to solve our problems managers will just have to learn to manage and a lot of trade unions will have to learn to be managed.'

The struggle against such elitist ideas is a long and complex one. There is no quick and easy method of replacing a reactionary government with a socialist one, of replacing reactionary candidates in the Labour Party with progressive ones, or of replacing bureaucratic trade union leaderships by 'working-class leaders armed with a real programme of class struggle'. No method, that is, which is quick and easy, and at the same time democratic.

The general strike, which *The Spartacist* calls 'the syndicalist panacea', is not a way to Socialism in One Easy Step, though it can be useful in raising the political awareness of the working class. Its limitations are clear, however. Any moderately successful strike of employees in the public sector – notably the miners and the dustmen – brings in its wake the threat of 'using troops' in order to 'avoid a breakdown in essential services'. How much more useful the armed forces would be during a general strike, when they could be used not only as strike-breakers but also as a disciplinary measure against the strikers. *The Spartacist* recalls one important instance in which an army turned against the workers:

'If the army is not defeated or won over politically, it will suppress the general strike.

One of the most important general strikes in history occurred in the 1925–27 Chinese Revolution. It was an explicitly political strike, designed to extract concessions from the imperialist powers. The strike was characterised by a division of labor whereby the Communist Party ran the strike and the national bourgeoisie commanded the army, through Chiang Kai-shek. When the bourgeoisie reached *its* compromise with the imperialists, it suppressed the CP and Chiang's army forced the strikers back to work at gunpoint. The Chinese revolutionaries learned the hard way that control of the labor movement is insufficient for revolution . . . Political and military as well as economic organisations are necessary. And winning over the soldiers, who are not subject to the discipline of the labor movement, requires a political party.'

The question is not so simple as this suggests. The Chinese workers had not simply failed to 'win over' the army, but had allowed control of the army to remain in the hands of a bourgeois elite. A soldier is trained to obey orders without question – 'theirs is not to reason why', they can leave the reasoning to their commanders. An army will fight in any cause, providing it has been sufficiently well trained. Jack London, writing at the turn of the century, gave this advice to the young man of his day:

'Young Man: The lowest aim in your life is to be a good soldier. The "good soldier" never tries to distinguish right from wrong. He never thinks, never reasons; he only obeys. If he is ordered to fire on his fellow-citizens, on his friends, on his neighbours, he obeys without hesitation. If he is ordered to fire down a crowded street when the poor are clamouring for bread, he obeys and sees the grey hairs of age stained with red and the life tide gushing from the breast of woman, feels neither remorse nor sympathy. If he is ordered off as one of a firing squad to execute a hero or a benefactor, he fires without hesitation, though he knows the bullet will pierce the noblest heart that ever beat in human breast.

A good soldier is a blind, heartless, soulless, murderous machine. He is not a man, he is not even a brute, for brutes kill only in self-defence. All that is human in him, all that is divine in him, all that constitutes a man, has been sworn away when he took the enlistment oath. His mind, his conscience, and his very soul, are in the keeping of his officer.

No man can fall lower than a soldier – it is a depth beneath which we cannot go.

Young man, don't be a Soldier or a Territorial . . . be a MAN.'

It seems that 'winning over the army' in reality means winning over the officers. Once you have the support of the shepherd and his dog, you can command the flock. Perhaps partly as a result of Chiang Kai-shek's betrayal in 1927, when the army was used as a tool against the workers and peasants, the People's Liberation Army in China today is quite different from any other army in the world, either in capitalist or in other 'socialist' countries.

'GUARD AGAINST ARROGANCE'

While the PLA is trained as a combat force, it is also encouraged to assist the workers in any scheme in which they can be helpful, which includes industrial and agricultural work. And instead of being entirely non-productive, and parasitical upon the workers, the army in China is as far as possible self-supporting; among the side-effects of this policy are a 'better attitude to labour', improved relations between the army and the people, and improved relations between officers and men. The method of training of soldiers is based on the three principles of 'officers teach soldiers; soldiers teach officers; and the soldiers teach each other'. Another piece of advice – given by Mao Tse-tung in *Methods of Work of Party Committees*, and put into practice by the Party, the people and the army in their everyday lives – concerns the attitude of the Government towards the governed, not only in politics, but in every sphere of life: 'Guard against arrogance. For anyone in a leading position, this is a matter of principle and an important condition for maintaining unity. Even those who have made no serious mistakes and have achieved very great success in their work should not be arrogant.'

Contrast this approach with the approach of the Engineering Employers' Federation, which in 1922 pleaded with the workers to respect 'managerial functions'. In their statement on the *Maintenance of Right and Employers to Exercise Managerial Functions*, the employers attributed to Lenin the claim that efficient working depended on the submission of employees to management decisions; their statement claimed:

'Four years ago Lenin learnt the same lesson from experience, but went very much further than we do or wish to do. After the Bolshevist revolution the factories were taken over by the workmen and the managing staffs dismissed or killed. The workmen proved totally incapable of carrying on the work, and in April 1918, Lenin addressed the Central Conference at Moscow on the subject. He said that they must re-engage managers and technicians at high salaries, that the first condition of production was unqualified submission to a single will, and that the workmen must render unquestioning obedience to the director of the works.'

This is a reflection of the employers' attitude to managerial functions, rather than a statement by Lenin. Under this arrangement, workers must grow a mentality similar to that of Jack London's soldier, leaving the elite in charge, and learning never to question the decisions of the elite, who are presumably infallible.

Not only does 'unqualified submission' assume infallibility on the part of the leadership (whether it be in a trade union, political party, or a factory), it also assumes that all except the elite are incapable either of thinking for themselves or of playing even a minor part in controlling their own lives. Neither of these assumptions is true. Evelyn King MP, writing about the BBC in *The Daily Telegraph* (8 October 1971), recognised that

'In an intellectually healthy community, change is the fruit of civilisation, but ideas, revolutionary or other, well up from below. Parliament must jealously ensure that the levers of power do not remain in the hands of an elitist minority able unchecked to impose their own views and censor other peoples. Democracy cannot submit to that solution of our problems and remain a democracy.'

This is true of the BBC; it is equally true of newspapers and mass media generally; it is true of industry, and of workers' industrial organisations; it is true of political parties and governments. Yet, as R. M. MacIver points out in his book *The Modern State*, all too often

'The will of the people, that "real will" which asserts its integrity and solidarity in sovereign decision, seems to dissolve into the interested and often sordid dominance of a narrow minority, exploiting for its own ends the practical conditions of organization and leadership. Behind the liberty of association is revealed the psychological necessity of control. Instead of the clear envisagement of political situations on the part of the people we discover, against a background of ignorance and inertia, the entanglement of personal attachments and repulsions, of local interest and discriminations. Instead of the people acting through representatives and officials, we find the officials and representatives controlling the "machine". The will of the people is set up as a mystical god, in whose name the political priests of a new oligarchy struggle and rule.'

POLITICAL ELITISM

In other words, democracy is a myth while 'ignorance and inertia' allow 'an elitist minority' to control the lives of the majority of the people. When the Tory Party is in power we can expect the elitist minority to be dominant. Nor can we expect anything different from the Labour Party, while the minority is permitted to believe in – and act upon – its own mistaken infallibility, by ignoring conference decisions, and so on. Writing in the Cambridge University Labour Club magazine, *Towards Effective Socialism*, in October 1971, Eric Heffer MP pinpoints the lack of rank-and-file control as the reason for the 'complete failure' of the 1964–70 Labour Government. He wrote:

'One of the tragedies of the situation was that many of those who had been associated with Nye Bevan were equally sucked into the right-wing vortex. In practice they became Gaitskellites, whilst continuing at times to use socialist phrases. The reason for this I believe is because they like the Gaitskellites are basically elitist in outlook. There have always been two basic streams of socialist thought. Not revolutionary or reformist, but elitist and non-elitist. Stafford Cripps in his Socialist League days was quasi-revolutionary in ideas, he contrasted to the Webbs who were deeply reformist. They were nevertheless both elitist in thinking. The elitists always know best. The Party are expected to accept their ideas, like manna from heaven. The rank and file of the Party and the Trade Unions must follow their gems of wisdom and if they refuse, then in the view of the elitists they are stupidly wrong. To put it another way, you can either have socialism-from-above, or socialism-from-below. Personally, I am a convinced socialism-from-below man. I well remember the words of Rosa Luxemburg, who once said "you cannot introduce socialism by decree". It can only come when the people want it, when they begin to push for it in a positive democratic way.'

It was 'socialism-from-above' which led Bertrand Russell, in a message to a national conference on Workers' Control (held at Nottingham, 1968), to remark that

'The Prime Minister and his friends have developed a quite new definition of socialism, which includes the penalising of the poorest, capitulating to bankers, attacking the social services, banning the coloured and applauding naked imperialism. When a government makes opportunism the hallmark of its every action, it is the duty of all socialists to cry "halt" and to help create an alternative based on socialist principles.'

It is an unfortunate truth that the Labour Party members, after building their activity into a crescendo immediately prior to an election, then sink under a wave of success (or failure) and blandly leave the Parliamentary Party to 'get on with it' for the next five years or so. Only when some disaster threatens (such as *In Place of Strife*) does the rank and file rouse itself sufficiently to register a complaint; otherwise it is content to leave ruling to the rulers. Hence – socialism-from-above establishes itself without protest. Russell's 'alternative based on socialist principles' is not going to rise spontaneously from the same leadership which was responsible for the Prices and Incomes Board, plans for industrial legislation, health-service cuts and so on. Yet, even when there is an opportunity to replace one of the authors of these capitalist policies, the Parliamentary Party turns it down. Roy Jenkins, after voting against his own party on the question of the Common Market, was nevertheless re-elected as Deputy Leader of the Party in 1970.

Bert Ramelson, in the *Morning Star* of 6 July 1971, pointed out the necessity for electing a Labour Government and *ensuring that it implements Left policies*. This means more than marginal rank-and-file activity at election-time. It means, says Ramelson,

'A recognition of the need to loosen the grip of the Right-Wing leadership of the Labour Party as has begun to take place within the trade union movement. In this the trade unions can and must play a big role. They should fight not only for the Labour Party to adopt Left policies but to elect leaderships who believe in those policies . . .

A recognition that only a constantly-developing vigilant extra-Parliamentary mass movement after as well as before the General Election will help a Labour Government to implement the agreed Left policies.'

This has not been done to date. The Labour Representation Committee in its Manifesto of 1906 stated that

'The aged poor are neglected. The slums remain; overcrowding continues, whilst the land goes to waste. Shopkeepers and traders are overburdened with rates and taxation, whilst increased land values which should relieve the ratepayers go to people who have not earned them . . . The unemployed ask for work . . . you are beginning to understand the causes of your poverty.'

Even the cautious optimism of the last sentence was an overstatement. Sixty-six years and several Labour Governments later, the poor are still poor, slums are multiplying instead of decreasing, land has not yet been nationalised, the unemployed are still asking for work. Of course, advances have been made, as anyone who has lived through those sixty-six years will tell you. But the *essential* problems remain, because Labour Governments have been allowed by the rank and file to play at capitalism, instead of getting down to the job of eradicating it.

Not only this, but the rank and file has sat by and watched while their elected leaders have been absorbed into the capitalist system, and have accepted all its trappings as well as its policies. How many Labour Members of Parliament opt out of taking the Oath? Or scorn the Black Rod-daily-circus, without which the House of Commons would no doubt collapse? How many subscribe to the traditional – if foolish – belief that the House cannot sit unless presided over by an ornate metal walking-stick, known as the Mace? How many refuse to pile into the House of Lords to hear the Queen's Speech at the start of the session, or turn down an invitation to a Royal Garden Party? Take a head-count of all those who turn out on such occasions, and you will know exactly who to mistrust! And how many take a conscientious stand against the Birthday (or any other) Honours List? The last place for any member of the Labour Party to be is on a Royal Honours List. It has been said that the Labour Party 'has not made up its mind' about the monarchy. This presupposes that there can be such a thing as 'monarchical socialism', although this is plainly a contradiction in terms.

As Willie Hamilton MP told the Foreign Press Association, referring to the monarchy:

'I regret to say that my own party leadership is among the most sycophantic of the people. If they don't want to preserve this institution, they do nothing to undermine it.

As long as we have got that kind of leadership in the Labour Party, then we deserve the kind of institution that we have got.'

It is a pity that these remarks were made over lunch in the Savoy Hotel, but that does not make them any the less valid.

Unfortunately, Labour Party sycophants do not confine themselves to the trappings of capitalism, but also embrace its policies. It was somewhat ridiculous for Harold Wilson, University Chancellor and ex-Prime Minister, to go through the motions of politely presenting Edward Heath, the incumbent Prime Minister, with an honorary degree. How much more ridiculous, and shameful, for a 'socialist' government, on achieving power, to accept as its inheritance a full complement of outworn capitalist policies from the defeated Tories. There was widespread dissatisfaction among Labour rank-and-file members at the failure of the Labour Government to implement socialist policies, and this dissatisfaction found voice in the 1970 Conference, after the defeat of the Party in the 1970 General Election. Ian Mikardo analysed the discontent in his closing speech to the conference as an 'argument about whether we are a party of power or merely a party of protest'. Rightly dismissing this argument, Mikardo pointed out that

'Power is not an alternative to protest, it is complementary to protest. Indeed it is the instrument through which protest issues in action . . .

We socialists protest against the injustice, the ugliness, the inefficiency and the inhumanity of the selfishly acquisitive society, and we seek power precisely to remedy these evils.

Some people seem to have been saying this week that radicalism and idealism are things we would all like to have, but they are things that we really cannot afford; they are luxuries because the first job is to win an election, and they say that job is made more difficult by our being radical and idealist, aye, and socialist as well.'

The object of a socialist government must be to achieve socialist aims. Such a government must be elected by the people in the full knowledge of what their programme is to be. The reason for the widespread discontent with the last Labour Government was that it failed to carry through any policies which might have been construed as a move in the direction of socialism, on the grounds that 'the economy had to be got right first'. In other words, the Labour leaders were pursuing capitalist policies to the extent that they were scarcely distinguishable from the Tories, and they would have continued on the same lines, had they been given the opportunity, even *after* the economy had been 'got right'. And, as Eric Heffer said, they would have continued to condemn the left wing as 'stupidly wrong'.

The Labour Party, both rank and file and leadership, must recognise the fact that no Labour Government to date has had the courage to take many steps in the direction of Clause 4, and the last one in particular virtually turned its back on Clause 4 altogether. The rank and file must prepare and discuss a new and *socialist* policy for the next Labour Government; it must see that its programme for the future is accepted by the Party Conference; and it must ensure that that programme is implemented by the leadership of the Party on the return of a Labour Government. This means that the Parliamentary Labour Party must accept that it has no divine right to ride roughshod over the Party or the people.

The Tribune Group of MPs put forward the following ideas for a new programme for the Party (September 1971) in the hope that it would 'form the basis for discussion within the party while future party policy is being formulated for the party manifesto at the next general election'. While this programme alone will not bring Clause 4 and other proposals for a socialist government to fruition, it goes some way towards tackling the problems at which the leadership of the Labour Party has so far jibbed:

'ECONOMIC POLICY

A Labour Government coming into office on such a programme must reorganise radically the methods and institutions of government. We set out here some of the policies that should be implemented by the next Labour Government:

1. The stranglehold of the Treasury must be broken. Economic planning and monetary policy must be controlled by a Ministry of Economic Affairs, with powers to make direct investment in publicly-owned enterprises, particularly in the development areas.

2. The Bank of England must be made truly subordinate to the government, and the political influence of the City financiers must be ended; industrial investment must be controlled according to social, regional and technological priorities rather than according to Stock Exchange values.

3. The government must take into public ownership the big insurance companies – always among the most formidable of "the commanding heights of the economy" – in order to control their investment funds, and should set up a government insurance corporation and a central investment bank.

4. Taxation structure should become much more progressive and redistributive than it is now; such a structure should include

effective taxation of wealth, capital gains and gifts, and a heavier tax on unearned income.

5. The continuous increase in the regressive poll-tax represented by the worker's contribution to his weekly stamp must be ended.

6. A Labour government must extend public ownership substantially. The aeronautical industry, the shipbuilding industry and the pharmaceutical industry are obvious candidates for public ownership and control, especially in view of the amount of public money involved in these industries.

We welcome the recent warning by the Labour Party's National Executive Committee that those investing in publicly-owned assets "hived off" by the Tories will get no compensation when the assets are taken back into public ownership.

7. A Labour government should also establish and own new industrial enterprises, especially where the government is the only customer or in the context of regional development.

8. A Labour government must establish a national minimum wage, to be reviewed annually.

9. The principle of equal pay must be fully implemented.

10. Policy on redundancy should include an automatic right to retraining.

Only a programme as bold as this would make it possible for the next Labour government to pursue those policies of planned economic expansion which are urgently required if the British people are to be enabled to use to the full their skills and the wealth that they have created.

INDUSTRIAL DEMOCRACY

None of these purposes can be achieved without radical reform and change within industry itself. There is no way of escaping from stop-go and of ensuring soundly-based and continuing economic growth, except by winning the active co-operation of the workers and their unions; and there is no way of winning that co-operation except by a total strategy based on social justice and equality.

Industrial democracy must cease to be merely a slogan: it will have to become the basis of industrial reorganisation. A number of trade union leaders and the Institute for Workers'

Control have already done excellent pioneering work on this subject.

These men should be invited into partnership by a Labour government and asked to co-operate in the creation of industrial democracy in plants and factories: the spreading of power and responsibility among those in the daily processes of production is the only foundation on which positive relations between a Labour government and the trade union movement can be surely based.

Any such association will necessarily require the following conditions:

1. The repeal of the Industrial Relations Act.

2. The introduction of a charter of trade union rights which would safeguard the freedom of the trade union movement and make provision for the democratic participation of the trade unions in the management of industry.

3. Unqualified acceptance by the government and industrial management of the principle that those in representative positions, at all levels in industry, must be directly responsible to the workers on the shop floor.

SOCIAL POLICY

Nowhere has the philosophy of Mr Heath's Conservative Government been more destructive than in the social services. The deliberate dismantling of the system of universal social services has been the main characteristic of Conservative policy.

But even before June 1970, under the Labour Government, serious inroads had been made into this system.

Whatever the reasons advanced at the time, the result has been a general weakening of the firm principles upon which the post-war Labour Government founded Britain's new social services. There has been a gradual moving away from the idea of universality, which established the right of every citizen to have proper care of his individual needs as a human being.

The principle of universality meant a decisive turning away from the Poor Law state. All that the Labour Government created in the period after 1945 is being destroyed: it is of the utmost urgency that this process should be reversed.

Policies based on "selectivity" must be critically re-examined;

the drift from our socialist principles must be arrested; better pensions must be provided – and they must be subject to an annual Parliamentary review of their levels and the prevailing needs.

HOUSING AND LAND

The Labour Party will strenuously oppose the proposals in the Government's White Paper on "Fair Rents". The rates of subsidy on council houses must be restored to a proper level at the earliest possible moment.

In this context, the future Labour Government must:

1. create the conditions necessary to make possible a programme of house-building of at least 500,000 a year;

2. transfer privately rented houses to public ownership;

3. establish a publicly-owned corporation both to construct houses and other buildings and to manufacture building materials; and transfer to public ownership a large section of the building industry.

This programme would be frustrated if the land-speculators continued to operate; development rights in all land must therefore be acquired for the people, and the land racket ended.'

WORKERS' CONTROL THROUGH PARLIAMENT?

Having established policies for the Labour Party to carry out when it is next elected to office, we must then ask whether it will be possible for the next or subsequent Labour Governments to introduce in a piecemeal way a socialist Britain which will give real control to the workers. In my opinion, this is not possible; it will be necessary to make a radical change in the way that representatives of the working people are elected, and also the kind of Parliament to which they are elected.

A Labour Government could change the form of government in the same way that governments now can change the boundaries of constituencies, and local government, and in the same way that the Labour Governments have occasionally brought forward proposals for the abolition of the House of Lords. If it is possible to change the constitution of government by only having a single chamber, it is also possible to change the whole content of a British parliament.

The Labour Party should, when it achieves power, set about restructuring the way that representatives are elected. Representatives could be elected directly by the workers from the various industries and services in the country, which of course must be publicly owned, to sit in a new kind of Parliament – an Industrial Parliament. In such a Parliament it would also be necessary for workers who are neither in industries nor services to be represented. Provision would have to be made for the representation of these other sectors of the nation: while the whole of the nation which contributed socially to the well-being and advancement of society would be represented there, others who, through no fault of their own, are not involved in industries and services – for example, the sick, the disabled, the elderly – should also have representation in such a Parliament of Labour. Apart from these exceptions, the basis of an Industrial Parliament would be the producer, who is also the consumer, and not as at present the consumer only.

It is sometimes argued that Parliamentarianism cannot lead to Socialism, because its supporters are inevitably reformists, who are committed to tying the workers' movement to a parliamentary role, and thereby stifling any rank-and-file dissent. Rosa Luxemburg argued this point of view. Mike Faulkner, writing on *Rosa Luxemburg, 1871–1971: An Appreciation* (in *The Marxist*, issue number 17), quotes a letter from Rosa Luxemburg to Klara Zetkin, in 1907, in which she disparages those who have

'completely pledged themselves to parliament and parliamentarianism and whenever anything happens which transcends the limits of parliamentary action they are hopeless – no, worse than hopeless, because they then do their utmost to force the movement back into parliamentary channels and they will furiously defame as "an enemy of the people" anyone who dares to venture beyond their own limits.'

Her opposition to parliamentarianism was rooted in her dislike of bureaucracy, which Mike Faulkner describes as 'a deeply felt antipathy to all centralised rules and discipline within the proletarian movement'. The key word in this description is *centralised*. Her opposition was not to discipline in itself, but

to the kind of discipline which was imposed from above. Zinoviev defends this 'democratic centralism', claiming that it is
'impossible to register the will of individuals'. In his statement
on behalf of the Third Communist International to the Industrial Workers of the World (IWW), he wrote:

'The Unions are thus a branch of the government – and this
government is the most highly centralised government that exists.

It is also the most democratic government in history. For
all the organs are in constant touch with the worker masses and
constantly sensitive to their will. Moreover, the local Soviets all
over Russia have complete autonomy to manage their own local
affairs, provided they carry out the national policies laid down
by the Soviet Congress. Also, the Soviet government represents
only the workers, and cannot help but act in the workers'
interests.

Many members of the IWW are opposed to centralisation,
because they do not think it can be democratic. But where there
are great masses of people it is impossible to register the will
of individuals; only the will of majorities can be registered, and
in Soviet Russia the government is administered only for the
common good of the working class.'

Local Soviets, he declared, can manage their own affairs, so
long as they do not overstep the mark – that is, 'provided they
carry out the national policies laid down by the Soviet Congress'. Rosa Luxemburg rejected this unquestioned obedience
and was critical of the ideas of the Bolsheviks concerning democratic centralism. Mike Faulkner quotes her preface to *Social
Reform or Revolution*, written in 1899, and adds his own interpretation of her words, in the light of later events:

' "As long as theoretical knowledge remains the privilege of a
handful of 'academicians' in the Party, the latter will face the
danger of going astray. Only when the great mass of workers
take the keen and dependable weapons of scientific socialism in
their own hands will all the petty-bourgeois inclinations, all the
opportunist currents come to nothing. The movement will then
find itself on firm ground."

The subsequent history of the revolutionary movement has
shown this to be true. Without the leadership of a revolutionary

party the workers can never take power; but unless the workers control the party and unless they are drawn fully into the administration of the state, they can never retain power. Since 1917 most communist parties throughout the world have gone the same way as the parties of the Second International; they have become divorced from the workers and have degenerated into bourgeois parties.'

CENTRALISM – DEMOCRATIC ?

Democratic centralism would perhaps be more aptly named '*bureaucratic* centralism'. Rosa Luxemburg believed that democratic centralism must inevitably mean control of the workers by a central bureaucracy, although Faulkner regards this attitude merely as an over-reaction to the bureaucracy of the German Party in which 'the leadership had come to see their parliamentary-role as all-important'. Although Mike Faulkner condemns the bureaucracy of the German Party, in which 'mass action *by* the workers came to be feared as it might disrupt the leadership's smooth plans *for* the workers', he nevertheless believes that Rosa Luxemburg 'failed to understand the importance assigned by Lenin to the vanguard political party integrally linked to the working class', and she was instead content to be over-optimistic about 'what could be achieved through the spontaneous action of the workers'.

But circumstances change situations. Even Zinoviev in his statement to the Industrial Workers of the World at the Third Communist International, was prepared to admit that 'Probably the coming proletarian revolutions in America and other countries will develop new forms of organisation. The Bolsheviki do do not pretend that they have said the final word in the Social Revolution'.

This is evident if one tries to apply the theories of 'democratic centralism' to an industrial parliament such as I have described. Democratic centralism entails indirect elections: the workers would elect a representative locally, and the local representatives would then meet and elect a representative to a higher level – perhaps a region – and the regional representatives would in turn meet and elect others to a national assembly. This kind of indirect democracy is not necessary in this country, because of its size. We already have direct representation from the people to a government, and there is no reason why this should not continue, through industry, when there is only one dominant class in control – the working class.

There must be room for expression of differences of opinion on policies to be pursued by the working class, but the state must be a working-class state and must always be representative of the working class. The speed and direction of policies must be decided by the representatives of the working class; there will be no private vested interests in such a parliament, so the representatives will not be elected to promote the policies of conflicting classes, but to represent the general interests of the working class only. Individuals will therefore be free to hold opinions and to express them openly, but there will be no need to create different parties for the purpose of expressing those opinions, because the single aim of Parliament will be to carry out the will of the working class.

Ultimately there will be no need for political parties, or even for a single political party, in a classless society. It is possible, and desirable, to have a parliament where all people have the right to stand for election, and there will then be no need for an elite to band themselves together in a vanguard party and decide who shall or shall not belong to that party and decide what shall be the policies of the state.

It was the opinion of Rosa Luxemburg that the very existence of a vanguard party would inhibit the involvement of the working class in political decisions, and she argued (in *Marxism or Leninism*) that Lenin, by promoting the idea of a vanguard party, was advocating

'the blind subordination of the different organs of the party to their central authority and the extension of the decisive powers of this latter onto the outermost periphery of the party organisation . . . a central authority which alone thinks, acts and decides for all.'

The working class in a capitalist state is unused to thinking for itself and taking decisions about its own future. In Britain, the working class takes its future into its own hands approximately once every five years, and thereafter delegates responsibility to whatever political party is in favour for the time being. This is called 'democracy', and it is an illusion created by the capitalist class and offered to the workers in exchange for the 'blind subordination' which Rosa Luxemburg refers to.

A working class which has lived in such conditions of submission needs initially a socialist leadership, in the form of a party, which will be responsible for raising the level of political consciousness among the workers, and bringing them to a point where the working-class majority sees the necessity of creating a working-class state. But such a political party must not be composed of intellectuals and bourgeois elements. In Britain, it need not be so, as the British working class has a great deal of political experience and democratic experience, which it can put to good use in the leadership of its own party. In addition, a true working-class party must differ from the traditional 'vanguard' party in a very important aspect: a workers' party must be open, in the sense that every worker is free to be a member if he chooses, and in the sense that every member is free to stand for election without having to rely for his success on obtaining the 'recommendation' of the party elite.

Marx, looking beyond the initial establishment of the dictatorship of the proletariat, foresaw a time when there would be no state machine or compulsory state bodies; a society in which people would live as free men and women where state force was no longer necessary; where people would behave in a decent social way to each other without the need for a state machine compelling them to do so. And at the same time as the internal need for state machinery began to wither away, there would also be a withering away of external threats, in the form of capitalist enemies, so that, as countries were taken over more and more by their workers, there would be less and less need for rigid vigilance by the state, in order to forestall aggression.

Workers' control or the dictatorship of the proletariat must therefore progress towards the 'withering of the state'; first, a working-class party under the complete control of the workers, then the gradual dissolution of 'government' in every form, and finally a stateless and classless society. Lenin, in *State and*

Revolution, describes this process, from capitalism to a stateless society, saying:

'Engels speaks here of the "abolition" of the *bourgeois* state by the proletarian revolution, while the words about its withering away refer to the remnants of the *proletarian* state *after* the socialist revolution. According to Engels the bourgeois state does not "wither away", but is *put an end to* by the proletariat in the course of the revolution. What withers away after the revolution is the proletarian state or semi-state.'

At no state in this development is it necessary for the working class to be controlled by an elite, and the danger is that the growth of elitism will arrest the development of workers' control, instead of aiding it.

There is one common problem amongst the countries with communist governments, and that is the amount and method of control which the workers shall exercise in managing the economy and the machinery of government. It would be worthwhile, therefore, to examine some of the experiences of the workers in these countries – the problems they have faced, and the attempts they have made to overcome them.

WORKERS' CONTROL – THE SOVIET UNION

In the *Morning Star* of 30 December 1971, more than fifty years after the establishment of a 'workers' state' in the Soviet Union, a short report appeared under the heading: 'Soviet move toward more control by workers'. The essence of the article was:

'The central committee of the Soviet Communist Party today again drew attention to the need to increase the participation of workers in management.

It did so in a decision specifically about the major iron and steel works at Cherepovets, in the Ukraine, but meant for much wider application . . .

The central committee said that some leading personnel used clearly administrative methods – issuing orders and instructions to solve problems that arose, without taking into account the moral-political consequences of their decisions. It singled out the former head of the open-hearth shop at the plant for abusing administrative methods, for his lack of tact and rudeness to his subordinates . . .

It also pointed out that there had been a certain formalism in carrying out Socialist competition without adequate participation of the rank and file in preparing and checking the progress of the competition.'

The word 'participation' occurs frequently in this report, as it does in the Supreme Soviet 'Statute on the Rights of Factory and Office Trade Union Committees', dated 27 September 1971, in which it is made perfectly clear that there is a dividing line between 'management' and 'workers', and the impression is given that the 'participation' of workers and trade unions is a privilege accorded to them, not always with the approval of the 'management'. The account of what officials are 'obliged' to do implies that officialdom has so far risen above the rank and file as to take note of rank-and-file opinion only on sufferance; the fact that they 'inform' workers of decisions taken by management, suggests that the degree of control given to – or taken by – workers is inadequate.

WORKERS' CONTROL – YUGOSLAVIA

Co-operation, no competition, should be the slogan in a socialist state. In a situation where management and workers are distinct entities, where management gives an unwilling ear to the proposals of the workers and then informs them of its decision, the workers are as easily reduced to the level of mere machines for producing goods as they are in a capitalist state. Then it is easy for personal competition and self-seeking to creep in, instead of workers progressing towards the 'genesis and development of a new human personality deeply imbued with and inspired by socialist humanism, to the development of man the producer, consumer and manager'.

This is one of the ideal aims of 'workers' self-management', as intended by the workers of Yugoslavia, where it was found that nationalisation did not immediately solve all the problems.

Twenty Years of Self-Management in Yugoslavia, a pamphlet by Milentije Pesakovic, expands this ideal:

'Speaking of the importance of the Law on Workers' Management, Josip Broz Tito stated at the time in the National Assembly that the enactment of this law is the most important historical act after the Law on the Nationalisation of the Means of Production. Nationalisation of the means of production did not actually mean the fulfilment of the watchword of the workers' movement: "Factories to the Workers, Land to the Peasants", which was no abstract propaganda slogan but a profound and meaningful principle and idea . . .

Self-management as a system of social relations should provide a continuous and effective check to the resurgence of bureaucratic tendencies and usurpation of power; in other words it should effectively prevent the transformation and deterioration of government by the working class into government of the working class.'

This sounds ideal. But does it in fact happen? Frederick Singleton, Chairman of the Research Unit in Yugoslav Studies at Bradford University, writing in *The Spokesman* (December 1971–January 1972) on *Yugoslavia's Market Socialism*, claimed:

'As a technocratic elite emerges, the gap between managers and the rank and file members of the workers' councils widens. Firms become larger as the demands of technical efficiency give rise to mergers and business associations . . .

What seems to me to be happening is that power in the enterprise is moving from the workers' council to the managing board . . .

As long as the enterprise is "delivering the goods" in the form of higher profits, the workers' council does not ask too many questions. In many workers' councils interest is only displayed when personal income distribution is under discussion. Other matters, concerning the general policy of the enterprise, investments, prices, etc., are left to the technical staff and the managers . . .

The managerial technocrat class begins to develop the features of an elite. The Socio-Economic Commission of the Trade Union Federation recently commented on "the unjustifiable increase in social differences" which is derived "not only in differentials in personal incomes, but also from unequal possibilities of schooling, employment, use of credits, the obtaining of publicly-owned flats, etc.".'

There is a great difference between the theory, as explained by Pesakovic, and the practice claimed by Frederick Singleton. The social differences described by Singleton are completely unjustifiable, and should be fought by the workers, instead of being accepted without protest. But, from the suggestion of Mr Singleton that the workers are simply 'not interested' in having an effective voice through the workers' councils, providing production, profit and pay are satisfactory, it appears that the political understanding of the workers is not yet high enough to ensure that they appreciate the importance of eradicating elitism right from the start. The working class can make mistakes, not only by actively supporting reaction (as they do in Britain, by periodically electing a Tory Government), but also by passively accepting as absolute and unchangeable the dictates of an elite.

WORKERS' CONTROL—HUNGARY

What can workers do, in a developing socialist environment, when bureaucracy deprives them of their control over that environment? In Hungary, they take strike action:

'I emphasise in the very beginning that the workers have a great many other means at their disposal besides this right [i.e. the right to strike]. For example, the veto right of the trade union which cannot be used without the workers being asked about it means a great deal more . . . The question arises: can problems be solved by a strike that were not successfully solved by the effective methods that are at the disposal of the working class? Nevertheless, the workers are entitled to strike. And it occurs that they actually stop working. There are such workshops where democracy is not esteemed, where the director, the trade unions and the third force existing in workshops, the Party, decide on questions without the workers. In such cases, because nobody else has rung the warning bell, the workers themselves make it ring. This is work stoppage. Every year there are three, four or five work stoppages, most often not on an enterprise level but on that of the workshop. This happens when the economic, the political and the trade union functionaries commit some stupidity simultaneously but this takes place rather seldom. Provisions are not implemented. The cup overflows. Higher forums intervene. And everything turns back into the regular channel to find agreement, naturally, in harmony with the interested workers.'

These are the words of Sandor Gaspar, the leader of the Hungarian trade union movement, in his book of collected speeches and interviews, *Role of the Hungarian Trade Unions in the Construction of Socialism*. Later in the book, he goes on to say that the Party, the State and the Trade Unions are not self-contained organisations, and none is subordinate to the others in the conduct of the workers' struggle (although he does say at the same time, that the Party *leads* the struggle). The trade unions, he says, were always regarded by Lenin as important to 'the unfolding of workers' democracy':

'To consult the workers on every substantial question, this is the basis for unfolding mass activity called for by Lenin. Therefore, the public activity of the workers on a society scale can realise itself only in the Socialist system. In the role of the trade unions, in their everyday activity, Lenin wanted to achieve the Marxist teaching that the masses should be active participants in the realisation of their own historic aims. Socialism – according to Lenin's conceptions – demands that a greater part of the workers should directly take part, and be effectively represented, in economy, management and also in the guidance of public life.'

WORKERS' CONTROL–CHINA

'To consult the workers on every substantial question . . .' This is being put into practice extensively in China, where the Cultural Revolution began in 1966 with the purpose of allowing the workers to criticise and improve the methods of work and of government, and identify the bureaucrats and bourgeois elements both at work and in the Party, and either convince them of their mistakes or remove them from office. In practice, the workers said, the amount of removal was small – it was usually enough to point out methods and actions which were anti-working class.

The existence of special 'schools' for officials of the Party and other leaders ensures that the leadership does not get too far removed from the masses, as they are obliged to return to manual work for a certain part of every year. Academics, students and professionals also learn from the workers, by assisting on farms and in factories, in addition to their usual work. During a visit to China in 1965, before the Cultural Revolution, I learned that all 'white-collar' workers were expected to do one month's practical manual work every year, while all the workers engaged in factory work, including the directors, put into practice the 'three togethers' – eat together, work together, live together. The directors' houses were similar to those of the workers, and they ate in the same canteen.

The general impression I got in the schools, factories, universities, theatres, communes, housing estates and amongst the people generally, was that they were all well aware of the social importance of the work or studies that they were doing, and the atmosphere was one of total involvement of the workers in the running of their environment. There are, for example, street committees which look after a small local area. Its activities extend from taking care of social amenities to making judicial decisions, or at least deciding when a case is serious enough to be referred to the local brigade security committee. Always the emphasis is on re-education rather than punishment, whether the offence is civil or political, and the most important lesson to learn is that an offence is 'bad' because it hurts the community, and is therefore an act of selfishness.

To quote a Chinese poem:

'If you plan for one year, sow corn,
If you plan for ten years, plant a tree,
If you plan for a hundred years, educate the people.

S

By sowing corn once, you will reap a harvest once,
By planting a tree, you will reap harvests ten times,
By educating the people,
You will reap harvests a hundred times.'

The point of view of the Chinese about socialism is certainly a long-term one, envisaging a continuous process of challenge by the workers in order to defeat incipient elitism. But, as Mao wrote:

'The wealth of society is created by the workers, peasants and working intellectuals. If they take their destiny into their own hands, follow a Marxist-Leninist line and take an active attitude in solving problems instead of evading them, there will be no difficulty in the world which they cannot overcome.'

WORKERS' CONTROL – CZECHOSLOVAKIA

This was true also of Czechoslovakia, prior to the armed intervention by the Soviet Union. The 1968 Action Programme of the Czech Communist Party made the following points:

'When attempting today to do away with equalitarianism, to apply the principle of actual achievements in the appraisal of employees we have no intention of forming a new privileged stratum. We want in all spheres of social life, the remuneration of the people to depend upon the social importance and effectivity of their work, upon the development of workers initiative, upon the degree of responsibility and risk. This is in the interest of the development of the whole society . . .

Nevertheless, *harmful characteristics of centralised directive decision-making and management have survived up to the day.* In relations among the Party, the state, and social organisations, in internal relations and methods within these individual partners, in the relations of state and other institutions to individuals, in the interpretation of the importance of public opinion and of people being informed, in the practical effect of personnel policy – in all these fields there are too many things souring the life of the people, while obstructing a professionally competent and scientific decision-making, and encouraging high-handedness. The reason may be sought, first and foremost, in that these relations in our political system have been built up for years as the instrument for carrying out the orders of the centre, and hardly ever made it at all possible for the decision itself to be the outcome of democratic procedure.'

Since this was written in 1968, the workers' councils – one of the means by which this centralism was to be overcome – have been dismantled, and centralism and bureaucracy re-established. *Rude Pravo*, on 29 October 1970, was once more advocating 'one-man management':

'[The socialist industrial manager] is empowered by the socialist state to direct and organise production in his enterprise in a qualified manner in accordance with the society-wide aims and in the interests of all members of the community . . . Whenever he makes an important decision he must consider not only the interests of the collective he leads, but also those of the entire national economy . . . Creating a continual harmony between society-wide interests and the interests of the enterprise collective is the feature of the decision-making process of a socialist manager.'

The manager therefore becomes part of an elite group of people, who are 'empowered' to make decisions on behalf of the workers. As Robert Vitak says, quoting this article in *The Socialist Register 1971*, 'it is still the managerial and not the democratic voice that will decide'.

The ruling elite sometimes manifests itself in the form of the 'vanguard' party, although – as George Lichtheim points out in his book on Lukacs, the vanguard concept is not one with which Marx could have agreed:

'In the Marxian perspective, the emancipation of the working class is the business of that class itself, and not of a revolutionary elite of intellectuals. The class no doubt has varying levels of consciousness, and socialists are called upon to work with the most advanced; but that is all. An elite which embodies a consciousness denied to the class is a concept which Marx would not have accepted.'

The inclination of the human race is towards selfishness and acquisition: that, at least, is the aspect of mankind which has been fostered throughout history. Certain countries are making efforts, with varying degrees of success, to eliminate or sublimate this aspect of human nature, and develop instead the instinct towards co-operation, mutual aid and peace. The concept of the elite is an assertion of the old character, as is the bureaucracy, the desire to govern, and exercise power over one's fellows.

'MAN'S INHUMANITY TO MAN'

T. B. Bottomore, writing on 'Industry, Work and Socialism' (an essay in *Socialist Humanism*, edited by Erich Fromm), analyses the relationship between control, work and human fulfilment in this way:

'The liberation of the individual from such conditions [i.e. exploitation, bureaucracy, elitism, etc.] which Marx saw as the objective of the growing working-class movement, would require changes in the social system as a whole and also within each productive enterprise. The independence and the power over others which the upper class in society enjoyed would be ended by the abolition of private property in the means of production and the consequent disappearance of social classes. But this was only one condition, though fundamental in Marx's theoretical scheme, for the creation of a classless society. It would also be necessary to overcome the division of labour, which enclosed men in narrow spheres of life and condemned large numbers of them to spend their days in dull, mindless, physically exhausting, sometimes harmful activities. The young Marx, like Fourier, saw a solution to the problem in regular changes of occupation; in a notorious passage of *The German Ideology* he observed that in communist society nobody would have "one exclusive sphere of activity", and the individual would be able to "hunt in the morning, fish in the afternoon, rear cattle in the evening, criticize after dinner", according to his inclination. Later on, Marx undoubtedly took a more critical view of these possibilities, and in a passage of *Capital* he distinguished between the sphere of production which would always remain a "realm of necessity", and the sphere of leisure time, "the true realm of freedom" in which "the development of human potentiality for its own sake" could take place; but he never abandoned the idea that necessary work could itself become, in some degree, a liberating and educative activity. Again in *Capital* he observes that "the limited detail worker of today" will be replaced in the future society by "the fully developed individual", who carries out a number of different social functions, and who has a different relation to his work because he has received a broad general and scientific education. The frequently quoted passage in which Marx criticized Fourier's view of work as an essentially pleasant activity is generally misinterpreted. Marx objected to the idea that work could be regarded simply as an agreeable, spontaneous activity, as a kind of game; he insisted on the element of painful effort in work, upon the constraints which it imposed, but at the same time he held firmly that it could be rewarding for the individual, in the way that a creative artist's work is rewarding, as a manifestation of human skill and determination, and of the human power to shape and control the natural world . . . Marx also takes account of the social aspects of work; in a classless and humane society, the individual would not only find *himself* in his work, but would also discover and express his cooperative relationship, his friendship, with other men.'

Through the development of workers' control, the working class will discover their best human relationships. They will use their power to control and change society in a humane way. Through their new economic and political relationships with workers throughout the world, they will lead mankind into a world where man's inhumanity to man will be banished for ever.

Appendix A

A Brief Account of Repression in Britain
Their Attack – Our Defence (Fred Silberman and Tom Wengraf)

1629–39 STAR CHAMBER
Cause: State's need to levy taxes for imperialist wars.
Attack: Revival of arbitrary power of State, through the courts, getting increasingly harsh.
Defence: Revolution.
Result: Cromwell's Commonwealth.

1800 COMBINATION ACTS
Cause: War against revolutionary France.
Attack: Trade societies declared illegal.
Defence: Trade societies go underground.
Result: After growing agitation, and breaches of the law, trade societies eventually legalised in 1824.

1811–16 LUDDITES
Cause: Rationalisation and redundancies.
Attack: Unemployment and wage cuts and large-scale spying on shopfloors.
Defence: Direct action against employers and their machines.
Result: Severe repression but eventual large increase in real wages and acceptance of workers' controls on quality.

1825 ANTI-UNION CAMPAIGN
Cause: Upsurge of trade union activity and strikes following 1824 legalisation of trade unions.
Attack: Employers demand that only licensed trade unions be allowed to raise funds.
Defence: Defence associations (forerunners of trades councils) swarmed London with delegates and petitions.
Result: 1825 Amendment Act did not require registration of trade unions, but imposed stringent new penalties on

'coercion of employers or fellow workmen by intimidation, molestation or obstruction'.

1833 ONE BIG UNION

Cause: Grand National Consolidated Trade Union represents threat.

Attack: Derby lock-out against all members of GNCTU. 1797
Act against administering unlawful oaths used to
prevent agricultural unionism, despite 1825 Act.
Tolpuddle Martyrs sentenced to seven years' trans-
portation.

Defence: London-Dorchester Committee lead 'monster union
procession' to present petition to Home Secretary.

Result: None (i.e. they won).

1834 WORKHOUSES

Cause: Landed elites back industrialists to rationalise and
develop large-scale capitalism.

Attack: Penal social security legislation (New Poor Law Act)
to eliminate the independence of the working class.
Also, more political power given to middle class.

Defence: Chartist and Anti-Poor Law movement. Mass meetings, workhouses burnt down, poor law guardians
attacked.

Result: Application of Poor Law suspended in militant dis-
tricts, but repressive laws remain for *selective* implementation, e.g. Tolpuddle transportations rescinded,
once GNCTU smashed.

1838–48 CHARTISM

Cause: Economic crisis and increasing European competition.

Attack: Unemployment and cuts in real wages.

Defence: Attempts to gain political power through reforms.
Chartist movement for universal suffrage, payment
of MPs, etc. Political strikes and direct action (plug
plot) discouraged by responsible leaders who opted
for petitions.

Result: Petitions had more signatures each time and were

treated with increasing contempt. Movement eventually collapses.

1866–71 ANTI-UNION CAMPAIGN

Cause: Growth of craft unions and their industrial pressure for political power.

Attack: Anti-trade union campaign. Royal Commission on Trade Unions aimed to incorporate leadership and isolate militants. Judicial attack in Hornby vs. Close on trade union funds.

Defence: Police ban on Hyde Park meeting ignored, railings broken down. Local riots elsewhere.

Result: Whigs bring in minimal reform bill. Tories defeat Government, but then Tories themselves forced by constant rioting to pass a more 'progressive' bill than that of the Whigs! 1871 Trade Union Act protected trade unions from being sued for damages. However, the accompanying Criminal Law Amendment Act imposed severe restrictions on 'threats, intimidation, molestation and destruction'. This gave considerable interpretive power to the police and the courts, strengthened further by the Conspiracy and Protection of Property Act 1875 which made 'watching and besetting a person's house or place of work or approach thereto' a crime. (i.e. no picketing.)

1889–94 ROYAL COMMISSION

Cause: Loss of British industry's monopoly position and crisis in British agriculture. General socialist agitation. New unionism (unskilled and white collar).

Attack: Widespread unemployment, followed by anti-union campaign and Royal Commission on Labour.

Defence: 1889 strikes by matchgirls, gas workers and London dockers (helped by £30,000 donation from Australian dockers). Widespread agitation. Trade unionists on Royal Commission successfully resist proposal to make collective agreements legally enforceable. 1893 formation of Independent Labour Party, under leadership of Keir Hardie.

Result: Royal Commission Report relatively innocuous. Decline of Liberal-trade union alliance, growth of independent political aspirations of trade union movement.

1900–06 TAFF VALE

Cause: Post-Boer War slump. In spite of several setbacks, trade unions beginning to be able to withstand lengthy lock-outs, e.g. South Wales miners, engineers.

Attack: Unable to get collective agreements made legally enforceable through Parliament, employers sought to attack trade union funds to discourage militancy. This was achieved in a number of judges' decisions whittling away at rights established in the 1870s, and culminating in the award of £20,000 civil damages for the Taff Vale Railway Company against the Amalgamated Society of Railway Servants for losses sustained through 'a conspiracy to induce workmen to break their contracts of employment'.

Defence: Unity through the TUC for a Labour Party to act as political wing of the movement. Politicisation of trade unions and trade unionists. Constant agitation.

Result: Real wages fall after Taff Vale as unions afraid to call strikes. By 1903, affiliation to Parliamentary Labour Representation Committee up to 1 million. Disagreement as to what sort of policies Labour Party should pursue, but in 1906 election twenty-nine Labour MPs won and most Liberals reluctantly committed to pro-union legislation. 1906 Trade Disputes Act gave trade unions immunity from being sued and protected members from liability for conspiracy in contemplation or furtherance of trade dispute. Legalised picketing 'to inform or persuade peacefully at, or near, a place where a person resides or works'.

1909 THE OSBORNE CASE

Cause: Establishment politically threatened by working class.

Attack: Through the courts, getting a judgement that trade unions did not have the right to collect and administer funds for political purposes. The Osborne Case (again against the Amalgamated Society of Railway Servants) was followed by a series of injunctions on other unions.

Defence: A wave of large strikes. Growth of Marxist Social Democratic Federation, unrest in Ireland and Scotland.

Result: Ruling class feels it safest to 'establish' a moderate Labour Party. Trade Union Act 1913 empowers unions to engage in political activities, subject to a ballot majority, and provision for contracting out of a separate political fund.

1914–18 WORLD WAR I MEASURES

Cause: War – a good excuse to cut trade union rights.

Attack: Strikes and lock-outs illegal under Munitions of War Act 1915, compulsory 'arbitration' and abandonment of protective practices (dilution etc.) agreed to by TUC.

Defence: Shop Stewards Movement and unofficial action.

Result: Sharp increase in workers' control on shopfloor and rise in political consciousness. 1916 Whitley Committee and 'joint-consultation' set out to incorporate movement into the system. When it suited them after the war, employers reverted to hard line. Fluctuating alienation of trade union bureaucracy from rank and file, continuing to present time.

1922 THE ENGINEERING LOCK-OUT

Cause: Employers need to regain control over workers after their wartime gains on the shopfloor.

Attack: The Engineering Employers lock-out to impose managerial prerogative.

Result: The lock-out lasted from 11 March to 13 June, when, their funds exhausted, denied social security under the Merthyr Tydfil decision of 1900 and with $1\frac{3}{4}$ million unemployed, the unions surrendered.

(Even so the AEU ballot was only 76 to 36 thousand for accepting the employers' terms.) Mutuality retained on piecework prices (in order to facilitate price cuts), but not on overtime and changes in conditions. York procedure aimed at throttling shop stewards' power and supporting trade union bureaucracy against them.

1926 GENERAL STRIKE

Cause: Export industries' crisis and employers' determination to cash in on 1924 defeat of MacDonald Lab-Lib Government by Tories.

Attack: Cut of miners' wages in open defiance of the triple alliance (miners, railwaymen and transport workers).

Defence: Nine-day General Strike, reluctantly called by TUC to pacify militants.

Result: Workers sold out by TUC. Government vaguely promised to 'reorganise' mining industry but this was never kept. Miners carried on struggle but eventually defeated after seven months. Trade Union Act of 1927 made sympathetic strikes illegal. (Not repealed until 1945.) Mond-Turner corporatism. Militants victimised throughout next ten years and severe drop in trade union membership.

1929–35 THE GREAT SLUMP

Cause: World crisis of capitalism.

Attack: Two million unemployed, cuts in social security and education, red bogies.

Defence: Hunger marches, petitions, appeals, demonstrations.

Result: Growth of Communist Party, especially among shop stewards. Otherwise nothing until rearmament and World War II re-established trade union strength.

1947 ATLEE'S SELL-OUT

Cause: Labour Government's unwillingness to lead country to socialism.

Attack: Acceptance of Marshall Aid, participation in Cold War and sterling convertability tied Britain to US

Defence: ?(Defeat of Labour Government?)
Result: Thirteen years of Tory rule, Gaitskellism, Wilsonism.

1945–51 RETENTION OF WARTIME ORDER 1305

Cause: Making capitalism work.
Attack: Conditions of Employment and National Arbitration Order 1305 requiring compulsory arbitration.
Defence: 1951 'Dockers in the Dock; Dockers out of the Dock' unofficial strike.
Result: Dockers arrested under Order 1305 released. Order 1305 withdrawn by Parliament.

1954–66 INCOMES POLICY

Cause: Constraints upon imperialism.
Attack: Incomes Policy, mergers, export of capital.
Defence: Industrial militancy, mainly 'unofficial'.
Result: Incomes policy smashed by dustmen. In 1969–70 increase in real wages at expense of profits. Labour Government moves right. Working-class apathy for parliamentary politics. The anti-union campaign. Tory victory of 1970. Industrial Relations Act 1972.

Appendix B

GEC 'Company Report', compiled by Draughtsmen's and Allied Technicians' Association, April 1971

1. MAIN SUBSIDIARIES

Source: GEC Statement of Accounts for year ended 31 March 1970.

It is unnecessary to name all the companies in the GEC empire, but the following list gives the number of companies in each activity or country.

Engineering	27 companies
Industrial	29 companies
Telecommunications, Electronics and Automation	48 companies
Cables and components	33 companies
Consumer products	16 companies
Other activities	6 companies

Overseas Subsidiaries

South Africa	11 companies
Rhodesia	3 companies
Zambia	1 company
Nigeria	1 company
Americas	12 companies
Asia	17 companies
Australasia	8 companies
Europe	35 companies

GEC has a total of 246 subsidiary companies.
There are also 54 associate companies.

2. COMPANY ACCOUNTS

Source: Labour Research Department, October 1969.
Sales, profits and dividends

	1966–7	1967–8	1968–9	1969–70
Sales		*£m.*		
General Elec. Co.[a]	180·1	197·5	497·7[d]	
Associated Elec. Ind.[b]	264·8	264·7	[e]	890·7
English Elec. Co.[c]	291·4	411·6	400·6	
Total	736·3	873·8	898·3	890·7
Trading profit				
General Elec. Co.[a]	22·9	27·5	59·3[d]	
Associated Elec. Ind.[b]	17·3	9·1	[e]	107·9
English Elec. Co.[c]	28·1	38·3	33·5	
Total	68·3	74·9	92·8	107·9
Ordinary dividends				
General Elec. Co.[a]	5·9	7·6	12·2[d]	
Associated Elec. Ind.[b]	5·6	4·5[f]	[e]	
English Elec. Co[c]	5·5	8·6	9·1	
Total	17·0	20·7	21·3	

Note: All figures have been converted to an annual basis to make them more comparable year by year. However the English Electric figures are still not comparable year by year as 1967–8 includes profits from Elliott-Automation, Ruston & Hornsby and Combined Electrical Manufacturers, for the first time, whilst the 1968–9 figure does not include profits from English Electric Computers which was merged with ICT to form International Computers (Holdings).

[a] Year to 31 March 1967, 1968 and 1969.
[b] Year to 31 December 1966 and 1967.
[c] Year to 31 December 1966, 1967 and equivalent 12 months of 15 month period 1 January 1968 to 31 March 1969.
[d] GEC and AEI for 12 months to 31 March 1969.
[e] Combined with GEC.
[f] Appears to be a reduction in dividend. In fact AEI shareholders also received £22m. in cash which at 7 per cent would give them an extra £1·5m. (making £6m.); and EE shareholders also received £51m. in cash and stock, which at 7 per cent would give them an extra £3·6m. (making £12·7m.)

GEC profits for 1969 can be broken down as in the table.

	£m.
Trading profit	107·946
Other income	8·251
Total profit	116·197
Depreciation	24·609
Directors	0·273
Audit	0·586
Interest payments	23·462
Provisions[a]	8·910
Pre-tax profit	58·357[b]
Tax	26·823
Net profit	31·534
Total assets	£162,355·000

[a] A total of £15 million was set aside for the rationalisation and reorganisation programme.

[b] *This pre-tax profit of £58·35m. is the figure which is always quoted by the company. The more realistic figure however is the total profit which takes account of certain costs such as provisions, directors' remunerations, depreciation, etc. and this gives a more accurate account of surplus.*

Directors
Source: GEC–EE–AEI Report and Accounts for the year ended 1970.

	Market value of shares 30 Sept. 1970	Dividends received in 1970
Lord Nelson of Stafford (Chairman)	£72,311	£2,184
Lord Aldington (Dep. Chairman)	£35,062	£1,059
W. J. Bird	£103,477	£3,126
K. R. Bond (Dep. Man. Director)	£553,680	£16,728
Lord Catto	£384,005	£11,600
R. H. Grierson	£108,881	£3,426
T. B. O. Kerr	£235,728	£7,171
D. Lewis	£3,810,662	£115,114
Sir Humphrey Mynors	?	?
Lord Poole	?	?
Sir Richard Powell	?	?
G. A. Riddell	£25,017	£757
Sir Jack Scamp	£105,912	£3,199
J. R. Sully	£24,120	£729
Lord Trevelyan	?	?
Sir Arnold Weinstock (Man. Director)	£5,535,778	£167,226
K. R. Bond and D. Lewis (jointly	£19,666,286	£600,162

No financial contributions are made to any political organisation.

Pay

The highest-paid director is the Deputy Chairman, Lord Aldington, with £40,000 p.a. (£770 per week). This constituted a rise
of *£400 a week* on his 1969 pay of £19,000 p.a. In 1968 Lord
Aldington was paid £10,000 p.a. Eight directors received salaries
of over £10,000 p.a.

3. EMPLOYEES

The average number of UK employees of the group was 206,000
and their aggregate pay was £234m. for the year – an average
per employee of £1,135 each (£21 17s. a week). At this rate it
would take the average employee thirty-seven years to earn what
Lord Aldington 'earned' in director's pay and share dividends –
and about 160 years to earn what Arnold Weinstock collected in
pay and dividends for 1969.

Total assets per employee   = £5,154
Total profit per employee   = £564
Trading profit per employee = £524

4. HISTORY OF GEC AND THE MERGER

The IRC gave substantial financial support to GEC's takeover of
AEI in November 1967. Prior to this takeover, the IRC supported
the merger of English Electric and Elliott-Automation to the
tune of £15m.

On 6 September 1968 GEC/English Electric announced their
intention to merge and on 13 September the IRC gave its official
support to the merger, having obtained certain assurances from
the two companies.

The result of the merger of GEC–EE–AEI was to 'create efficiency' and this was achieved through rationalisation in the form
of widespread redundancies. To date, four major redundancies
have been announced, involving 16,220 employees. These are
listed in the table.

T

Redundancies – all employees

February 1968	AEI Telecommunications, Woolwich, London	5,500
	AEI Telecommunications, Sydenham London	400
	Research Laboratories, Blackheath and Harlow	200
9 May 1968	Witton, Birmingham	1,650
	Wythenshawe, Manchester	300
	Plastics Factory, Aldridge, Birmingham	430
4 February 1969	Willesden, London	1,100
	Witton, Birmingham	1,100
	Newton-le-Willows	1,100
	Rugby	140
5 August 1969	Richard Whiffen, Ashton-under-Lyne	140
	Whetstone (Labs), London	230
	Walthamstow, London	810
	Netherton, Liverpool	1,400
	Accrington	285
	Stafford	305
	Thornbury, Bradford	50
	Fazakerly, Liverpool	305
	Mosley Road, Manchester	930
	Trafford Park, Manchester	810
+ in 1970	Wythenshawe, Manchester	750
	Mosley Road, Manchester	1,000
	GEC, Walthamstow	50
	AEI, Trafford Park	100
	EE, Netherton	500
	EE, Napier, Liverpool	500
	Total	19,120

Source: 'Labour Research', October 1969 and Minutes of National Joint Advisory Committee of GEC.

The list above is by no means a complete one.

'In the middle of 1967 the three companies had 268,000 workers between them (GEC 63,000, AEI 85,000 and English Electric 120,000); by mid-1970 the combined companies employed approximately 235,000.' (Jones and Marriott, *Anatomy of a Merger*, p. 322)

It would appear that the rationalisation programme has accounted for a decrease in staff of approximately 33,000 employees. Half of these were *direct* redundancies as detailed above, whilst the other half has been accounted for by natural wastage, i.e. slow down in recruitment programme, retirements, people leaving, etc.

Since 1964 the whole face of the British electrical manufacturing industry has changed, and the spate of mergers shows no sign of abating. The GEC colossus with sales for 1970 forecast at £1,000m., trading profit at over £100m. and currently with assets of over £770m. and 206,000 UK employees shows no sign of not adding more companies to its empire. The IRC in their 1968-9 Report already credit GEC with 40 per cent of the 'entire UK electrical/electronics industry' and they go on to say 'there remain many opportunities for further reorganisation'.

Future Company Prospects

There is no indication that the upheavals in the electrical manufacturing industry have finished. Before being wound up, the IRC were looking for further rationalisation. The only firm forecast in the GEC Annual Report is more sales and higher profits. The report suggests that further reorganisation is likely in power engineering, diesel engines and consumer products.

BIOGRAPHY OF CHAIRMAN AND DIRECTORS OF GEC

Lord Nelson of Stafford: Chairman of GEC.
Also Director of: the Bank of England, Babcock and Wilcox, Atomic Power Construction Co. Ltd, British Aircraft Corporation, Marconi International Marine, National Bank of Australasia, International Computers Ltd, International Nickel Company of Canada. Also Chancellor of Aston University.

In an interview with *The Engineer*, 6 November 1969, Lord Nelson made the following comments:

'The most important aspect here is the utilisation of resources in industry and the proper utilisation of resources in the University and the organisation courses must be geared to these . . .

What I don't like to see, quite frankly, is a half-empty shop in the works and finding out that half the personnel are on day-release.

We can't afford to have capital equipment lying about doing – nothing . . .'

Lord Aldington: Deputy Chairman GEC.
Also Chairman of: National & Grindlays Bank Ltd, Exporters

Refinance Corporation Ltd, United Power Company. Also Vice-Chairman of Sun Alliance and London Insurance Ltd. Also Director of: John Brown & Co., National Discount Co. Ltd, English China Clays, Lloyds Bank, William Brandts and Sons. Former Deputy Chairman of Conservative Party Organisation 1959–63.

Lord Catto: Director GEC.
Also Managing Director of Morgan Grenfell & Co. Ltd. Also Director of Australian United Corporation Ltd, Australian Mutual Provident, Andrew Ule & Co. Ltd, *News of the World*.

R. H. Grierson: Director GEC.
Also Chairman of H. Grierson & Co. Ltd, Scientific Enterprise Associates.

Sir Humphrey Mynors: Director GEC.
Also Chairman of Finance Corporation for Industry Ltd. Also Director of Imperial Tobacco Group Ltd, Legal & General Assurance Soc. Ltd, Pilkington Bros. Ltd.

Lord Poole: Director GEC.
Also Chairman of Lazard Bros. & Co. Ltd. Also Director of S. Pearson & Sons Ltd, Whitehall Securities Corporation Ltd. Conservative Party Organisation: Treasurer 1952–5, Chairman 1955–7, Dep. Chairman 1957–9, Jnt Chairman 1963–4.
   Note that Lord Aldington (Deputy Chairman of GEC) succeeded Lord Poole as Chairman of the Conservative Party.

Sir Richard Powell: Director GEC.
Also Director-General of the Institute of Directors since 1954. Director of Bovis Holdings.

Sir Jack Scamp: Director GEC.
Also Director of Fairfields, Urwick, Orr & Partners, New Opportunities.
   Has been appointed to many Government committees, and pay enquiry teams.
   Also Associate Professor of Industrial Relations at Warwick University.

Lord Trevelyan: Director GEC.
Also Director of Matheson & Co., British Petroleum Co. Ltd, British Bank of the Middle East.

Sir Arnold Weinstock: Managing Director of GEC and by far the most important person in the combine. It is said that he is in virtual control of his empire – GEC does not hold board meetings as Weinstock regards them as time-consuming (*Anatomy of a Merger*, p. 225).

Aged 44. Educated at the London School of Economics (he is now a member of the Court of Governors of the LSE). After the war he engaged in finance and property development. Married the daughter of Sobell, who ran Radio and Allied Industries, a company producing radio and TV sets, and became a director of the company. When it was taken over by GEC in 1961 he became a director of GEC, and managing director in 1963. Between 1961 and 1967, the profits of GEC were from £10m. to £24m. He holds over 4,600,000 ordinary 25p shares of GEC worth about £6m. His pay from GEC in 1969 was over £27,000. Weinstock is also on the board of London Weekend Television.
Source: Who's Who, 1970.

The following quotes from Weinstock clearly illustrate his carefree attitude towards workers and the fact that profits come before anything else:

'People are like elastic, the more work they have to do the more they stretch.'   *The Financial Times*, 27 May 1969

'There will be no more borrowing. Clearly, therefore, we shall have to do lots of things such as reducing stocks and debtors and selling assets from which no return is being made.'
Letter to Managers, 9 January 1969

'The test of whether or not industry is acting in the national interest is the quite simple test of whether it is efficient. And the only criterion by which efficiency can be judged in a competitive private enterprise system or even in a public enterprise system – is the test of profitability.'
R. Jones & O. Marriott, *Anatomy of a Merger*, Jonathan Cape

Appendix C

Draft – 16th April 1970.
Revised Procedure Agreement for Manual Workers
Proposed by Engineering Employers' Federation

I. PREAMBLE

1. This Agreement is between the Engineering Employers'
Federation and federated engineering employers on the one hand,
and the signatory Unions and their members employed as manual
workers by federated engineering employers on the other.

2. The Agreement provides for the following:
   (a) the establishment of a National Industrial Relations
   Council covering manual workers in the engineering
   industry.
   (b) the appointment of shop stewards and joint works committees, and
   (c) procedures for dealing with grievances, claims and other
   questions arising in federated establishments.

II. GENERAL PRINCIPLES

1. Signatory unions shall be accorded recognition for their
members covered by this Agreement in accordance with its provisions.

2. It is in the interests of federated engineering employers and
their workpeople that manual workers covered by this Agreement should be members of an appropriate signatory union in
order that negotiations can be conducted on a fully representative
and authoritative basis.

3. This Agreement places an obligation on all the parties to
observe at all stages the appropriate procedure, as laid down in
Section VI, for dealing with questions arising. Until the appropriate procedure has been carried through there shall be no
strikes, lockouts, industrial or any other coercive action of any
kind by any of the parties.

4. Internal union or inter-union disputes shall not be the subject of industrial or coercive action against the employer by the workpeople involved. Such disputes shall be determined in accordance with union or inter-union procedures and with any decisions of the TUC.

III. NATIONAL INDUSTRIAL RELATIONS COUNCIL

1. A National Industrial Relations Council shall be established for the engineering industry within six months of the date of this Agreement.

2. The Council shall be charged with the following functions together with such additional functions as the Council shall from time to time decide:

(a) The determination of conditions of employment and minimum pay standards for the engineering industry.

(b) The specification of those matters which shall be the subject of determination nationally and those which shall be determined domestically together with the specification from time to time of any nationally agreed criteria on which factory bargaining shall take place.

(c) The review of procedures for dealing with questions arising and effecting such changes as may from time to time be necessary.

(d) The appointment of national joint committees on appropriate matters, e.g. safety and training.

(e) The interpretation or application of any national agreement.

3. The employer representatives on the Council shall be appointed annually by the Federation and shall be notified thereafter to the General Secretary of the Confederation.

4. The union representatives on the Council shall be appointed annually by the Confederation from the unions parties to this Agreement. Their names shall thereafter be notified to the Secretary of the Federation.

5. The Council shall be responsible for prescribing the constitution and procedure necessary to enable it to carry out its functions.

IV. REGULATION OF EMPLOYER / EMPLOYEE RELATIONS

(a) General

1. The Federation and the unions appreciate the importance of the development and maintenance of good industrial relations at factory level and on the proper operation of the procedure for dealing with questions arising. They accordingly accept the need to have men of experience in the engineering industry who are properly qualified and trained in the duties they are called upon to perform in negotiating on behalf of employers and their workpeople.

2. It is the responsibility of each employer to ensure that appropriate training is given to those nominated to negotiate on his behalf and of the unions to provide appropriate training for their shop stewards.

(b) Appointment of Shop Stewards

3. Workpeople employed in a federated establishment shall have the right to elect shop stewards from among the members of the unions employed in the establishment to act on their behalf in accordance with the terms of this Agreement.

4. Shop stewards shall be subject to the control of their unions and shall act in accordance with all relevant agreements.

5. Shop stewards shall be afforded reasonable facilities to deal with questions raised in the shop or portion of the shop which they represent. In all other respects, shop stewards shall conform to the same working conditions as their fellow workers.

6. No employee shall be eligible to act as a shop steward unless he is at least 21 years of age and has at least one year's continuous service in the establishment immediately prior to nomination (except in the case of a completely new establishment and where otherwise mutually agreed).

7. Where requested by the workpeople concerned federated employers shall provide mutually acceptable facilities for the election of shop stewards by ballot.

8. On appointment, the name of each shop steward, the shop or portion of the shop which he represents and the trade union to which he belongs shall be notified officially by the trade union

concerned to the employer for acceptance. The employer shall acknowledge receipt of such information.

9. A shop steward shall be entitled to represent the interests of the members of his trade union in the shop or portion of the shop in which he is employed. By agreement between the employer and the trade unions involved a shop steward may also represent all the workpeople employed in that shop or portion of that shop.

10. By agreement between an employer and the shop stewards in the establishment arrangements may be made for the appointment and recognition of a chief shop steward, or stewards.

These arrangements, including the scope of activity and the stage at which such a chief shop steward or stewards shall be entitled to participate in discussions on questions arising, shall be matters for mutual agreement at domestic level. Such arrangements may, for example, take one of the following forms:

    (i) Recognition of a chief shop steward who is permitted to participate at a specified stage of negotiations on all claims affecting manual workers, regardless of whether or not the workers concerned in a claim are members of his union.

    (ii) Recognition of a chief shop steward who is permitted to participate at a specified stage of negotiations on all claims affecting manual workers, members of his union.

V. JOINT WORKS COMMITTEES

1. In every federated establishment employing 250 or more manual workers a joint works committee consisting of employer representatives and shop stewards shall, at the request of either side, be established to act in accordance with the terms of this Agreement.

2. The shop stewards shall be representative of the various classes of workpeople employed in the establishment. There shall be mutually agreed arrangements to ensure that this is achieved. Mutually agreed arrangements shall also be made for the election of the shop steward members of the joint works committee.

3. If a question falling to be dealt with by the joint works committee in accordance with the procedure laid down in Section VI of this Agreement arises in a department which has not a shop steward on the works committee, the committee may, as regards that question, co-opt a shop steward from the department concerned.

4. The provisions of this Section of the Agreement shall be without prejudice to the operation of mutually acceptable domestic arrangements.

5. Any problems arising as to the constitution or functions of a works committee shall be dealt with in accordance with the procedure laid down in Clauses 4 to 10 of Section VI of this Agreement.

VI. PROCEDURE FOR DEALING WITH GRIEVANCES, CLAIMS AND OTHER QUESTIONS ARISING

(a) General Provisions

1. The parties to this Agreement re-affirm their acceptance of the principle that effective joint consultation has a vital part to play in the avoidance of disputes. It is also accepted that, except as expressly restricted by the terms of this or any other agreement, the management of the operations, including the allocation of work and the direction of the workforce, is the responsibility of the employer.

2. Any claim, grievance or other question which either the workpeople or their employer desire or are obliged to raise in terms of this Agreement, shall be discussed in accordance with the procedure set out in Clauses 4 to 10 of this Section of the Agreement.

3. Where an employer seeks to change:

(a) an existing system of wage payment or a condition of employment, which is either agreed or is customarily applicable to employees in an establishment or part thereof, or

(b) an individual worker's condition of employment, unless the change required is in accordance with agreed or established practice in the establishment or part thereof, the existing term or condition shall be maintained until agreement has been reached or the procedure laid down in Clauses 4 to 10 of this Section of the Agreement has been exhausted.

Nothing in the foregoing shall require the employer to invoke the procedure when carrying out his responsibilities within the framework of agreed or established conditions. In such circumstances the decisions of the employer shall be implemented immediately without prejudice to the right of the workpeople concerned to raise such issues in the procedure thereafter.

4. In each federated establishment there shall be in written form a mutually agreed domestic procedure for dealing with grievances, claims and other questions arising. Whilst the details of this procedure shall be a matter for domestic determination the following principle shall be incorporated therein:

(a) that apart from general questions, any question arising shall first be raised by the worker or workers directly concerned with his or their immediate supervisor;

(b) that the domestic procedure shall contain an agreed number of stages providing, wherever possible, for specified time limits within which any question or type of questions arising shall be discussed;

(c) that clear provision, based on the terms of this agreement, shall be made regarding the rights, obligations and functions of shop stewards, and where recognised, of chief shop stewards;

(d) that clear provision shall be made as to the level of management to be involved at each procedural stage;

(e) that the joint works committee, where established in terms of this Agreement, shall constitute the final stage of the domestic procedure through which all unresolved questions arising – individual, sectional and factory wide – shall be processed before the external stages of procedure provided for in Clauses 5 to 10 of this Section of the Agreement may be invoked.

5. Failing settlement in accordance with the domestic procedure provided for in terms of Clause 4 of this Section of the Agreement the question at issue may be referred, on behalf either of the employer or of the workpeople directly concerned, to a works conference.

The parties at the works conference shall comprise representatives of the employer and of the employers' association together with representatives of the workpeople directly concerned and the full-time local official of their union.

Arrangements for a works conference shall be made between the trade union or unions concerned and the employers' association, and shall be held within seven working days of receipt of application unless otherwise mutually agreed.

Where mutually agreed by the employers' association and the full-time official(s) of the union(s) concerned, it shall be competent for a question, unresolved at the meeting of the works committee, to be referred direct to the local conference stage provided for in the following Clause.

6. Failing settlement at works conference, the question at issue may be referred, on behalf either of the employer or of the workpeople directly concerned, to a local conference to be held between the employers' association and local representatives of the trade union or unions concerned.

Local conference shall be held within seven working days of receipt of application unless otherwise mutually agreed.

7. Failing settlement at local conference on questions other than those in which the interpretation or application of a national agreement is an issue, the procedure shall be regarded as exhausted but there shall not be any form of industrial action until (a) 7 days' notice of the action contemplated has been tendered to the other party by the executive of the trade union or unions concerned or the Federation, as appropriate, and (b) Federation and executive officers of the trade union or unions concerned have jointly reviewed the decision of local conference. A meeting for this purpose shall be arranged without delay and preferably within the period of notice specified above.

8. Failing settlement at local conference of a question which involves the interpretation or application of a national agreement, that question may be referred on behalf either of the employer or of the workpeople directly concerned to central conference which shall be composed of members of the Conference Committee of the Federation and executive officers of the union or unions concerned.

Central conference shall be held on the second Friday of each month at which questions referred to central conference prior to fourteen days of that date shall be taken.

9. A stoppage of work, either of a partial or general character, such as a strike, lock-out, a go-slow, a work-to-rule, an overtime ban or any other restriction on output, shall not take place until the procedures provided for in this Section of the Agreement have been exhausted.

10. Notwithstanding the other provisions of this Section, a temporary arrangement may be agreed without prejudice to either side, pending a final determination of the question.

(b) Special provisions relating to discipline, and termination of employment

11. Any domestic procedures or arrangements relating to discipline or termination of employment, including dismissal on account of redundancy, shall include the following:

(a) Where an employer has to consider a reduction of the workforce, a period of four weeks shall be allowed for consultation and to enable any proposal of the employer to be questioned before any formal notices of termination are given. These provisions shall not apply in cases where, because of an emergency, action has to be taken at short notice but the workpeople shall have the right, through the procedure laid down in Clauses 4 to 10 of this Agreement, to question the action taken.

(b) Where, for reasons other than industrial misconduct or redundancy, an employer gives notice of dismissal to an individual worker whom he has continuously employed for two years or more and the worker gives notice to his employer within 24 hours of his intention to question that decision through the procedure, his contract of employment shall not be terminated until a period of four weeks has elapsed from the date when the employer gave notice, unless during that period the employer's decision is accepted or the procedure laid down in Clauses 4 to 10 has been exhausted.

Bibliography

P. A. BARAN AND P. M. SWEEZY *Monopoly Capital: An Essay on the American Economic and Social Order* Monthly Review, 1966

ROBIN BLACKBURN AND ALEXANDER COCKBURN (eds) *The Incompatibles: Trade Union Militancy and the Consensus* Penguin, London 1967

British Labour Statistics Department of Employment and Productivity, 1971

MICHAEL BARRATT BROWN *Opening the Books* Institute for Workers' Control, Nottingham 1968

T. CLIFF AND C. BARKER *Incomes Policy, Legislation and Shop Stewards* Industrial Shop Stewards' Defence Committee, London

KEN COATES (ed.) *Can the Workers Run Industry?* Sphere Books, London 1968

KEN COATES *The Crisis of British Socialism* Spokesman Books, Nottingham 1971

KEN COATES *Essays on Industrial Democracy* Spokesman Books, Nottingham 1971

KEN COATES, T. TOPHAM AND BARRATT BROWN *The Trade Union Register*

KEN COATES (ed.) *A Trade Union Strategy in the Common Market* Spokesman Books, Nottingham 1971

The Debate on Workers' Control A Symposium, Institute for Workers' Control, Nottingham 1970

KEN FLEET *Whatever Happened at UCS?* Pamphlet No. 28, Institute for Workers' Control, Nottingham 1971

ERICH FROMM (ed.) *Socialist Humanism* Allen Lane, The Penguin Press, London 1967

SANDOR GASPAR *Role of the Hungarian Trade Unions in the Construction of Socialism* Tancsics Publishing House, Budapest 1971

BRIAN HINDLEY *Industrial Merger and Public Policy* Hobart Paper No. 50, Institute of Economic Affairs, London 1970

LENIN *State and Revolution* Lawrence & Wishart, London 1918

LENIN *Lenin on Britain* Lawrence & Wishart, London 1934

CHARLES LEVINSON *Capital, Inflation and the Multinationals* George Allen & Unwin, London 1971

GEORGE LICHTHEIM *Lukács* Fontana, London 1970

R. M. MACIVER *Modern State* Oxford University Press, London 1964

RALPH MILIBAND AND JOHN SAVILLE (eds) *The Socialist Register 1971* Merlin Press, London 1971

GERALD NABARRO *NAB 1* Robert Maxwell, Oxford 1969

WILL PAYNTER *British Trade Unions and the Problem of Change* George Allen & Unwin, London 1970

MILENTIJE PESAKOVIĆ *Twenty Years of Self-Management in Yugoslavia* Medunarodna Politika, Beograd 1970

D. N. PRITT *The Labour Government: 1945–51* Lawrence & Wishart, London 1963

BRYN ROBERTS *The Price of TUC Leadership* George Allen & Unwin, London 1961

Royal Commission on Trade Unions and Employers' Associations (Chairman: Lord Donovan) HMSO, London 1968

Sovereignty and Multinational Companies Fabian Tract No. 409, Fabian Society, London 1971

TUC *International Companies* (Report of a Conference), Trades Union Congress, October 1970

SIDNEY AND BEATRICE WEBB *The Origins of Trade Unionism*

Index

Ruskin House Series in Trade Union Studies

Workers' Control

Ruskin House Series in Trade Union Studies

International Trade Unionism
Charles Levinson